BECOMING AN EFFECTIVE SUPERVISOR

BECOMING AN EFFECTIVE SUPERVISOR

A Workbook for Counselors and Psychotherapists

by

Jane M. Campbell, Ph.D.

USA	Publishing Office:	ACCELERATED DEVELOPMENT
		A member of the Taylor & Francis Group
		325 Chestnut Street
		Philadelphia, PA 19106
		Tel: (215) 625-8900
		Fax: (215) 625-2940
	Distribution Center:	ACCELERATED DEVELOPMENT
		A member of the Taylor & Francis Group
		47 Runway Road, Suite G
		Levittown, PA 19057
		Tel: (215) 269-0400
		Fax: (215) 269-0363
UK		ACCELERATED DEVELOPMENT
		A member of the Taylor & Francis Group
		27 Church Road
		Hove
		E. Sussex, BN3 2FA
		Tel: +44 (0) 1273 207411
		Fax: +44 (0) 1273 205612

BECOMING AN EFFECTIVE SUPERVISOR: A Workbook for Counselors and Psychotherapists

1 2 3 4 5 6 7 8 9 0

Printed by Sheridan Books, Ann Arbor, MI, 2000.
Cover design by Ellen Sequin.

A CIP catalog record for this book is available from the British Library.
∞ The paper in this publication meets the requirements of the ANSI Standard Z39.48-1984 (Permanence of Paper).

Library of Congress Cataloging-in-Publication Data available from publisher.

ISBN 1-56032-847-9 (paper)

CONTENTS

ACKNOWLEDGMENTS

I wish to thank a number of people for their help and support in writing this book. First and foremost, I wish to thank the hundreds of participants in my supervision workshops who taught me the realities of post-degree supervision for licensure purposes. Additionally, this book would never have been written without the encouragement of my friend, colleague and copresenter, Barbara Herlihy. I wish also to thank Sandra Lopez, LMSW-ACP, for her help with social work supervision, particularly introducing me to the work of Shulman, Middleman, and Rhodes. Her insightful conclusions about the difficulties faced by clinical supervisors in agency settings, contributed greatly to my own growth as a supervisor and to the content of the book. Another thank you needs to be extended to my first assistant, Stephanie Hillman, who gave me encouragement and ideas for structuring the workbook during the initial planning phase. Sue Lombardi, LPC, worked tirelessly on many drafts of the manuscript and it is to her I owe thanks for many of the tables and forms throughout the workbook and in the Appendices. Also, I have heartfelt appreciation for her husband, Robert, his computer expertise, and his great patience with my lack thereof, and for James Benshoff, PhD, who reviewed the manuscript and gave excellent suggestions for organizing of the workbook and structuring the exploration questions. I wish to thank Jill Osowa, Editorial Assistant at Accelerated Development, for her help on numerous revisions, spending hours reviewing my writing and improving my sentence structure. And last but not least, I wish to thank Dr. Joe Hollis, former editor of Accelerated Development, who supported me through the early stages of the book and gave me courage to continue when the task seemed overwhelming.

PREFACE

In 1992, while on the faculty of University of Houston-Clear Lake, I was asked to teach a 40-hour continuing education course for Licensed Professional Counslors (LPCs) and Licensed Marital and Family Therapists (LMFTs) who wished to become approved supervisors for licensure purposes. I asked my colleague, Barbara Herlihy, to join me as a cofacilitator, and then, when social workers in Texas also needed a course in supervision to become approved supervisors, I cotaught the course with Sandra Lopez, LSW-ACP.

The majority of participants in these workshops were experienced counselors and clinicians with no formal training in supervision. These practitioners wanted to learn how to be the most effective supervisor possible but had limited time to expend on such a task as they balanced the demands of their jobs and their clients with that of being a supervisor. They wanted material that was easily accessible, readable, and provided them with the essential elements required to be effective as a supervisor. I discovered, however, that most of the material on counseling and clinical supervision was spread over a number of textbooks and academic journals and that the resources were written for graduate supervision courses in university settings. Very little printed information was available that addressed the specific issues and problems of counseling and clinical supervisors in agencies, schools, and hospitals.

Thus, I was challenged to come up with creative ways to condense volumes of material about supervision and to present it in such a way as to keep people interested, stimulated, and desirous to learn more. This workbook is the result of that effort. My copresenters, Barbara Herlihy and Sandra Lopez, have contributed extensively to my knowledge base, but it is the workshop participants who have refined my thinking about supervision and have guided the workbook's development. I have had the opportunity to meet hundreds of experienced and talented practitioners who have taught me everything I know about supervision in the trenches. It is to this group that my work is dedicated. The future of the profession is in their hands. I hope this workbook will make the task easier.

WHAT IS SUPERVISION?

Becoming a clinical or counseling supervisor can be a challenging experience for the mental health practitioner. While supervision is a relationship that is similar in many ways to counseling or psychotherapy, it has a different structure and purpose. *The primary purpose of clinical supervision is to ensure the quality of client care while the trainee or supervisee is learning.* The supervisor must constantly weigh the needs and welfare of the client with the supervisee's need to learn and grow professionally. Supervision requires the evaluation of the supervisee's professional and therapeutic competence as well as suitability for the profession. Therefore, supervision is a hierarchical relationship with evaluation as a key component.

To be an effective supervisor, the practitioner must develop separate skills from those required for the practice of counseling and psychotherapy. Simply because one is a skilled counselor or psychotherapist does not necessarily mean one will be a good supervisor. Because supervisors accept the ethical and legal responsibility for the work of the supervisee with clients, an additional burden of responsibility is placed on the counselor or psychotherapist serving in a supervisory role. Pressures from the work setting, ethical and legal concerns, and a host of practical problems related to practicing in today's health care climate also affect the supervisor and the supervisory relationship. Mental health professionals are already challenged by the mandate to maintain ethical standards and to follow state laws while operating within licensing guidelines and institutional policies. Factors such as survival in the work setting, conflict resolution, and the impact of larger cultural, socioeconomic, and political issues also affect the supervisory process. Thus, practitioners who become clinical supervisors need to demonstrate competence not only in working with clients but in working with organizational systems as well.

With post-degree supervision for licensure or certification purposes, the task of being a supervisor can be even more difficult, especially for busy practitioners. In this capacity, the supervisor serves as the last gatekeeper for evaluating the skills, expertise, and ethical behavior of the supervisee before independent practice. It is an important role and should not be taken lightly. As more and more states are requiring licensure for all mental health professionals, there is an increasing demand today for competent, trained clinical supervisors in all settings, including schools, agencies, hospitals, and private practice. The National Board for Certified Counselors (NBCC) has just established an Approved Clinical Supervisor credential, and The American Association of Marriage and Family Therapists has had a special supervision credential since 1987. Some states, such as Texas, are requiring potential supervisors in counseling, marriage and family, and social work to be certified and to take a formal, 40-hour course in supervision

Therefore, just as there was a need for training in the techniques of Counseling and psychotherapy, the same is true for supervision. The majority of practitioners who have not received any training in supervision might believe that because they are capable, accomplished, and experienced counselors or therapists, they therefore can supervise. They fail to understand that there is no perfect relationship between being a good therapist and being a good supervisor.

Borders and Usher (1992) have made a strong argument for the value of post-master's supervision by stating that counselor growth and development upon graduation is related to supervised, not unsupervised, experience. However, little is known about supervision practices or the training of these supervisors outside academic settings (Borders, Cashwell, & Rotter, 1995, Bernard, 1997).

According to Baronchok and Kunkel (1990), few therapists receive formal training in supervision as part of their degree program. Smaller still are the numbers of supervisors who themselves receive formal supervision of their ongoing work with supervisees. As a result, Worthington (1987) expressed concern that supervisors may simply be perpetuating the mistakes of their own supervisors.

One problem for practitioners who want to become effective supervisors is the lack of material available to train supervisors outside of academic settings. This workbook is designed to fill that gap. It is not meant to replace a textbook, but to provide a practical, hands-on tool to facilitate the teaching of supervision to mental health practitioners regardless of degree or setting. Although each area, such as school counseling, social work, marriage and family therapy, and psychology, has information specific to its field, there are certain universal supervision concepts, models, and methods to be learned. *The goal of the workbook is to help the practitioner move from the theory of clinical supervision to its practice.* It is hoped that readers, on completing the workbook, will feel more comfortable and effective in their role as supervisor and that their interest will be piqued to explore the topic further.

How to Use the Workbook

This workbook is suitable for either the beginning or the more advanced supervisor. It can also be used to teach a formal course in supervision or serve as a structure for home study. While the primary audience for this workbook is practitioners with master's degrees in counseling, social work, and marriage and family therapy engaged in supervision for licensure or certification purposes, it could also be used by psychologists, pre- and postdoctoral-level supervisors and in academic settings.

The workbook contains an introduction to the key points of each content area, followed by exploration questions. A brief list of suggested readings accompanies each chapter. The exploration questions are designed to stimulate the examination of practical issues in real-life situations and to help integrate learning. Space is provided in the workbook itself to answer each question, but the amount of space should not be used as a guideline as to how extensive or brief your answers should be. It may be necessary to use additional sheets of paper to complete the questions. It is hoped that the questions included will encourage the supervisor, regardless of experience, to further learn and grow by identifying areas of weakness and areas for improvement. At the end of each exploration section, an action plan question is included to help move the reader from thought to action. To this end, it is recommended that you create a supervision file, labeling each folder in the file to match the workbook chapter headings, and then use this file to organize materials, forms, handouts, ideas and action plan suggestions specific to each folder topic. An additional suggestion is to file a copy of each section of exploration questions for easy review.

Because the workbook is designed for use by mental health practitioner regardless of their degree or discipline, several terms have been chosen to indicate this universal approach. When used in the workbook, the word *practitioner* refers to the counselor or therapist who is delivering service to the client. The term *client*, rather than *patient*, was selected to refer to those receiving counseling or psychotherapy services, regardless of the setting. The term *supervisor* refers to the counselor or therapist formally designated with the responsibility to train and evaluate the expertise and skills of the supervisee. Referring to them as *clinical supervisors* is meant to distinguish their role and function from that of an administrator. The term *supervisee* refers to the counselor or therapist in training under the supervisor.

What Is the Nature and Purpose of Supervision?

Clinical supervisors are responsible for transmitting the skills, knowledge, and attitudes of their profession to the next generation of practitioners. In addition, supervisors are required to "oversee" the work of less experienced counselors or therapists to ensure that their clients receive quality care. According to Liddle, Breunlin, and Schwartz (1988), supervision is the major vehicle through which a profession evolves. Similarly, Kaiser (1992) indicated that "supervision and the supervisory relationship are the medium through which therapy is taught" (p. 294). Supervision provides an opportunity for the supervisee "to capture the essence of the psychotherapeutic process" (Holloway, 1995, p.5).

Many individuals have attempted to describe and define the supervisory relationship. Loganbill, Hardy, and Delworth (1982) defined supervision as "an intensive, interpersonally focused one-to-one relationship in which one person is designated to facilitate the development of therapeutic competence in the other person" (p. 4). Bradley (1989) expanded this definition to include oversight of the counselor-in-training's work for the purpose of "facilitating personal and professional development, improving competencies and promoting accountability in service and programs" (p. 26). Further research and literature in social psychology indicates that supervision is a process of social influence with the goal of changing the attitudes and behavior of the supervisee (Claiborn, Etringer, & Hillerbrand, 1995). This goal can be accomplished through monitoring, assisting, redirecting, and amplifying the supervisee's clinical work (Haber, 1996). Watkins (1997) stated that "supervision is about helping the therapist become better and more effective with regard to conceptual ability, intervention, assessment, and implementation, among other areas" (p. 5).

Bernard and Goodyear (1998) viewed supervision as a training intervention that extends over an agreed-upon period of time. A senior member of a profession typically provides supervision to a junior member of the same profession. The supervisory relationship may be voluntary (sought out) or involuntary (required by law), as in the case of licensure requirements. In addition, the relationship is hierarchical and evaluative in that the supervisor is a gatekeeper, screening those who wish to enter the helping profession (Bernard & Goodyear, 1998; Watkins, 1997). It is important that both the supervisor and supervisee understand this fact, because if the relationship is not handled appropriately, conflict surrounding power and authority may arise (Sherry, 1991).

Given the large impact that supervisors have on the future of the profession and the well being of clients, it is critical that the reader not only understand, but also be able to fully utilize the supervisory relationship in order to meet the needs of both the supervisee and the clients. This task becomes more onerous when the goal of supervision is state licensure and when, upon completion of requirements, the supervisee will be able to work autonomously. Regardless of the setting, this fact means that the supervisor is the final gatekeeper involved in evaluating the ethical, professional, and therapeutic competence of the supervisee and his or her suitability for independent practice.

What Are the Qualities of Effective Supervisors?

Effective supervisors need a broad range of competencies in a variety of areas. Borders and Leddick (1987) stated that supervisors should be confident but not dictatorial, be respected and seen by others as capable, and be advocates for their supervisees. They also stated that the counselors, especially those in schools, need to provide positive models for dealing with power and authority in the system. This would also be true of supervisors in agencies and hospitals. A study by White and Russell (1995) concerning the essential elements of marriage and family therapy supervision generated over 800 variables that influence the outcome of supervision. Using a systems perspective, they identified five factors that contribute to variations in conceptualization and the practice of effective supervision: (a) the setting, (b) the supervisor and supervisee, (c) the relationship between supervisor and supervisee, (d) the activities in supervision, and (e) the interactions in supervision. The results of this study speak to the complexity of the supervisory process.

Some of the personal attributes that have been consistently identified as helpful in supervisors and supervisees are humor, empathy, respect, genuineness, ability to confront, immediacy, concern for supervisee's growth and well being, concern for the client's welfare, availability for self-inspection, flexibility, courage, tolerance, and openness to various styles of learning. According to Virginia Satir (1988), the better the supervisor's self-esteem, communication ability, personal congruence, and role flexibility, the more likely that the supervisory relationship will foster exploration, learning, and development.

The following is a list of the qualities, characteristics, and behaviors of the effective supervisor compiled from multiple sources (Blocher, 1983; Bordin, 1983; Bradley, 2000; Conway & Ellison, 1995; Corey, Corey, & Callanan, 1993; Haber, 1996; Lambert & Ogles, 1997; Loganbill et al., 1982; Magnuson & Wilcoxon, 1998; Shanfield, Matthews, & Hetherly, 1993), including responses from participants in previous supervision workshops conducted by myself between 1994 and 1997.

Effective Supervisory Behaviors

➤ Clarifies expectations and style of supervision
➤ Maintains consistent and appropriate boundaries
➤ Has knowledge of theory and current research
➤ Teaches practical skills
➤ Teaches case conceptualization
➤ Provides frequently scheduled supervision
➤ Is accessible and available
➤ Encourages the exploration of new ideas and techniques
➤ Fosters autonomy
➤ Models appropriate ethical behavior
➤ Has a personalized therapeutic style
➤ Is personally and professionally mature
➤ Is willing to serve as a model
➤ Perceives growth as an ongoing process
➤ Is able to assess learning needs of the supervisee
➤ Provides constructive criticism and positive reinforcement
➤ Is invested in the supervisee's development
➤ Creates a relaxed learning environment
➤ Cares about well being of others
➤ Has the ability to be present and immediate
➤ Has an awareness of personal power
➤ Has the courage to expose vulnerabilities, make mistakes, and take risks
➤ Is nonauthoritarian and nonthreatening
➤ Accepts and celebrates diversity.
➤ Has the ability to communicate effectively
➤ Is willing to engage in fantasy and imagination
➤ Is aware of and accepts own limitations and strengths
➤ Is willing to negotiate
➤ Works collaboratively

Personal Qualities and Characteristics

➤ Sense of humor
➤ Integrity
➤ People oriented
➤ Trustworthy
➤ Honest
➤ Tenacious
➤ Open and flexible
➤ Competent
➤ Credible
➤ Considerate
➤ Respectful
➤ Understanding
➤ Sensitive
➤ Objective
➤ Congruent
➤ Tactful
➤ Genuine
➤ Curious

- ➢ Intelligent
- ➢ Warm
- ➢ Supportive
- ➢ Tolerant
- ➢ Encouraging
- ➢ Available

It may be evident from the above that the list of *ineffective* supervisory qualities and behaviors may contain the following descriptions: unavailable, inconsistent, inconsiderate, dogmatic, closed, prejudiced, inflexible, arrogant, critical, and disinterested.

Note that these characteristics of an effective supervisor mirror those of the effective helper. For example, in a summary of research on supervision, Lambert and Ogles (1997) found that those supervisors who exhibited qualities such as expertise, trustworthiness, and the ability to create facilitative conditions such as empathy, genuineness, concreteness, and positive regard were rated more effective as supervisors. According to Russell and Petrie (1994), regardless of the specific theoretical model or the level of the supervisee, a supportive, facilitative supervisory environment is deemed critical to effective supervision and supervisory growth. Therefore, those personal qualities that contribute to creating a nurturing environment are the most essential. Perhaps the terms "respect" or "being respectful" capture the essence of those qualities necessary to the effective supervisor. Shanfield et al. (1993) concluded that excellent supervisors placed the supervisee's concerns at the center of their supervisory activities. While lists of behaviors and qualities can be generated for both the effective and ineffective supervisor, just as in counseling and psychotherapy, little is known about what kind of supervision is going to be effective with a particular supervisee in any given situation. It is still up to the supervisor to figure out what specific qualities, behaviors, methods, and techniques are going to be most effective with each supervisee. A more extensive discussion of this important consideration will follow in chapter 6.

What Is the Role of Goal Setting in Supervision?

One of the first tasks required of effective supervisors is to establish the goals for supervision. Holloway (1995) stated that before beginning, the supervisor must make a list of competency areas required of the supervisee, clearly describing the content of each area. To accomplish this task, supervisors should refer to requirements described for the state license or national certification being sought by the supervisee. Supervisors should also consider the needs of their setting and discipline, and their own sense of what a competent and ethical counselor or psychotherapist needs to know to practice in today's world. In other words, to be successful, supervisors need to know where they are going in order to plan how to get there.

A number of authors in the field of supervision have suggested descriptors of important competencies or content areas to consider. Loganbill et al. (1982) suggested eight domains: competence, emotional awareness, autonomy, theoretical identity, respect for individual differences, purpose and direction, personal motivation, and professional ethics. Stoltenberg, McNeill, and Delworth (1997) listed intervention skills, assessment techniques, interpersonal assessment, client conceptualization, individual differences, theoretical orientation, treatment goals and plans, and professional ethics. A study by Cook, Berman, Genco, Repka, and Shrider (1986) identified a number of skills and knowledge areas considered important by agency administrators when hiring mental health practitioners. Rated high were skills in individual and family counseling and psychotherapy, knowledge of individual differences, written skills, knowledge of ethics and multicultural populations, and group skills. Other suggestions might be intake procedures, screening, treatment planning, case management, crisis intervention, report writing and record keeping, consultation and referral (Powell, 1993). All supervisors need to take time to create their own lists of essential content areas required of a competent and ethical licensed professional before they begin to supervise.

EXPLORATION ➤ Defining Supervision

1. In your own words, how would you define supervision?

2. Formal definitions of supervision stress the dual goals of providing clients with quality care and helping with the professional development of the supervisee.
    a. In your own experience in supervision, was there any problem that developed between these two stated goals? Describe the problem and give an example.

    b. At this time, what problems, if any, do you see developing for you as a supervisor between these two stated goals of supervision? Can you give an example?

3. Write a short paragraph summarizing your experiences in post-masters degree supervision.

a. What would you say was the purpose of this supervision in your own professional development? Can you give an example?

b. Do you feel you received excellent supervision?

c. Did any of your supervisors have specialized training in supervision?

d. Did your site have a training program or did you learn by experience?

e. What was one thing you liked about your supervision experience?

f. What was one thing you didn't like?

4. Can you think of how your own personal experiences in supervision might influence your supervision of others?

EXPLORATION ➤ Qualities of the Effective Supervisor

1. When you were in graduate school, what did you need from your supervisor?

2. Did your needs change when you were working towards licensure?

3. Suppose you were looking for a supervisor now:
   a. What qualities of the supervisor would be important to you?

   b. What do you currently need from a supervisor?

c. Review your answers. Do you see any descrepencies between what you say you currently need from a supervisor and the qualities you are searching for in a supervisor? Describe.

4. Review the list of behaviors and qualities of the effective and ineffective supervisor listed earlier in this chapter.
   a. Select eight or ten qualities and behaviors you think are most important. List them below.

   b. Select several qualities that are not as important to you.

5. From your own experience as a supervisee,
   a. Make a list of qualities that you feel describe an effective supervisor.

b. Now list the qualities of an ineffective supervisor (again, from your own experience as a supervisee).

c. Review these answers: What does this indicate will be your primary focus as a supervisor?

6. Review your thoughts at this point about the effective supervisor. Take one quality. In specific behavioral terms, can you describe one or two things you would have to do as a supervisor in order to be effective? For example, for the quality of: "Being available and reliable," the behavior might be: "Make arrangements for the supervisee's access to you, prioritize time for supervision in your busy schedule and set a consistent time for it."

EXPLORATION ➤ Identifying Goals for Supervision

1. Before you begin the workbook, take a few minutes to ponder the most significant question you will have to answer as a clinical supervisor. Even if you are not currently involved in supervision for licensure purposes, still take time to answer this important question: What will my supervisee need to demonstrate for me to sign off without reservation on their final application form for licensure or certification? In other words, can you describe at least four or five things you expect from a licensed professional in your field? (This question is adapted from Magnuson, 1996.)

2. A number of suggestions for important content areas to include in teaching supervision were given in the earlier section on goal setting, such as ethics, assessment techniques, intervention strategies, group and individual skills, crisis intervention, conceptualization of client problems, record keeping, and intake procedures. Review all of these suggestions and create your own list of content areas you expect the supervisee to be competent in when they finish supervision? Use your list to complete the following table and then rank-order the content areas as to importance. For example, ethics 1, assessment 2, etc. Continue on a separate sheet of paper if necessary.

COMPETENCIES	
Content area	Rank order as to importance

b. Examine the list. What areas do you emphasize most? Least?

c. Compare this list to your answers given in question 1 of this section concerning what things you would expect from a licensed professional. Is there anything you left out of the above list? Describe.

3. Create a short summary of your supervision goals and keep it available to refer to as you continue with the workbook.

➢ Conclusions

What conclusions might you draw from these exercises that may be helpful to you in working with your supervisee?

➢ Action Plan

What do you need to do as a result of these conclusions?

➢ Chapter Highlights

❑ The supervisory relationship, while similar in some respects to counseling and psychotherapy, has unique characteristics.

❑ Supervision is a hierarchical relationship with evaluation as a key component.

❑ The practitioner must develop distinct skills to be an effective supervisor.

❑ Supervision is the means through which the field of counseling and psychotherapy is taught.

❑ Supervisors are responsible for facilitating the professional and personal development of supervisees.

❑ Goal setting is a key factor in effective supervision.

Suggested Readings

Bernard, J., & Goodyear, R. (1998). *Fundamentals of clinical supervision.* Chapter 1: The importance, scope, and definition of clinical supervision. Boston: Allyn and Bacon.

Borders, L. D., Cashwell, C. S., & Rotter, J. C. (1995). Supervision of counselor licensure applicants: A comparative study. *Counselor Education and Supervision, 35,* 54–69.

Borders, L. D., & Leddick, G. (1987). *Handbook of Counseling Supervision.* Introduction & Chapter 3: Goals for supervision. Alexandria, VA: Association for Counselor Education and Supervision.

Borders L. D., & Usher, C. H. (1992). Post-degree supervision: Existing and preferred practices. *Journal of Counseling and Development, 70,* 594–599.

Bradley, L. (2000). *Counselor supervision.* Chapter 1: Overview of counselor supervision; Chapter 11: Supervision training: A model; & Chapter 8: Supervision for counselors in schools. Washington, DC: Accelerated Development.

Holloway, E. (1995). *Clinical supervision: A systems approach.* Chapter 1: The essence of supervision. Thousand Oaks, CA: Sage.

Kaiser, T. (1997). *Supervisory relationships: Exploring the human element.* Chapter 1: The importance of the relationship. Pacific Grove, CA: Brooks/Cole.

Lambert, M.J., & Ogles, B. M. (1997). The effectiveness of psychotherapy supervision. In *Handbook of Psychotherapy Supervision.* New York: Wiley.

Liddle, H., Breunlin, D., & Schwartz, R. (1988). *Handbook of family therapy training & supervision.* Chapter 1: Family therapy training and supervision: An introduction; & Chapter 9: Systemic supervision: Conceptual overlays and pragmatic guidelines. New York: Guilford.

Magnuson, S., & Wilcoxon, S. A. (1998). Successful clinical supervision of prelicensed counselors: How will we recognize it? *The Clinical Supervisor, 17,* 33–47.

Powell, D. J. (1993). *Clinical supervision in alcohol and drug abuse counseling: Principles, models, methods.* Introduction; Chapter 1: A historical review of supervision; Chapter 2: A working definition of supervision; & Chapter 4: Traits of an effective clinical supervisor. New York: Lexington Books.

Shulman, L. (1993). *Interactional supervision.* Part I, Chapter 1: Introduction to interactional supervision. Washington, DC: NASW Press.

Watkins, C. E. Jr. (Ed.). (1997). *Handbook of psychotherapy supervision.* Chapter 1: Defining psychotherapy supervision and understanding supervisor functioning. New York: Wiley.

2

WHAT DO
SUPERVISORS DO?

After supervisors identify the essential topic areas necessary for a licensed practitioner in today's world, the next step is to decide how to approach supervision in order to accomplish these stated goals for competence. A number of authors in the field of supervision have suggested the need to break down each topic area into components, and, like teachers, to place them in an organized supervision curriculum.

What Are the Components of Supervision?

Bernard's discrimination model was one of the first models created to help supervisors organize their thinking about supervision and the vast amount of material involved in their work with the supervisee (Bernard, 1979). In this model, the components of supervision are divided into three areas: (a) process skills or intervention skills; (b) conceptualization skills, including knowledge and the assessment and the use of that knowledge; and (c) personalization skills, referring to the personhood of the supervisee—his or her personality, culture, race, and way of being (Bernard, 1997). Lanning (1986) added the category of professional behavior to this model, referring to the ethical behavior and professionalism of the supervisee.

While planning a supervision curriculum for the National Board for Certified Counselors (NBCC)-Approved Clinical Supervisor credential, Borders et al. (1991) noted that three essential components are needed in order to ensure the competence of the supervisee. These components include (a) theoretical and conceptual knowledge, (b) skills and techniques, and (c) self-awareness. Bradley (2000) used the terms knowledge, practice, and personal, to describe these same components. She suggested that the specific content of the three areas would vary by setting and state licensure requirements. For example, school counselors and those in private practice may formulate very different lists. It should be noted that Bradley's components mirror those suggested by Borders et al. (1991) in their supervision curriculum, and can be summarized in the following way.

The first component, knowledge, refers to theoretical and conceptual knowledge of counseling and psychotherapy theory and research. Knowledge of material is typically gained by reading and attending lectures, seminars, and continuing education (CEU) courses. The supervisor may want to give short didactic presentations, handouts, or assigned readings to impart information. Regardless of the method, supervisors should encourage supervisees to continue learning throughout their career. For example, effective counselors and therapists must periodically update their knowledge base at least every 10 years. In addition, the supervisor should encourage their supervisees to become involved in professional organizations; attend local, state, and/or national conferences; and participate in other activities that foster a sense of professional identity.

The second component, practice, or the overall clinical performance of the supervisee, encompasses skills, techniques, clinical judgment, and the manner in which content knowledge is integrated into each session with clients. Supervisors can use a variety of techniques and methods such as live observation, taping, cotherapy, staffings, and training workshops to contribute to developing the practice component. More information on this will be given in the chapter on methods and techniques.

The final component is the importance of a supervisee's personal characteristics and self-awareness on their work with clients and the supervisory relationship. Characteristics such as honesty, genuineness, flexibility, sensitivity, openness, objectivity, and empathy are generally considered effective personal characteristics necessary for "good" therapeutic relationships. Often the supervisee will possess many of these qualities prior to beginning their clinical work. However, the supervisor may want to use activities such as journaling, role playing, modeling, psychodrama, and assigning participation in a psychotherapy group or personal psychotherapy to develop the supervisee's personal awareness.

Haber (1996) presented a different description of the components of supervision. He used the metaphor of a professional house to describe the components of the supervisory relationship from a systems perspective. The first floor of the house includes the development of the personal self, maturity, and personal characteristics. The second floor is the work context that includes the rules, roles, and relationships of one's work setting. Included here would be support systems at work, such as the relationship with one's supervisor. The third floor refers to ideology and encompasses one's theories, methodology, professional ethics, and values. The attic refers to the cultural component that includes cultural values, gender issues, family, and life cycle expectations.

Haber's (1996) illustration emphasizes the fact that the supervisory relationship is embedded in other relationships and systems and does not stand alone. Thus, it is important for the supervisor to attend to the process variables (the how, what, where, and when of supervision) as well as to the content, tasks, and roles. In fact, these process issues may be more important and influential in effective supervision than the technical and content aspects of supervision. For example, the supervisee's difficulties in working with clients may represent deficits in all three areas of knowledge, skills, and personal awareness. Examining the how, what, where, and when of the problem may be more fruitful than attempting to decide if the problem exists in one particular area.

In summary, the supervisee's development can be viewed as a continuous, nonlinear process of learning and growing that will span his or her entire career. The supervisor sets the stage for this process. Dividing the content of supervision into the three components, knowledge, practice, and personal can be used to guide goal setting, planning of intervention strategies, and evaluation. The supervisor may want to emphasize a particular area more strongly at different points over the course of the supervisory relationship. However, regardless of the choice of terminology for these components, the real problem will be identifying in which area the supervisee is having the most problems and determining how to resolve these difficulties.

What Are the Roles of the Supervisor?

In order to be effective, the supervisor may need to assume many different roles and draw from a variety of intervention strategies, techniques, emphases, and components of supervision (Sherry, 1991). Unfortunately, these roles may overlap and sometimes conflict.

A number of supervisory roles have been identified: teaching, supporting, modeling, challenging, consulting, evaluating, and mentoring. For example, Loganbill et al. (1982) described the main roles of the supervisor as monitoring client welfare, enhancing supervisee growth, promoting stage development, and evaluating the supervisee. In contrast, Holloway (1995) referred to these "roles" as the functions of the supervisor and described them as follows: (a) monitoring and evaluating, (b) instructing and advising, (c) modeling, (d) counseling, and (e) supporting and sharing. Another way to conceptualize the role of the supervisor is put forth by Bernard and Goodyear (1998), who suggested drawing a parallel to parent–child or sibling relationships. Hess (1980) used the metaphor of master and apprentice and described six different roles for the supervisor as follows: lecturer, teacher, case reviewer-master therapist, consultant, monitor-evaluator, and therapist.

To be effective, the supervisor must decide which role to assume during a supervision session. In making this decision, the supervisor must consider where the supervisee stands developmentally, what the client's needs are, and many other things prior to assuming a particular role. As Bernard and Goodyear (1998) suggested, role flexibility is essential to effective supervision; different situations and supervisees call for different roles, techniques, and interventions. Similar to the work undertaken as a counselor or therapist, the supervisor must be willing to make adjustments in the relationship process to meet each supervisee's learning needs. Holloway (1995) refered to this as the artistry of supervision.

Effective supervisors are continually balancing client welfare, supervisee training needs, professional guidelines (ethical, licensure, and legal), and organizational or contextual needs (Sherry, 1991). Tension may build as they attempt to balance these needs. One suggestion for easing this tension is to talk directly with the supervisee about these multiple roles and then, together, to process their impact on the supervisory relationship.

It may be evident from reviewing Table 2.1 that there is an essential agreement about the three main roles or functions of the supervisor among leading authorities in the field: teacher, counselor, and consultant, with some adding the important role of evaluator.

TABLE 2.1. Supervisory Roles or Functions

Holloway (1995)	Hess (1980)	Neufeldt (1994)	Bernard & Goodyear (1998)	Bradley (2000)
Monitor/evaluator	Monitor			Evaluator
Advisor/instructor	Teacher	Teacher	Teacher	Teacher/trainer
Model		Model		
Consultant	Colleague		Consultant	Consultant
Support/share	Therapist	Support	Therapist	Counselor

The teaching or training role is utilized when the supervisee needs content knowledge. The supervisee may need to learn a considerable amount of information, including clinical content, agency policies, organizational procedures, professional ethics and guidelines, laws, administrative tasks, and record keeping. To facilitate learning, the supervisor will first need to provide the supervisee with a structure as to how to approach learning all these important materials, to provide them with information and examples, to encourage them to ask questions, and to continually summarize and review.

This task often seems to be an easy one to accomplish for the supervisor who possesses a broad base of knowledge. However, teaching and learning are not always connected. Although it may be relatively simple for the supervisee to learn facts and theories and to understand research findings, it may be more difficult to apply this knowledge in practice or in more complicated situations. Learning involves doing, repeated practice, taking risks, self-scrutiny, and making mistakes. Ultimately, whether or not the supervisee learns the information provided or integrates these new insights with previous knowledge is in his or her hands. Altucher (1967) assumed that learning to be a counselor or psychotherapist is an anxiety-producing experience with both emotional and intellectual components. He identified two main areas of learning difficulty for the supervisee: (a) lack of experience and knowledge and (b) the supervisee's characteristic pattern of behavior that may affect relationships with both the client and the supervisor. Each of these would require different ways of intervening on the part of the supervisor. Therefore, it is suggested that both the supervisor and the supervisee try to delineate what the problem in learning may be. It is also advised that supervisors examine their own patterns of responses to the supervisee's learning difficulties.

To be effective, the supervisor should seek out innovative methods to communicate knowledge besides traditional handouts and reading assignments. Modeling, role playing, and experiential methods (e.g. art, family sculpting, Gestalt) may facilitate the transfer of learning from knowledge to practice. For example, modeling may be used to demonstrate how to set ethical and contextual boundaries, how to manage authority and power within the work setting, and how to apply specific intervention techniques. Family sculpting may help the supervisee find solutions to problems with difficult clients. Role playing and role reversal can be used to the same end.

The counselor function of the supervisor refers to the common therapeutic factors that are used to facilitate the supervisee's personal growth, such as support, advanced empathy, and personal sharing. However, the focus of the counseling function in supervision is to build rapport, help with the release of anxiety, and facilitate insight. Although many refer to this function as a counselor function, it is really reflective of the supportive function or role of the supervisor. For example, you may momentarily use counseling and therapeutic skills to facilitate your supervisee's self-exploration and development of self-awareness as they work with clients or patients. Supportive interventions are particularly helpful when the supervisee makes mistakes, as it fosters a more open learning environment and promotes risk taking.

The consultant role is utilized by the supervisor to encourage the problem-solving skills of the supervisee and to facilitate professional development as well as involvement or affiliation with other colleagues. It is particularly difficult to describe this function. Much more is known about the supervisor as teacher and counselor (Bernard, 1997). However, in post-degree supervision with more advanced supervisees, the consultant role is perhaps the most important role or function.

Consultation as a supervisory function is used primarily in four areas: (a) personal problems in work with clients, (b) professional development, (c) the acquisition of new skills, and (d) program development, maintenance, and evaluation (Bradley, 2000). Since consultation is seen primarily as a nonevaluative relationship, the supervisor as consultant moves from directing and structuring supervision to mutually establishing goals and objectives with the supervisee. For example, to promote self-development, ask the supervisee to generate their own personal goals and objectives, instead of telling the supervisee what to do. A more detailed discussion of this important function is given in chapter 5, in the section about interpersonal skills essential to effective supervision.

The last function, evaluation, can be the most problematic for the beginning supervisor. Evaluation is a key component of supervision, and as such must be discussed directly with the supervisee from the beginning. Counselors and therapists by nature and by training may be uncomfortable with concepts of hierarchy, approval, and power. They may seek to minimize these factors in their work with clients. To resolve the difficulty in supervision, the supervisor may seek to ignore evaluation as a concern. However, the supervisee is probably acutely aware of this unspoken evaluative function. Deciding not to address the issue directly may influence the quality of the working alliance and possibly that of client care. Certainly, the supervisor may wish to change the emphasis on evaluation over the course of supervision, stressing it more highly with beginning supervisees than with the more advanced ones.

How Does a Supervisor Select a Preferred Style?

There are a number of factors that should be considered when selecting a preferred style of supervision, including one's personality characteristics, leadership style, work values, and learning style. There are a number of models and instruments available to help the supervisor examine style preferences. For example, The Supervisory Styles Inventory of Friedlander and Ward (1984) measures three dimensions of supervisory style felt to be important: attractiveness, interpersonal sensitivity, and task orientation. (A copy of this instrument is included in Appendix C of Bernard and Goodyear's (1998) *Fundamentals of Clinical Supervision*.) Another instrument, The Supervisor Emphasis Rating Form-Revised (SERF-R) by Lanning & Freeman (1994) looks at the choice of supervisory style from such aspects as professional behavior, use of process and conceptual skills, and personalization—the sharing of one's personal beliefs and feelings.

D'Andrea (1989) described a "person process model" of supervision which takes into account the personal characteristics of the supervisee using Loevinger's model of ego development: preconformist, conformist, and postconformist levels. It is suggested that understanding the supervisee's level of ego development can help increase the effectiveness of the supervisor. For example, supervisees at the preconformist level are seen as less mature, more impulsive and insensitive, more concrete, less abstract in their thinking, and not really good on a team. They would do better with one-on-one supervision, using behavioral techniques such as shaping, reinforcement, and contracting. Those at the conformist level are more open and less defensive, more concerned with how others think, and good team players. They do better in group supervision, as they want feedback and need less structure than the preconformist-level supervisee. Postconformist-level supervisees are intellectually more mature, empathetic, creative, and self-initiating. The most effective techniques to use at this level are consulting and collaboration, which present the supervisor with opportunities for creativity and self-initiation.

Additional supervisory style inventories as well as an excellent discussion of this topic may be found in Middleman and Rhodes (1985). These authors indicated one distinct difference in viewpoint that can be influential in selecting a style: Does the supervisor view the trainee as internally or externally driven in motivation? Supervisors who see their supervisees as internally driven encourage risk taking and making mistakes as part of learning. They stress the importance of the relationship and are open to giving and receiving direct feedback. In other words, the supervisee is seen as self-motivated and self-directed. Overall, the concern is for the process—*how* things are done. The supervisor serves more in a consultant role and the relationship is more supervisee-centered. However, when the supervisee is seen as externally driven, there is more concern with guidance and structure and the accomplishment of tasks. For example, the supervisor will stress the use of structured activities for learning, modeling, and monitoring of tasks. The supervisor serves more as a teacher or coach and the focus is more supervisor-centered.

Middleman and Rhodes (1985) also discussed two systems theory concepts: field-independence and field dependence, as they apply to selecting a supervisory style. Field-independent people prefer freedom and autonomy, the ability to create one's own structure and goals and self-evaluation. Other characteristics may be originality, creativity, experimenting, and tolerance for ambiguity. Field-dependent supervisors value working within clearly articulated organizational guidelines and structure, enjoy working in groups on set tasks, and value instruction and guidance from others.

Other important areas to explore when selecting a supervisory style are the supervisor's own personal work values, personality characteristics, learning style, and preferences. There are a number of instruments available that could be useful for this purpose. Two such instruments are the Myers–Briggs Type Indicator (Briggs & Myers, 1993) and the Values Scale (Nevill & Super, 1985). Both instruments are used in career counseling and copies can be obtained by contacting Consulting Psychologists Press.

One suggestion that might be beneficial in selecting a style is for both the supervisor and the supervisee to take the Myers–Briggs Type Indicator (Briggs & Myers, 1993). This well-known instrument is based on Jung's psychology of types: extroverted and introverted; sensing and intuition; thinking and feeling; judgment and perception. The assumption is that these types will affect people's personality preferences, how they take in and process information, what they pay attention to, how they make decisions, and their overall lifestyle choices. While research may criticize whether the test in fact measures truly dichotomous preferences or qualitatively distinct types (Barbuto, 1997), the supervisor can still use the information to stimulate their thinking about style preferences. Additionally, the supervisee could be requested to take the Myers–Briggs and a dialogue then opened concerning differences and similarities in learning style, communication, and other important relationship factors. The same could be true of taking the Values Scale.

Learning style is also an important factor to consider when deciding on a preferred style of supervision. Powell (1993) mentioned several differences in learning style, such as analytical style of thinking, conceptual thinking ability, abstract reasoning, and ability to form hypotheses. Some people learn best by talking about cases and hearing responses (oral processors), while others learn most effectively by reading and writing assignments. Active learners learn best by hands-on practice, while vicarious learners learn by watching modeling by the supervisor. Noting and understanding these differences in learning style will help guide the choice of methods and techniques. For example, beginners, overwhelmed by information and material, may need structure. Those whose low analytic ability make it hard for them to process information and draw their own conclusions would benefit from written work sheets with structured questions.

In closing, while Ellis and Ladany (1997), in their review of research on supervision, questioned the reliability and validity of many of the available supervision instruments, practicing supervisors might find one or two of these instruments helpful in organizing their thinking and stimulating discussion with their supervisee. Whatever the supervisor's preferred style, it is still recommended that they try to achieve a balance between their own preferences and those of the supervisee.

EXPLORATION ➤ The Components of Supervision

1. Bradley (2000) lists three main components of supervision: knowledge, practice, and personal.
   a. Assign percentages to each of the three areas according to their importance to you in supervising counselors or therapists.

   b. Next, rank-order them as to their importance for a beginning supervisee.

   c. Finally, rank-order them as to importance for a more advanced supervisee.

   d. Summarize your answers in the following table.

Area	Percentages	Importance in rank order	
	Importance to you	To a beginning supervisee	To a more advanced supervisee
Knowledge	_____	_____	_____
Practice	_____	_____	_____
Personal	_____	_____	_____

2. Review your answers given above.
    a. Do you prefer to emphasize a particular area?

    b. What area do you tend to neglect or emphasize the least?

    c. How do you see this influencing your supervision?

    d. How might your supervision be different if you emphasized these neglected areas?

3. Take each component, knowledge, practice, and personal, and make a list of topic areas you would wish to include under each component.

4. Locate your personal list of required competencies from the "Exploration" section of chapter 1.

   a. Compare your list of competencies to your answer in Question 3. What do you notice?

   b. Decide under which components—knowledge, practice, or personal—you would place each competency, and complete the table below.

Competency	Knowledge	Practice	Personal
Ethics	X	X	X

   c. Now, take each competency and write out descriptors or examples of activities you would wish to use in each category. An example is given below to help guide you with this activity. Save your responses to use in chapter 6 and again in chapter 9.

Competency	Knowledge	Practice	Personal
Ethics	Knowledge of the ethical standards	Applies knowledge to client problems	Good boundaries; Professional judgment

d. What did you learn from this exercise?

3. Utilizing the metaphor of a house suggested by Haber (1996), take a separate sheet of paper and draw a house, labeling each floor per Haber's suggestions: self, work context, theoretical models, and culture. Fill in your own professional house.

EXPLORATION ➤ The Roles of the Supervisor

1. Review the discussion on supervisory roles. What do you see as the most important role or roles of a supervisor? Describe.

2. Looking back at your own experience as a supervisee . . .
   a. What particular role or roles did each of your supervisors assume? Describe and give an example.

   b. How did this meet or not meet your training needs?

   c. How might this awareness help you generate new ideas for working with your supervisee?

3. Imagine that you are a supervisor and your supervisee seems to be struggling to apply a particular theory to a current case. Can you describe how you might want to address this in supervision?

4. Now visualize a scenario in which the supervisee is having difficulty working with a client and you suspect that there are some personal issues involved. Describe how, as a consultant, you might want to approach this problem. What might you want to say or do?

EXPLORATION ➤ Selecting a Preferred Style

1. Think about your personal style and preferences as a supervisor.
   a. Can you describe in your own words how you want to "be" in a supervisory relationship?

   b. How do you imagine your supervisee might respond to your interpersonal style and preference?

   c. How might you expect your style to limit or enhance your supervisee in getting their training needs met?

2. Knowing your preferred learning style is considered important in selecting a supervision style,
   a. do you know how you learn best? Describe.

b. Choose one of the following:

➤ Do you first like to know the general overall purpose of something and to then break it down into little parts?

➤ Do you like things broken down into separate smaller parts, and then to have someone else put it together for you?

➤ Do you like to have someone show or tell you in general terms what they want, and to then figure it out on your own?

3. Imagine you are planning to go on vacation. How would you prepare for it? Describe what you would do. (For example, do you just like to go and see what happens or do you spend weeks or months planning, calling, or writing to get information, making reservations well in advance? Do you like to do all the planning yourself, use an agent and then review or alter his or her suggestions, or just use an agent's suggestions, no questions asked?)

The following questions are adapted from Middleman and Rhodes (1985, Appendices B, C, & D).

4. Which of the following statements most closely fits your preference in a supervisor?

   I prefer a supervisor who . . .

   a. Gives detailed instructions as to how the work should be done, makes most of the decisions, expects me to learn by watching how he/she does the work, emphasizes the task aspect of the work, gives very specific instructions and feedback for any changes, closely monitors my work, strictly follows rules and procedures, and has extensive personal experience as a practitioner and shares that experience (both the successes and failures). (Teacher)

   b. Emphasizes the relationship aspects of supervision, spends time exploring my personal feelings and responses to clients, shares their own personal feelings and responses to my work and to me, and emphasizes the importance of self-awareness, personal thoughts, and personal feelings in my development. (Counselor)

   c. Emphasizes the role of the organization and rules in solving problems, challenges me to integrate ideas and information from a number of different sources, evaluates my success based on mutually determined goals and objectives, encourages my independent functioning and decision-making ability, and is able to bend the rules when necessary. (Consultant)

5. Using the descriptions below of field-dependent and field-independent supervisors, which one most closely describes you?

   a. Field-dependent:
      ➤ Seeks feedback and opinions of others before making up their mind
      ➤ Enjoys working in groups even if the process is time consuming
      ➤ Enjoys working with a colleague rather than working alone
      ➤ Works best when guidelines are spelled out clearly
      ➤ Prefers to know what their supervisor thinks before proceeding
      ➤ Likes structure and predictability at work
      ➤ Likes to conform to the group and avoids conflict

   b. Field-independent:
      ➤ Enjoys working alone, rarely asking others for help
      ➤ Viewed by others as an independent thinker
      ➤ Is able to focus on work even when there are a lot of distractions
      ➤ Is more concerned with solving problems than with pleasing people
      ➤ Dislikes depending on others to complete a project or solve problems
      ➤ Is comfortable in making decisions

➤ Finds self-evaluation more important than the evaluation of others
➤ Tends to grow impatient with groups and committees
➤ Is able to express anger when impatient or stressed

6. Middleman and Rhodes also stressed the importance of whether you as a supervisor see your supervisee as internally or externally driven. Select the description below that most closely describes you.

   a. Goals for supervision should be mutually arrived at, and should include the areas of greatest concern to the supervisee. Supervisees will do best with a supervisor who inspires them and who, after teaching them the basics, lets them learn on their own. Effective supervisors are flexible, provide a work environment that facilitates the self-awareness of supervisees, and provide opportunities for processing their thoughts and feelings. (Internally driven)

   b. Goals should be based on what the supervisor believes is most important for the supervisee to know in order for them to do the work. Supervisees need direction and a structured work plan describing what is expected. They do best when having access to someone who knows what to do and who can direct them on how to solve their problems. Effective supervisors are well organized and experienced and can systematically guide the development of the supervisee. (Externally driven)

7. Review the answers to the previous three questions and think about how you see these preferences affecting your choice of style. Write a short paragraph summarizing your learning. Keep your answers available to review in the next sections on models and methods.

8. Ask one or two of your colleagues to answer these same questions. Compare your answers with theirs and then discuss together what each would prefer in a supervisor in order to learn. Use specific examples.

9. Imagine you have a supervisee who prefers a learning style opposite to yours. What might you need to do differently to effectively work with this person? Can you describe using concrete behavioral terms?

10. How do you imagine that the answers given here might affect you in other work roles beside supervisor? For example, with your clients? With your own supervisor?

➤ Conclusions

What conclusions might you draw from these exercises that may be helpful to you in working with your supervisee?

➤ Action Plan

What do you need to do as a result of these conclusions?

➤ Chapter Highlights

❏ Supervision takes place in a larger system that will affect supervisory style, roles, and relationships.

❏ The supervisor must balance the needs of the supervisee along with those of the client.

❏ Different situations and supervisees call for different roles, techniques, and interventions.

❏ A number of factors should be considered when selecting a preferred style of supervision.

❏ The effective supervisor must be flexible, innovative, creative, and open to change in their style.

Suggested Readings

Bernard, J. M. (1997). The discrimination model. In Watkins, C. E. Jr. (Ed.), *Handbook of psychotherapy supervision*. New York: Wiley.

Bernard, J. M., & Goodyear, R. K. (1998). *Fundamenals of clinical supervision*. Appendix C: Supervision instruments. Boston: Allyn and Bacon.

Borders, L.D., Bernard, J.M., Dye, H.A., Fong, M.L., Henderson, P., & Nance, D.W. (1991). Curriculum guide for training counseling supervisors: Rationale, development, and implementation. *Counselor Education and Supervision*, 31, 61–78.

Bradley, L. (2000). *Counselor supervision*. Philadelphia: Accelerated Development. Chapter 1: Roles of the supervisor & activities of counselor supervision; & Chapter 9: Advocacy in counseling supervision.

Haber, R. (1996). Dimensions of psychotherapy supervision. New York: Norton. Chapters 1, 2, & 3.

Holloway, E. (1995). *Clinical supervision: A systems approach*. Thousand Oaks, CA: Sage. Chapter 2: Tasks and functions of supervision.

Keirsey, D., & Bates, M. (1984). *Please understand me* (5th ed.). Del Mar, CA: Prometheus Nemesis Books.

Myers, I. B. (1993). *Introduction to type: A guide to understanding your results on the Meyers-Briggs Type Indicator* (3rd ed.). Palo Alto, CA: Consulting Psychologists Press.

Middleman, R. R., & Rhodes, G. B. (1985). *Competent supervision: Making imaginative judgments*. New Jersey: Prentice Hall. Chapter 4 & Appendices A, B, C, & D.

Powell, D. J. (1993). *Clinical supervision in alcohol and drug abuse counseling: Principles, models, methods*. New York: Lexington Books. Part I; Chapter 2: A working definition of supervision.

Usher, C., & Borders, L.D. (1993). Practicing counselor's preferences for supervisory style and supervisory emphasis. *Counselor Education and Supervision*, 33, 66–79.

WHAT ARE THE MODELS OF SUPERVISION?

3

There are two main categories of supervision models available to the supervisor: psychotherapy-based supervision models and supervision-specific models. Psychotherapy-based models of supervision use the assumptions, methods, and techniques of a particular theory to train the supervisee; some examples of such theories include behavioral, cognitive-behavioral, psychodynamic, systemic, solution focused, and brief therapy. The second category of models are developed specifically for supervision and training, and include developmental models, parallel process or isomorphism model, interpersonal process recall (IPR), and interactional supervision. Since the main point of this workbook is that the assumptions, goals, and practices of supervision are different from those of therapy, and supervisors, in order to be most effective, must move beyond their training in specific psychotherapies to incorporate training in models specific to supervision, it makes sense to focus one's attention on models specific to supervision. Therefore, while this chapter includes a brief summary of a few psychotherapy-based models and their potential application to supervision, supervisors should take time to read more extensively about models specific to supervision. (See the suggested reading list at the end of this chapter.)

How to Select a Model of Supervision

Before beginning to supervise, it is important for supervisors to start with their own models of counseling or psychotherapy, to identify their beliefs about change, and to "conceptualize and articulate a workable therapeutic approach" (Liddle, 1988, p. 167). To do so, a supervisor must be able to answer a number of important questions. For example, what are one's beliefs about the change process? How do people change? What factors are important to be successful with different populations? Are there some universals that apply or does each person and problem differ? Another task required to build a model of change is to identify some key variables that represent a focus for clinical work. Powell (1993) termed this the descriptive dimension, meaning how one's beliefs about change are manifested in practice. For example, one key variable could be time frame (here and now vs. there and then). Another is whether one is focused on changing the person or on solving problems, and whether the emphasis is on processing feelings or exploring thoughts and behaviors. A third variable might be the importance of insight versus action. A number of questions are included in an "Exploration" section of this chapter to help beginning supervisors identify personal beliefs and important variables significant in the change process.

Psychotherapy-Based Models of Supervision

It would be beyond the scope of the workbook to attempt to describe all the available models of counseling and psychotherapy, so only a few were selected to highlight their application in supervision. Supervisors would naturally want to review their own favorite counseling and psychotherapy-theoretical models and explore ways and means to apply concepts and techniques from these models in supervision.

Behavioral Models

There are many applications of behavioral therapy to supervision, particularly in defining goals and establishing evaluation criteria. Bradley (1989, p. 128) listed the components of behavioral supervision as follows:

> ➤ The need to establish a relationship with the supervisee,
> ➤ The ability to analyze skills and assess learning,
> ➤ The need to set goals in supervision,
> ➤ The construction and implementation of strategies to accomplish these set goals,
> ➤ The use of a final evaluation to gauge success.

In behavioral models, the supervisor takes on the role of teacher, helping the supervisee to create goals for learning and to design methods to assess their own performance. Behavioral theory explains that to be successful, all training goals and objectives must be described or operationalized in terms of observable performance and should be within the reach of the supervisee. The employment of checklists, written contracts, and written evaluation techniques are all significant aspects of behavioral therapy with application in supervision.

Perhaps one of the best examples of the application of behavioral concepts in training and supervision is that of microcounseling and microtraining, developed by Allen Ivey in the early 1970s. Microtraining provides a systematic framework for teaching individual counseling skills, such as paraphrasing, reflection of feelings, attending, confrontation, open-ended questions, and how to organize a counseling interview. The microtraining approach is considered one of the most thoroughly researched and systematic programs for training counselors in interviewing skills (Ivey, 1999; Daniels, Rigazio-DiGilio, & Ivey, 1997). Ivey's book, *Intentional Interviewing and Counseling* (1999), is an excellent resource of information on skills training for beginning supervisees.

Bandura's (1986) social-cognitive theory, which incorporates a combination of behavioral and cognitive concepts including reinforcement, rehearsal, practice, vicarious learning, and modeling, could be very productive in the supervision experience. For example, the supervisor could model for the supervisee a method for handling a particularly difficult client or situation, and then request that the supervisee role play the same situation applying the suggested intervention.

Key Concepts Helpful to the Supervisor

> ➢ Use behavioral descriptors to objectify goals and define success.
> ➢ Familiarize oneself with self-management methods (checklists, relaxation techniques, etc.).
> ➢ Apply social learning principles such as modeling, role reversal, role playing, and practice.

Cognitive Models

Rational emotive therapy (RET), a cognitive approach, also has many noteworthy applications to supervision (Wessler & Ellis, 1983; Woods & Ellis, 1997). With RET, the relationship between the thinking, feeling, and doing parts of the supervisee can be examined simultaneously. It is assumed that the trainee's thoughts about themselves and their expectations will affect the meaning they give to each client's actions. These attributions can create problems of *irrational thinking* in the supervisee. Goals such as the need to be perfect, the need to be liked by everyone, the need to appear competent in all areas, the need to be in control at all times, and the need to avoid conflict, all contribute to irrational thinking on the part of the supervisee. This, in turn, affects the supervisory relationship (Wessler & Ellis, 1983). The goal of RET supervision is to educate the supervisee about irrational thinking patterns so that they can then employ this information with clients. In this model, the supervisor would serve primarily as a teacher, using techniques like demonstration, modeling of techniques, and assigned reading to educate the supervisee. When reviewing tapes and cases, supervisors would apply their own consultant skills to assist the supervisee in uncovering any irrational thinking patterns that might undermine their success with clients in the future (Wessler & Ellis, 1983).

David Burns (1999), a cognitive therapist who popularized the work of Aaron Beck, identified several categories of cognitive distortions that may also filter the supervisee's perception: (a) all-or-nothing thinking: seeing things in black and white; (b) magnification or minimization: blowing things out of proportion or discounting their importance; (c) overgeneralization, seeing one event as a neverending pattern of defeat, such as "I always do that"; (d) mental filtering: dwelling on negatives (part of perfectionistic thinking), (e) jumping to conclusions: making consistent assumptions about what people are thinking or what is going to happen, and (f) labeling: giving yourself a negative label, such as "I really am stupid or a failure."

As a supervisor, it may be helpful to identify the use of generalizing types of words such as *always, never,* or *everyone,* typically used by supervisees when they speak about their work. The use of such words may indicate the presence of perfectionistic thinking and negative self-talk. The supervisor could apply cognitive restructuring techniques, requesting that the supervisee substitute more realistic, less distorted thinking as they discuss their work with clients.

Key Concepts Helpful to the Supervisor

➤ Become aware of distorted or negative thinking on the part of the supervisee that contributes to negative feelings and behavior.
➤ Identify self-defeating patterns that affect client care as well as the supervisee's growth.
➤ Become familiar with cognitive and cognitive-behavioral concepts and techniques to work with depression and anxiety, two problems most common to clinical practice.

Psychodynamic Models

The psychodynamic approach to supervision examines the dynamics of the therapeutic relationship and how the supervisee's own experiences and feelings may block client insight and growth (Dewald, 1997;

Ekstein & Wallerstein, 1972). In this model, the supervisor acts more as a therapist, believing that the best way for supervisees to learn techniques is to undergo personal therapeutic work with their supervisor. Concepts such as transference and countertransference, resistance, and intrapsychic conflict are all explored in psychodynamic supervision.

Transference refers to the unconscious attempt on the part of the supervisee to recreate with the supervisor the relationship they had with their mother or father and thus to act this relationship out in supervision. It is described as an emotional response towards the supervisor by the supervisee which reflects past experience and which may not be appropriate to the present situation. With countertransference, just as supervisees may transfer feelings from their childhood experiences to the supervisor, the supervisor can also transfer unresolved issues with family members onto the supervisee. Some common countertransference responses experienced by supervisors include the need to be needed, the need to be liked, and the need to be powerful. Resistance in psychodynamic terms is thought to represent an underlying intrapsychic conflict within the supervisee that must be uncovered and resolved. In the supervision experience, resistance may take the form of the trainee's rejection of the supervisor's suggestions or interpretations of client dynamics. Resistance, transference, and countertransference form the basis of all work in psychodynamic supervision.

Key Concepts Helpful to the Supervisor

➤ Understand the role of personal issues in the supervisory relationship.
➤ Encourage insight, self-exploration, and continual reality testing.
➤ Understand the presence of intrapsychic issues such as resistance, transference, and countertransference.

Adlerian Model

In his model of psychotherapy, Alfred Adler combined psychodynamic principles along with specific action techniques (Mosak, 1995). He saw the problems of adult patients to be the result of personal fictions or faulty perceptions that stemmed from childhood experiences. Since patients were seen as discouraged by these fictions, and therefore not "sick," it was important at some point in therapy to stop the analysis and move from insight to action in order to encourage the patient to try out new thoughts and behaviors to solve their problems (Sweeney, 1998). Thus, as an Adlerian, the supervisor takes on a consultant role, helping supervisees to explore faulty thinking and offering support for trying new behaviors.

There are a number of Adlerian techniques that apply to supervision, particularly those designed to encourage action. One such technique is to *act as if*. For example, supervisees could be asked to act as if they were experts with their clients. The idea is that if they feel differently, they will behave differently with their clients. A second Adlerian technique is the Lifestyle Inventory, an assessment tool that includes a series of structured questions on family background and experiences, especially sibling relationships (Sweeney, 1998). A discussion of the application of this instrument to supervision is given in chapter 10, on personal development. Other examples of Adlerian action techniques that could be used in supervision are catching one's self, the push-button technique, and creating visual images.

Key Concepts Helpful to the Supervisor

- ➤ View the supervisee as discouraged and needing encouragement to take risks.
- ➤ Explore personal fictions that may hinder the supervisee's professional growth and development.
- ➤ Encourage the supervisee to act differently, to take risks.
- ➤ Assess family background and influences with the Lifestyle Inventory.

Existential Psychotherapy Model

Existential psychotherapy is considered more of an orientation or approach to therapy, rather than a school or method. Existentialism is concerned with understanding the nature of human beings and the four ultimate concerns of human existence: the inevitability of death, the freedom to make our lives what we will, the isolation and aloneness of living, and the seeming meaninglessness or lack of obvious purpose to life (Yalom, 1980). Here, the goal of therapy is to help clients face the anxiety that emerges from a conscious or unconscious attempt to cope with these concerns (Yalom, 1989). To the existential psychotherapist, anxiety is at the core of all problems and is considered a normal and natural part of living and being human.

One area where existential theory can be particularly beneficial to the supervisor is in working with crisis, trauma, death, and dying. Existential therapy provides the supervisor with the means to address larger issues in the context of supervision, such as the meaning of life, death, and suffering, the role of purpose and meaning in life; their role in mental health and life satisfaction; and the feelings generated by these issues. Existential therapy also supports facilitating the supervisee's questioning of his or her own professional identity and role in the helping profession. For example, post-degree supervisees, as they work toward licensure, may have many questions about whether this is the right career choice, whether they can be effective, and whether counseling or psychotherapy really helps people at all. In such cases of professional self-reflection, the existential approach can provide a structure within which this type of questioning can be most productive.

Key Concepts Helpful to the Supervisor

- ➢ Understand that the awareness of death gives meaning to life but also creates anxiety.
- ➢ Understand anxiety as a normal part of the human condition.
- ➢ Address core topics in supervision such as the meaning and purpose of life and death.

Family Therapy Models

Family therapy can be seen either as a model of psychotherapy or as a separate discipline. Training in the field of family therapy relies heavily on supervision as the means to teach both theoretical knowledge and skills. The complexity of working systemically with families has propelled the development of new supervision methods and techniques, including the use of video, live supervision behind the mirror, and bug-in-the-ear (Liddle et al., 1988). Family therapy has consistently been on the forefront of critical thinking about training, and in particular the training of supervisors (Anderson, Rigazio-Digio, & Kunkler, 1995). In fact, the American Association of Marriage and Family Therapy has had a separate credential for supervisors since 1987. Family therapy supervision can be more complicated than individual supervision because the focus is on a family rather than on a single client. In family systems theory, the problems of one member in the system are seen as affecting others in that system. Thus, a change in one member of a family can lead to changes in other family members and thereby in the family as a whole. Supervisors, by thinking systemically, can broaden their understanding of client problems. Systems theory can also help to set goals for supervision or the planning and development of programs and services (Bradley, 2000; Holloway, 1995). Topics for supervision might include how to manage the anxiety generated by live supervision, how to use a systems approach to explore family dynamics, how to address several members of a family at one time, and how to work as a cotherapist or part of a team.

There are a number of family systems models, including strategic, structural, constructivist, narrative, and transgenerational. Each model has its own specific techniques. Some techniques that can be helpful in supervision are genograms, circular questions, paradoxical interventions, triangulation, reframing, boundary setting, and homework. Usually, the techniques and principles of any one particular model are taught via live supervision by teams of supervisors behind one-way mirrors, using phones, or a bug-in-the-ear (a microphone placed in the trainee's ear). Freestanding family therapy training centers now exist that offer excellent continuing educational training to mental health professionals, and supervisors are encouraged to take advantage of such training.

Key Concepts Helpful to the Supervisor

➤ Understand that change to one person in the system brings change in others.
➤ Work with a whole system, not just an individual.
➤ Use live supervision techniques whenever possible, especially with beginners.

Brief Therapy and Solution-Focused Models

Brief therapy, or short-term therapy, combines theoretical assumptions from a number of therapeutic models, such as client centered, behavioral, cognitive, psychodynamic, systems, and human development. Brief therapy is best described as a state of mind or attitude on the part of the practitioner concerning therapy and the change process (Budman & Gurman, 1988; Strupp & Binder, 1984). For instance, the emphasis is on strengths, resources, developmental factors, the nonobservable aspects of change (the role of the outside environment), the importance of the therapeutic relationship as a vehicle for change, the importance of setting realistic goals and keeping a problem focus, and the use of activities, such as homework assignments (Budman & Gurman, 1988; Ecker & Hulley, 1996; Strupp & Binder, 1984). Therapy begins with the first contact; there is no lengthy assessment and history taking, and interactions between therapist and client become part of the therapeutic experience.

Solution-focused therapy, a form of brief therapy, can be extremely helpful when applied to supervision for two reasons: It helps to empower the supervisee and it allows both the supervisor and supervisee to benefit from working collegially. One major assumption of solution-focused therapy is that the supervisee has the resources and strengths to solve their own problems (Juhnke, 1996; Thomas, 1992). To empower the supervisee, the supervisor assists in creating what are called successful scenarios. Attention is directed towards what the supervisee did *well* with clients, his or her successes, and contributing strengths and talents. In this model, the supervisor moves out of the expert role into a more consultative and cooperative role, showing respect for the resources of the supervisee, to encourage, compliment, and validate. Another helpful concept of solution-focused therapy is the focus on action, believing that understanding the roots and causes of problems (i.e., insight) is not necessary to solve them. Any change, no matter how small, is better than no change (DeShazer, 1985). Thus the motto of solution-focused therapy is *move your feet* or do something different (O'Hanlon & Weiner-Davis, 1989). The idea of stressing small change can be reassuring and encouraging to supervisees. There are a number of solution-focused techniques with direct application in supervision. These will be discussed in more detail in chapter 6.

Key Concepts Helpful to the Supervisor

➤ Supervisees have the resources to solve their own problems.
➤ One does not necessarily have to know the roots and causes of problems to solve them.
➤ There is no such thing as resistance, only a difference in goals or viewpoint.
➤ Any action, no matter how small, is better than no action.

EXPLORATION ➢ Building Your Own Model of Change

1. To organize your thinking, make the following lists. Do not try to organize these lists. Just free-associate and brainstorm for a while before writing things down. Then, review each list to see which items stand out.

   a. List books, authors, teachers, and other professionals (perhaps your own therapist or a colleague) who are important to you. To assist in this project, go to your bookshelf; what books do you have in your office? Whose writing has been influential?

   b. What former teachers or supervisors do you often think of or whose ideas you still use in your work with clients?

   c. Off the top of your head, make a list of CEU workshops or conferences you have attended. If you have been in practice for a long time, simply focus on those that you easily recall or have attended in recent years.

2. Now, answer the following questions:
   a. Whose ideas would you say have been most provocative and shaped most strongly how you work now with your clients?

   b. What ideas or intervention strategies from attending workshops or conferences do you still use?

   c. Which writers or theorists have you actually seen work with clients, either in workshops or on videotape?

3. To stimulate your thinking on what factors are most important in your philosophy of change, a sample list of possible variables is included here. Place an X on each of the continuums below to indicate where you belong.

Insight/awareness—————————————————————————Action
There-and-then (the past)—————————————————Here-and-now (the present)
Focus on personality—————————————————————Focus on problem
Changing the person——————————————————Solving specific problems
Heredity (biological)——————————————————Environmental factors

Feelings————————————Behaviors————————————Thoughts
Importance of feelings——————————————Importance of thoughts
Emotional catharsis————————————————Cognitive restructuring
Therapist centered——————————————————Client centered
Therapist is the expert————————————————Client is the expert
Individual————————————————————————Systems
Universals——————————————————————Situation specific
Relationship important————————————————Techniques important
Medical model——————————————————Phenomenological model

List other differences:

4. What do you notice from this exercise? What does it say about your model of change?

    a. How might this affect your model of supervision? Describe.

    b. How might it affect your choice of intervention strategies? Give an example.

5. One old argument in psychotherapy involves whether you first change attitude and then behavior or whether you first change behavior and then attitude. Which way do you lean on this argument?

6. One generic description of the change process is the following: Awareness + understanding + action = change.
   a. Do you agree with this formula?

   b. Is there a part of this statement to which you give more weight?

   c. Is there a part you would leave out entirely?

7. Most practitioners today describe themselves as eclectic, meaning they borrow concepts and techniques from a number of theoretical models.
   a. Do you describe yourself as eclectic?

   b. What does that term mean to you?

c. Even though technically eclectic, most practitioners ground their work in one or two theoretical models. For example, one of the most popular blends today is psychodynamic theory with cognitive behavioral techniques. Are there one or two primary models that guide your choice of approach to clients and their problems? Describe, giving two examples.

8. Review your answers to all the questions given in this exploration section. How you would describe your theoretical roots and dominant mode of practice at this time? Write out a short paragraph or two summarizing your thoughts and ideas. Retain this summary to use as you build your own model of supervision.

EXPLORATION ➤ Psychotherapy-Based Models of Supervision

1. There are many levels of knowledge concerning theories of counseling and psychotherapy. There are theories you have never heard of at all. There are theories you heard about in lectures or textbooks. There are theories that you have studied and in which you have received training. Some theories have been integrated into your own model of psychotherapy, and one or two are the primary models under which you now practice. Using these very broad categories, rate your knowledge of the following theories and models of psychotherapy.

Model	Not at all familiar with the model	Somewhat familiar with the model	Familiar with the model	Know a lot about the model	Consistently use the model
Behavioral					
Cognitive					
Cognitive-behavioral					
Psychodynamic					
Adlerian					
Existential					
Family therapy					
Brief therapy					
Solution-focused					

Rate yourself on these additional models as well.

Model	Not at all familiar with the model	Somewhat familiar with the model	Familiar with the model	Know a lot about the model	Consistently use the model
Jungian					
Reality therapy					
Gestalt					
Multimodal					
Client centered					
Transtheoretical					
Experiential					
Eclectic					

2. Now, rate yourself on your familiarity with the skills and techniques of each of these theoretical models.

Skiils and techniques of these models	Not at all familiar with these skills and techniques	Somewhat familiar with these skills and techniques	Familiar with these skills and techniques	Know a lot about these skills and techniques	Consistently use these skills and techniques
Behavioral					
Cognitive					
Cognitive-behavioral					
Psychodynamic					
Adlerian					
Existential					
Family therapy					
Brief therapy					
Solution-focused					

Rate yourself on these additional models as well.

Skills and techniques of these models	Not at all familiar with these skills and techniques	Somewhat familiar with these skills and techniques	Familiar with these skills and techniques	Know a lot about these skills and techniques	Consistently use these skills and techniques
Jungian					
Reality therapy					
Gestalt					
Multimodal					
Client centered					
Transtheoretical					
Experiential					
Eclectic					

3. Review your answers.
   a. What do you notice about your knowledge of the theories of counseling and psychotherapy and the practical application of skills and techniques?

b. Do you have one or two specific models you use in your own practice?

c. Are there any models you might want to explore in more depth? Describe.

What Are the Models Specific to Supervision?

Four models have been conceptualized specifically for supervision: IPR, parallel process or isomorphism, interactional supervision, and developmental. Of the four, developmental models are the dominant ones appearing in the supervision literature, and even though research on their application to post-degree supervision is sparse, they will receive the most attention here. Parallel process and IPR, while referred to here as models of supervision, can concurrently be considered techniques for supervision to be applied regardless of theoretical orientation. Interactional supervision is important to review as it focuses on the interaction between the supervisee, supervisor, and the environment, and the distinction between clinical and administrative supervision.

IPR

Interpersonal process recall, or IPR, combines psychodynamic, behavioral, and phenomenological concepts to train beginning counselors (Kagan, 1980a; Kagan & Kagan, 1997). The goal of IPR is to increase the trainee's self-awareness and understanding of client dynamics. There are a number of innovative applications of IPR to post-degree supervision; for example, IPR methods can be employed to process the events of a supervision session or to process client tapes. With IPR, the supervisor serves in the role of a consultant, asking a series of inductive questions to focus the supervisee's attention on his or her own feelings, thoughts, and behaviors as they work with their clients. Kagan (1980a) chose the term "inquirer" to describe this consultant role. Because IPR questions are designed to encourage self-exploration, they are less likely to be interpreted as threatening to supervisees. For example, "What were you feeling right then when the client did . . . ?" A number of examples of IPR questions and their application to reviewing audiotapes and videotapes are included in chapter 4. For additional information and materials on IPR, please contact Microtraining Associates, Inc., PO Box 9641, North Amherst, MA 01059-9641.

Key Concepts Helpful to the Supervisor

➢ Recognize the importance of processing relationship dynamics in supervision.
➢ Consider the importance of the underlying thoughts and feelings of the supervisee in responding to the verbal and nonverbal behavior of clients.
➢ Use the role of inquirer to reduce supervisee's anxiety about processing his or her work with clients.

Parallel Process Model or Isomorphism

Most supervisors, regardless of their theoretical orientation, support the existence of a parallel process phenomenon in supervision (Raichelson, Herron, Primavera, & Ramirez, 1997). The term *parallel process* was created to describe a relationship dynamic found specifically in supervision. It defines the action in which supervisees will unconsciously reflect feelings experienced in client sessions during supervision (Doehrman, 1976). For example, if a supervisee feels overwhelmed by the helplessness or dependency of a client, they will present themselves as helpless and stuck in supervision. Typical parallel process patterns concern issues of helplessness, dependency, control, and anger, and are similar in nature to the concepts of transference and countertransference. Working with parallel process issues, the supervisor takes on the role of both teacher and counselor, bringing relationship issues to the foreground, and stimulating the supervisee's awareness. In the above situation, to facilitate understanding of parallel process issues, the supervisor would say: "What are you experiencing now as you talk to me about this client? What are your feelings? How is this similar to what you experience as you work with this client?" To be successful, the supervisor must demonstrate effective communication skills, like giving and receiving feedback, active listening, and self-disclosure (Delucia, Bowman, & Bowman, 1989). Parallel process theory also reminds the supervisor of the need to look closely at his or her own personal responses to both the supervisee and their respective clients. Exploring parallel process can be easily integrated into a variety of supervisory methods such as live observation, group supervision, or review of videotapes. Any number of techniques, such as role playing, journaling, and the empty chair, can be used to stimulate awareness and to facilitate parallel processing.

Marriage and family therapists use the term *isomorphism* to describe a phenomenon similar to parallel process (Liddle, Becker, & Diamond, 1997; Liddle et al., 1988). Isomorphism means to have similar or identical structure or form (Webster's New College Dictionary, 1999). However, with isomorphism, comparisons and similarities would be drawn between systems and structures, not between individual dynamics, as in parallel process. For example, the supervisor would question similarities between the client system and that of the supervisee using such terms as *triangulation, enmeshment,* or *client resistance.* Both isomorphism and parallel process provide the supervisor with a rationale and the means to process relationship issues throughout supervision.

➤ Recognize the importance of relationship dynamics among supervisor, supervisee, and client.
➤ Use parallel process to analyze difficulties with supervisees.
➤ Understand that the parallel process model has broad application in supervision.

Interactional Supervision

Interactional supervision was developed in the field of social work (Shulman, 1993). The central concept of this model, borrowed from systems theory, is that the supervisee's interaction with various systems, such as the agency setting and the population served, will influence the supervisor's own role and function. There are three basic assumptions underlying these interactions: (a) there are a number of common relationship dynamics and core skills central to supervision; (b) these relationship dynamics and skills are universal to whatever type of supervisory interaction; and (c) these relationship dynamics and skills are parallel to those found in any other helping relationship (Shulman, 1993). Interactional supervision identifies the relationship skills necessary for productive clinical supervision, including empathetic understanding, acknowledgement of feelings, confrontational techniques, and how to combine administrative and clinical functions. Because of its efficacy of bringing to the foreground, the interaction between supervisor, supervisee, agency setting and populations served, interactional supervision is highly recommended for clinical supervisors who are also administrators in agencies, hospitals and schools.

Key Concepts Helpful to the Supervisor

➤ Note the role environmental context plays in supervision.
➤ Understand similarities and differences between administrative and clinical functions.
➤ Emphasize the importance of relationship skills in supervision.

Developmental Models of Supervision

Developmental models are perhaps the most widely used and researched models in supervision. Even though at this time there is little empirical research to demonstrate support for these models, they make intuitive sense and can provide a framework to organize thinking about the supervisory process (Neufeldt, Beutler, & Banchero, 1997; Stoltenberg,

McNeill, & Crethar, 1994). In developmental models of supervision, the supervisee is seen to grow and change over time as a result of the supervisory process. "Since supervision is essentially a developmental process, it follows that developmental theory could offer an appropriate foundation for our needs" (Loganbill et al., 1982, p. 20). There are a number of developmental models now available; while they may differ in the terms used to describe supervisory growth, all developmental models use concepts analogous to those of human development. At each stage or level, supervisees are viewed as expanding their knowledge, competence, and repertoire of skills as they grow professionally. Thus, mature supervisees possess very different qualities and characteristics than when they began supervision. Dependent, childlike, unaware, impulsive, and egocentric are all descriptors used to characterize the beginning or entry-level supervisee. The supervisee then progresses from this childlike, dependent state to a more adolescent level, which is characterized by a desire for autonomy and challenge to authority. Just as in adolescence, the supervisee at this level of development will experience confusion and conflict, seek independence, reject suggestions, and ignore direction from the supervisor. The last stage is adulthood, where the supervisee is viewed as more self-aware, self-confident, and ready for independent practice. Hawkins & Shohet (1989) use the term *master craftsperson* to describe this last stage.

One popular developmental model that could be used by post-degree supervisors is the Integrated Developmental Model (IDM) (Stoltenberg, McNeil, and Delworth, 1998). IDM described the needs of the supervisee at each level of development, the role of the supervisor during that developmental level, and the competencies required by both. Level-one supervisees (beginning their master's-level training) are viewed as dependent and in need of structure. At this level, the supervisor serves in the role of teacher. Level-2 supervisees (master's-level interns) are recognized as experiencing conflict between their dependency and their desire for autonomy. At this point in development, the supervisor needs to act more as a coach. Inexperienced supervisors will often find level-two supervisees more of a challenge. Level-3 supervisees (post-master's degree and doctoral level supervisees) are described as much more stable in their professional development. At this level, supervisees are much more desirous of mutual sharing, challenge, and confrontation on the part of the supervisor. The supervisor serves more in a consultant role, with most of the structure provided by the supervisee. Level 4 refers to the master counselor, and supervision, if it occurs at all at this level, is mostly collegial in nature.

Within each stage of development, a number of content areas have been identified, including assessment techniques, ethics, client conceptualization, and professional identity (Loganbill et al., 1982;

Stoltenberg, McNeil, and Delworth, 1998). The supervisee may reach different levels of competency in each content area depending on a variety of factors, such as age, gender, previous training, previous experiences in supervision, and previous work experience (Powell, 1993). Bernard and Goodyear (1998) suggested that, in order to assess developmental level, the supervisor use a combination of direct and indirect methods, such as observation, as well as collection of information on background and experience. This information could then be used to form a tentative hypothesis as to the supervisee's developmental level and competencies. However, as a cautionary note, the supervisor must be vigilant regarding the role of multicultural issues in this evaluation of the supervisee's competence and his or her stage of development.

As with any stage models, it is often difficult to correctly assess developmental level. Because almost all research on supervision takes place in academic settings, descriptors of beginning supervisees and their needs are more readily available than those of the intermediate and advanced supervisee. In fact, a study by Chagnon and Russell (1995) found it easier to describe characteristics of the beginning or more advanced supervisee than those of the intermediate stage. Differences in training programs, their purpose, length, and quality of training, can add to this difficulty. Post-masters degree supervisees who have completed a 45- to 60-hour master's program, should undertake their post-degree supervision for licensure having completed at least the beginning, or Level-1, phase of development; most will have had a minimum of two semesters of practicum or internship experience, with some having two years. Thus, they have reached the intermediate, or Level-2, phase of development, ready after a short time, if not immediately, for more autonomy and independence and less structure-building from the supervisor. This would certainly be true of supervisees in predoctoral internships who probably have had even more training experience. Other supervisees, particularly those working in drug and alcohol counseling, may be expected to learn a majority of their practice skills while working in the field (Powell, 1993). Hence, they will be closer to the beginning, or Level-1, phase of supervision.

Movement through these developmental stages is not an automatic or smooth progression. It is accepted that development is dependent on the supervisee's experience in supervision and their ability to learn and grow from these experiences. Hogan (1964) described supervision as a dynamic process in which the supervisee moves back and forth between stages, especially when changing settings or supervisors, developing new skills, or facing a particularly difficult client. It is assumed that the supervisory relationship will have different qualities at different stages of development, so supervisors must be flexible and open to a variety of methods and techniques; they must understand and accept that what works with one supervisee may not work with another.

Key Concepts Helpful to the Supervisor

➢ Understand the presence of developmental factors in supervision.
➢ Use developmental models to plan for supervision.
➢ Recognize difficulties in the placement of post-degree supervisees in developmental stages.

Does the Supervisor Develop Also?

Supervisors, as well as supervisees, experience developmental stages. Watkins (1993) identified four primary issues that many supervisors face as they progress through their stages of development:

1. competency versus incompetence (concern about their performance or role);
2. autonomy versus dependency (struggle with need for independence);
3. identity versus identity diffusion (clarity or confusion about their role);
4. self-awareness versus unawareness (awareness of issues unique to supervision).

In general, beginning supervisors, like supervisees, may experience anxiety about their role. At this stage, beginning supervisors will often be more focused on meeting their own needs rather than those of the supervisee. For example, the supervisor may focus on playing the role of the expert, working directly with the supervisee's clients (Hess, 1986). The supervisor with no specific training in supervision may simply fall back on the supervision methods their own supervisor used. As they gain experience, the supervisor will begin to lose their anxiety about role, will find it easier to focus on the learning needs of the supervisee, and will be better able to use different intervention strategies and techniques on their behalf (Hess, 1986). The final stage of supervisor development will be characterized by feelings of confidence. At this stage, the supervisor respects cultural and personal differences, understands the role of the supervisor, and applies a variety of methods and techniques (Haber, 1996). In other words, the advanced supervisor is more easily able to share control with the supervisee, especially in setting goals and evaluation. They are less concerned about the supervisory relationship and are able to

		Supervisee		
		Beginning supervisee	Intermediate-level supervisee	Advanced-level supervisee
Supervisor	Advanced supervisor Confirmation of identity and role			
	Intermediate-level supervisor Exploration			
	Beginning supervisor Expert Structured			
	Supervisor role	Teacher/monitor	Evaluator/challenger	Colleague/consultant
		Dependent	Conflictual	Autonomous
		Goals set by supervisor	Mutual goal setting	Goals set by supervisee

FIGURE 3.1. Developmental Models: Supervisor/Supervisee Levels and Relationships

focus on the supervisee's agenda rather than on their own. Hess (1986) refers to this stage as the *confirmation of supervisor identity* stage.

In summary, one can assume that the developmental level of the supervisor will interact with that of the supervisee and affect the quality of the relationship and selection of methods and techniques. Thus, it is important for both the supervisor and the supervisee to assess their own developmental level before beginning the supervision process. For post-degree supervisors, peer supervision or consultation could be used as a means to assess developmental level. Figure 3.1 is provided to facilitate this process.

Key Concepts Helpful to the Supervisor

➤ Understand that supervision is a transformational process where both the supervisor and the supervisee grow and change personally and professionally.
➤ Recognize that supervisors as well as supervisees go through developmental stages.
➤ Acknowledge that both the supervisor and the supervisee require supervision in order to grow.

EXPLORATION ➤ Supervision-Specific Models

Model	Not at all familiar with the model	Somewhat familiar with the model	Familiar with the model	Know a lot about the model	Consistently use the model
IPR					
Parallel process/ Isomorphism					
Interactional supervision					
Developmental					

1. Did any of your supervisors use one of these models in supervision? If so, describe how it was used and the impact on your supervision experience, growth, and development.

EXPLORATION ➤ Developmental Models of Supervision

1. Developmental models are thought to make intuitive sense and provide supervisors with a useful way to approach supervision. Think back to your own experience as a supervisee and apply one of the developmental models such as Stoltenberg, McNeill, and Delworth's IDM model.

   a. Which stage of development do you think you reached by the end of your master's program?

   b. Would you say you "developed"? Can you describe in what ways? Give examples.

   c. If you engaged in supervision for licensure or credentialing purposes, what stage of development were you in when you began this post-degree supervision?

d. What stage of development were you in when you completed your post-degree supervision? Describe what occurred during supervision that helped you move to this final stage of supervisory development.

e. Review your list of essential areas of competency identified in the exploration section of chapter 1. Take this list and rate yourself on your competency level in each area at the beginning of your post-degree supervision experience and at the end.

2. Using Watkins' model of supervisory development,
    a. at what stage of supervising development do you place yourself? Mark the continuum with an X.

Beginning————————————————Intermediate————————————————Advanced

    b. how would you describe your skills and experience as a supervisor at this time?

c. Now think about your supervisee or potential supervisee. Where would you place him or her on the continuum? What factors would you use to describe this placement?

Beginning————————————————Intermediate————————————————Advanced

d. How do you see the answers to these two questions affecting your role and style as a supervisor?

➤ Conclusions

What conclusions might you draw from these exercises that may be helpful to you in working with your supervisee?

➤ Action Plan

What do you need to do as a result of these conclusions?

➤ Chapter Highlights

❏ Supervisors must understand their own model of change and they must be able to articulate it and demonstrate it to others.

❏ A supervisor's model of change helps focus the time and energy of both the supervisor and supervisee and guides the type of information important to collect and the strategies employed.

❏ Supervision-specific models recognize that the supervisory relationship has distinctly different natural purposes and goals from psychotherapy.

❏ To be effective, supervisors must become familiar with training models specific to supervision.

❏ Supervisors, just as supervisees, go through developmental stages.

❏ The developmental stage of the supervisor and supervisee interact and affect the quality of the supervisory relationship and the selection of methods and techniques.

Suggested Readings

Baldwin, M. (1983). *Satir: Step by Step*. Palo Alto, CA: Science and Behavior Books.

Bernard, J., & Goodyear, R. (1998). *Fundamentals of clinical supervision*. Boston: Allyn and Bacon. Chapter 2: Psychotherapy-theory based models & Development approaches to supervision (especially note parallel process or isomorphism as the focus of supervision, pp. 63–66); & Chapter 11: Supervisor development and training.

Bradley, L. (2000). *Counselor supervision*. Philadelphia: Accelerated Development. Part II: Models of supervision.

Budman, S. H., & Gurman, A. S. (1988). *Theory and practice of brief therapy*. New York: Guilford.

Burns, D. D. (1999). *Feeling good: The new mood therapy*. New York: Avon Books.

Carlson, J., Sperry, L., & Lewis, J. (1997). *Family therapy: Ensuring treatment efficacy*. Pacific Grove, CA: Brooks/Cole.

Corsini, R. J., & Wedding, D. (Eds.) (1995). *Current psychotherapies*. Itasca, IL: F. E. Peacock.

Goldenberg, H., & Goldenberg, I. (1994). *Counseling today's families*. Pacific Grove, CA: Brooks/Cole.

Hanna, S. M., & Brown, J. (1995). *The practice of family therapy: Key elements across models*. Pacific Grove, CA: Brooks/Cole.

Kaslow, F. W. (1986). *Supervision and training: Models, dilemmas, and challenges*. New York: Haworth Press.

Liddle, H. A., Breunlin, D. C., & Schwartz, R. C. (1988). *Handbook of family therapy training & supervision*. New York: Guilford. Section 2: Family therapy models: Approaches to training.

O'Hanlon, W. H., & Weiner-Davis, M. (1989). In search of solutions: A new direction in psychotherapy. New York: Norton.

Powell, D. J. (1993). *Clinical supervision in alcohol and drug abuse counseling: Principles, models, methods.* New York: Lexington Books. Part II: Models; & Chapter 6: A developmental approach to supervision.

Quick, E. K. (1996). *Doing what works in brief therapy: A strategic solution focused approach.* San Diego: Academic Press.

Shulman, L. (1993). *Interactional supervision.* NASW Press. Part I; Chapter 2, An interactional approach to supervision.

Stoltenberg, C. D., McNeill, B. W., & Delworth, U. (1997). *IDM supervision: An integrated development model for supervising counselors and therapists.* San Francisco, CA: Jossey-Bass.

Strupp, H., & Binder, J. L. (1984). *Psychotherapy in a new key: A guide to time-limited dynamic psychotherapy.* New York: Basic Books.

Watkins, C. E., Jr. (Ed.) (1997). *Handbook of psychotherapy supervision.* New York: Wiley. Part II: Approaches to psychotherapy supervision; Chapter 12: Supervision from a developmental perspective (IDM); Part III. Training models for psychotherapy supervision; & Chapter 17: Interpersonal process recall: Influencing human interaction.

4

WHAT ARE THE METHODS AND TECHNIQUES OF CLINICAL SUPERVISION?

There are several different formats for supervision: individual, group, peer, and team (Borders et al., 1991). Within each of these formats, there are a number of methods and techniques available.

In individual supervision, the supervisor typically works alone with the supervisee in a one-to-one relationship. Supervision can take place at a set weekly time or used prior to or directly following a client session. Timing of the supervision session will influence content. Supervision occurring immediately before a client session will focus on specific strategies, while supervision after a client session will be more concerned with theoretical conceptualization (Bernard & Goodyear, 1998). The primary method used in individual supervision is case consultation, which relies on the supervisee's self-report. However, a number of other methods and techniques are available for individual supervision, such as live supervision, audio- or videotaping, cotherapy, written assignments, role playing and role reversal.

One or two supervisors, working with either large (8–12) or small (4–6) groups can lead group supervision. Usually group supervision is seen as a supplement to, not a replacement for, individual supervision, especially for licensure purposes. State licensure requirements usually dictate the size and use of groups for post-degree supervision. For example, in Texas, a Licensed Professional Counselor (LPC) supervisor is restricted to a maximum of 6 supervisees and may use group supervision for no more than half the total supervised hours. Limiting the size of the group can be important to its effectiveness; a rough rule for containing the group size might be to allow 15 to 20 minutes per participant or no more than 6 people for a 1½-hour group. The frequency of group meetings can also affect the group experience; groups that meet weekly offer more intense personal learning, whereas those meeting monthly are more like training seminars. Methods available to group supervisors include case presentations, the use of audio- or videotaping, modeling and demonstration, and experiential techniques such as role playing, gestalt, psychodrama, art, movement, and family sculpting.

There are a number of advantages with group supervision, the most obvious being the savings of time and money. Additionally, group supervision may contribute to the supervisee's growth toward independence and may defuse problems of power and hierarchy in the supervisory relationship (Powell, 1993). Group supervision can also help supervisees normalize their anxiety, examine irrational thinking patterns, and explore personal responses to the supervisor as well as to their clients. Supervisees can gain support from the other members of the group and can feel more comfortable with taking risks. It can be beneficial to require that a personal journal be kept to process group experiences to promote self-awareness.

While the benefits of groups are numerous (Corey, 1995; Yalom, 1985), the supervisor needs to have training in how to work with groups and good leadership skills before venturing forth in this direction. Bradley (1989) suggested that the level of training and experience of the supervisor in group methods is more important to effective group supervision than the type of supervisee. Thus, the supervisor needs to be an experienced group leader who understands the nature of groups, group dynamics, and the role of conflict, who is familiar with the developmental stages of groups, and who is comfortable with confrontation. An effective group supervisor also needs to be knowledgeable about the differences between training groups and groups for counseling or psychotherapy. Additionally, since many supervisors use group supervision to teach particular methods and techniques such as psychodynamic, Gestalt, or psychodrama, and use the group members and their issues to demonstrate these techniques, it is often difficult for the supervisor to draw the line between what is supervision and what is psychotherapy. In order to avoid ethical problems with dual relationships, supervisors will need to clearly define the goals and expectations for the group and their role and function within the group, and to continually monitor the boundaries between supervision and therapy. Appendix A provides a sample group leadership skills evaluation form.

Peer and team supervision are similar to consultation in that they usually do not include the evaluative component. Peer supervision is more informal than team supervision and can be done either individually or with groups. Methods include case consulting, reviewing of tapes, or actually working with someone else's clients. Using rating forms and structured questions for observation and feedback augments the success of this peer format (Carmichael, 1992). Peer supervision is probably the most useful way for busy practitioners to receive ongoing support and feedback. Developing a peer supervision group of other clinical supervisors would be well worth the effort, as it can contribute greatly to success as a supervisor. Sharing this workbook and the accompanying exercises with other supervisors would be an excellent way to begin this process.

Team supervision is used primarily in hospital or agency settings, where a number of mental health professionals from different disciplines, such as a psychiatrist or psychologist with social workers and counselors, are involved with a client case. Supervision can be live (behind the mirror) or take place in staffing or training seminars. Case presentations, reviewing tapes, demonstration of techniques, cotherapy, and role playing can all be used.

What Are the Main Methods of Supervision?

With each format—individual, group, peer and team—a variety of methods and techniques could be selected. Methods would include case consultation, written activities, audio- and videotapes, live supervision, and cotherapy. Techniques available would be modeling and demonstration, role playing, gestalt empty chair, family sculpting, psychodrama, art therapy, and guided visualization.

What Is the Most Common Method of Supervision?

Case consultation is perhaps the most popular and best-known method of supervision used in all four formats. Wetchler, Piercy, & Sprenkle (1989), in a survey of marriage and family therapists, listed case consultation as the primary mode of supervision by over half the group. Typically, when employing this method the supervisor meets weekly with the supervisee to discuss their cases. In schools and agencies with large numbers of clients to serve, and limited resources with which to help them, this method is considered to be the most effective for monitoring purposes. Timing and content may vary, especially with new supervisees or in times of crisis. For example, immediately prior to a session with a client, the focus of consultation will be on specific interventions, while afterwards it will likely focus on conceptualization (Bernard & Goodyear, 1998).

There are a number of benefits from using the case consultation method. For example, it can often help the supervisee organize information, conceptualize problems, and decide on intervention strategies. It can also assist the supervisee in looking at the larger context of a problem, such as the role of cross-cultural issues, it can help with development of a theoretical model of change, and it can help integrate theoretical understanding with practice (McCollum & Wetchler, 1995). Case consultation also promotes the development of self-supervision (Haber, 1996).

However, there are also a number of important drawbacks to relying exclusively on the case consultation method. The success of self-report methods depends on "the observational and conceptual abilities of the supervisee as well as the insightfulness of the supervisor" (Bernard & Goodyear, 1998, p. 92). Self-reporting by supervisees can also be subject to deception, especially when they are faced with problem situations. To avoid such difficulties, especially in the beginning of the supervisory relationship, it is recommended that supervisors include at least one more direct method of gaining information about clients, such as the use of taping or live observation. For example, Goodyear and Nelson (1997) suggested combining case presentations with written progress notes and taping.

How to Structure the Case Conference

When using case consultation, it is necessary to think in advance about one's goal and purpose in order to decide what information to include, and to create a structure for the session. The case presentation format should be built around the particular needs and concerns of the supervisor in his or her setting. For example, supervisors must decide if they want a quick overview of most or all of the supervisee's cases, or if they want specific detailed information about particular ones. After deciding what is needed, it is possible to use case consultation in a variety of ways: to explore assessment skills and conceptualization, to examine the application of particular theories and techniques, to process relationship issues such as parallel process or transference, and to promote self-awareness on the part of the supervisee. In the beginning, the supervisor may wish to structure the format for case consultation, whereas with more advanced supervisees should themselves suggest the goals and content of the sessions.

One very effective method is to organize each case presentation around specific questions to help guide the supervisee. A number of case consultation formats are available in the literature on supervision (Bernard & Goodyear, 1998; Bradley, 1989; Feltham & Dryden, 1994; Haber, 1996; Powell, 1993). However, the following are some topics that might be included: identifying data, presenting the problem, important history, and environmental factors. Tentative assessment or diagnosis, the plan of action and goals, concerns or problems surrounding this case, relationship issues, ethical concerns, and multicultural issues are all popular additions to this format. Certainly, however, this framework should be adapted to the particular theoretical model and needs of the setting. For a sample case consultation format, see Appendix B.

What Are the Benefits of Audiotaping and Videotaping?

Although research has demonstrated the effectiveness of taping, particularly when used to teach skills, it is not seen as widely in post-degree supervision as in case consultation (Wetchler et al., 1989). However, taping an actual supervision session and reviewing the tape with the supervisee can provide a means to examine important relationship issues. The idea of taping in the work environment may at first seem overwhelming and troublesome. However, the benefits outweigh any difficulties. It is recommended that supervisors make at least one tape of themselves supervising and get at least one tape of a client session from each supervisee.

Each method of taping has its merits and drawbacks. Audiotaping is technically easy, more readily available, and cheaper. The focus of audiotaping can be on the overall pace of the session, nonverbal voice cues, general rapport, and intervention skills (Goldberg, 1985). Videotaping is more expensive and technically more complicated, but it can be an even richer source of material for supervision. However, since inexpensive, easy-to-use cameras and combination TV/videos are now available, videotaping is becoming more accessible for supervision. Both methods will give supervisors the luxury of reviewing sessions as many times as desired, while processing any number of different issues. Three of these have been described by Breunlin, Karrer, McGuire, & Cimmarusti (1988): reviewing the content of the session, reviewing the affective and cognitive aspects of the session, and processing relationship issues with the supervisee in the here and now. Since tapes can be stopped and rewound and then replayed, the supervisor can encourage the supervisee to try out new responses or intervention ideas. However, as with other methods, to reap maximum benefits, supervisors will need to be familiar with taping, to think through their goals for its use, to have some structure in mind for reviewing the tapes, and to prepare both the supervisee and the client involved.

How to Prepare for the Taping Session

The first area to address is the technical aspect of using audio- and videotaping. Nothing is more frustrating than to attempt to listen to a tape with no sound or picture. Therefore, before beginning, become familiar with all equipment, make a practice tape to assure quality, and take steps to prepare both the client and the supervisee. A signed release must be obtained from the client, outlining the purpose for taping and what procedures are in place to protect client confidentiality. Anxiety related to taping on the part of the supervisee or the client should be processed before proceeding. Even though most master's degree programs today provide students experience with direct supervision techniques such as live observation or taping, some anxiety may still be present. There are three potential areas of anxiety for supervisees; technical aspects including equipment and room availability, concern regarding client confidentiality, and worry about the supervisor's critical evaluation of their performance. Supervisors should remember that the more comfortable and enthusiastic the supervisee is with the value of taping, the more comfortable the client will be. A checklist to serve as a guide for taping is included as Appendix C.

How to Review Tapes

There are a number of possible methods to choose when reviewing tapes for supervision purposes. The supervisor may choose to review the tape alone before the supervision session and give verbal or written feedback to the supervisee, to use voice-over to critique the session on the tape itself, or to review the tape during the supervision session. Written assignments can be added to supplement the tape review. When reviewing the tapes, respect confidentiality: do not play the tape at work or home, where others can hear or see it. Also, if reviewing a number of tapes, please vary the structure of the session to prevent boredom.

Whatever the method, stopping the tape at regular intervals is necessary to optimize learning. Whiffen (1982) suggested that the attention span for reviewing tape is approximately 4 minutes. The use of a remote control can also be an aid, allowing that both supervisor and supervisee to stop the tape as needed. To save time, if the whole tape is to be reviewed, request that the supervisee rewind the tape completely before supervision; if reviewing only a portion of the tape, have the supervisee wind the tape to the selected section ready to begin. Both supervisor and supervisee need to set the goals and structure for the tape review together. Breunlin et al. (1988) stated that starting with goals that are limited in scope and thus obtainable by the supervisee work best for optimal learning. Bernard and Goodyear (1998) recommended that the supervisee come to the session having already selected a section of the tape to play and prepared to discuss with the supervisor why this portion was chosen.

Possible topics for review are as follows

➢ Select a section of tape that focuses on something the supervisee did well or a situation in which problems were encounterd (Goldberg, 1985). It could be an example of the supervisee's best work or an example where he or she had some difficulty or got stuck with the client; have the supervisee explain why.

➢ Highlight a part of the session where the supervisee demonstrated particular skills such as assessment, confrontational feedback, or handling feelings (Borders, 1989).

➢ Examine the dynamics of the relationship (issues such as transference and parallel process), ethical dilemmas, and multicultural issues.

➢ Analyze the tape from a particular perspective or theory such as systems theory or psychodynamic, or analyze it from a parallel process point of view (Bernard & Goodyear, 1998).

➢ Examine all or parts of the tape from a cognitive-behavioral viewpoint, examining one's thinking about the session and the attributions and meaning given to events, and processing one's self-talk in the session (Morran, Kurpius, Brack, & Brack, 1995).

➢ Review a tape examining the presence of three typical patterns from one's family of origin to handle anxiety: triangulation, overfunctioning and underfunctioning, and pursuit and distance (Getz & Protinsky, 1994).

As mentioned previously, the supervisor must be aware of the role of anxiety when reviewing tapes. By asking the supervisee to summarize their feelings about the session and their level of satisfaction beforehand, it may defuse some of the anxiety and dread. Having the supervisee comment first when stopping the tape also helps them to feel more comfortable and in control (Powell, 1993). The supervisor should make an effort to moderate the number of critical responses, keeping the feedback specific to whatever the goals were in making the tape—stopping the tape constantly to give corrective feedback can overwhelm the supervisee and defeat the purpose of learning. For example, if the supervisor wants to explore how the supervisee organizes information and creates a tentative working hypothesis, then they should restrain critical commentary to that purpose. Then, at the end of the viewing, other comments and overall suggestions for improvement could be offered. To maximize learning, always take time at the end to ask the supervisee what they gained from viewing the tape.

Another method for reviewing the tape is to promote self-supervision. The supervisor might ask the supervisee to imagine that they were the supervisor and then describe what suggestions they would make (Haber, 1996). Perhaps the best model to use for this purpose is IPR. With IPR, both supervisor and supervisee are encouraged to stop the tape periodically and ask a series of structured questions to help the supervisee process relationship dynamics with the client and increase self-awareness. For example, the supervisor might ask, "I noticed at this point, that you did. . . . What were you feeling right then? What were you thinking? " or "I wonder: If you had said . . . what do you think the client might have felt? Thought? Done?" (Kagan, 1980b, p. 183). Additional questions can be added, such as: "Where were you going when you asked . . . ? What were your hopes? Anything you wish you had done differently?" It is a good idea to have these questions available on a separate sheet to give to the supervisee while reviewing the tape.

What Are Live Supervision Methods?

There are several methods available for live supervision: behind the mirror, in the room, cotherapy, and telecommunication. Live supervision has different benefits for the supervisor depending on how it is used. Live supervision techniques such as behind the mirror, bug-in-the-ear, phone-in, etc. are the primary methods of training in family therapy, usually with beginning supervisees in academic settings. Live supervision is well regarded because it allows the teaching of basic skills while protecting the quality of care for the client (Wetchler et al., 1989). Taping is often combined with live supervision to maximize learning. With advanced technology, supervision can now be done between sites using telecommunications. Computers are now even being placed in the room to assist with feedback (Smith, Mead, & Kinsella, 1998).

For the busy practitioner in private practice or in agencies or schools without rooms with mirrors or advanced technology, there are two methods of live supervision still open to consideration: sitting in the room with the supervisee while they work with a client, and cotherapy. Regardless of method chosen, however, the activities need to be structured previous to the session, permission needs to be gained from the client or group, and steps need to be taken to ensure that confidentiality is protected.

When present in the room, the supervisor can choose either to simply observe or to engage in actual supervision. The purpose of observation at the beginning of supervision is to assess the supervisee's basic skills and to set goals for learning; in the middle, the purpose becomes monitoring the supervisee's progress, and at the end, it is to evaluate overall competence and abilities. When observing, the supervisor should sit discretely out of the direct line of view and make no comments during the actual session, delaying processing the experience with the supervisee until immediately afterwards. Structured checklists and good note taking help guide both observation and feedback. One cautionary note in using this method is that sitting in a client session and observing without participating increases the anxiety of both supervisee and client and may affect the overall quality of the session (Powell, 1993). To counteract this possibility, insure that the client is prepared in advance and that the supervisor's purpose in being there has been clearly explained, have the supervisee and client decide where they will be most comfortable having you sit, and, if possible, observe more than one session.

With live supervision, the supervisor takes a more active role while in the room. A number of possibilities exist: the supervisor may interrupt periodically to make suggestions, stop the session and take over to model a particular technique, or use role playing and psychodrama techniques such as doubling or serving as the alter-ego (speaking unspoken thoughts of client or supervisee). Another popular technique in family therapy is to stop after half the session and process with the supervisee while the client family is still in the room, or have the supervisee trade places with the supervisor behind the mirror (Schwartz, Liddle, & Breunlin, 1988). Haber (1996) suggested that to clarify roles and boundaries, a chair be set aside in the room for the supervisor to move to whenever commenting or giving corrective feedback to the supervisee. No matter what method is used, Powell (1993) wisely suggested limiting comments and interruptions to a maximum of four per session to avoid appearing to take over.

Haber (1996) divided live supervision into three phases: presession, session, and postsession. During presession (approximately 15 minutes), the supervisor is oriented to the case, the background, the goals for the session, and the planned approach; to save time, this could all be done in writing. The actual session may last half hour to 50 minutes. Allowing for postsession processing time is considered critical to the success of the method. Thus, planning to spend overall one and 1½-hours will give maximum benefit. Even overwhelmed practitioners, if convinced of the value of live supervision, can negotiate this at least once during a year's supervision experience. However, if this seems impossible, combining written methods and taping with live supervision can reduce the time required without sacrificing the benefits

Cotherapy is another form of live supervision. Kirby (1996) referred to this as *apprentice* cotherapy, suggesting that cotherapy is really a misnomer because the supervisee is not the supervisor's professional equal. Using cotherapy is an excellent, time-efficient method in supervision. It can help alleviate the supervisee's performance anxiety. It allows the supervisor to explain and model techniques while simultaneously learning about both the needs and style of the supervisee. However, for many supervisors the difficulty will be managing the dance between wanting to be in charge of the session and the need to give power away in order to promote the supervisee's independence.

What Are the Techniques of Supervision?

There are three main categories of supervision techniques that can be used with any supervision format or method: written, modeling, and demonstrative and experiential. Within each category, there would be numerous examples, so only a few can be highlighted here.

Written Techniques

Written techniques in supervision include a log of activities, case progress notes, process notes, and journaling. Asking supervisees to keep a journal to process their thoughts and feelings while in supervision can enrich the overall experience. Another idea is to request that supervisees give a written, as well as an oral, presentation of a case. This presentation could certainly be done in the beginning of a supervisory relationship in order to familiarize the supervisor with the thinking and conceptual skills of the supervisee. Verbatims are another example of a written technique in which supervisees are asked to write up a case, including dialogue, and then include written responses to a series of stimulus questions. Written techniques can be combined with reviewing tapes, live supervision, or cotherapy by asking the supervisee to process his or her experiences in writing or to respond to a series of structured questions. These assignments could be structured to focus attention on the conceptualization of client problems and the selection of intervention strategies, and to increase self-awareness. For example, the supervisor might ask the supervisee to answer specific questions in writing before presenting a case orally in supervision. The questions might go as follows (adapted from Goodyear & Nelson, 1997, p. 333):

1. What were you most aware of in this session?
2. What thoughts or feelings did you have as you worked with this person?
3. What do you believe is going on here?
4. What do you think the client wanted or needed from you during this session?
5. What do you need from me now as your supervisor?

Modeling and Demonstration

Modeling and demonstration can be used in a variety of supervision formats, including group supervision, reviewing tapes, or case consultation. Modeling and demonstrations should be combined with other cognitive-behavioral techniques such as rehearsal, behavior shaping, reinforcement, and practice. It is best for supervisors to first point out what specifics they would like the supervisee to note in the demonstration, and to then follow the modeling up immediately with a practice session using a role play. With any demonstration, time should be taken to process any learning gained from the demonstration along with potential application to current client problems.

Experiential Techniques

Experiential techniques bring underlying dynamics to the surface and facilitate awareness on the part of the supervisee. The use of experiential techniques can increase the level of understanding and empathy on the part of both supervisor and supervisee. They can be especially beneficial with group supervision or to enrich case consultation. Any number of experiential techniques such as the use of the empty chair (Gestalt), role play, psychodrama, family sculpting, expressive art or movement therapy, relaxation, and visualization can be adapted for supervision. They can be very helpful to the supervisor in several ways:

> ➤ to help enliven case consultation;
> ➤ to provide the supervisor, especially if relying solely on case consultation, with additional, more direct information about the skills and abilities of the supervisee;
> ➤ to help the supervisee to gain new perspective on a situation and to help the supervisee get unstuck with difficult clients;
> ➤ to create a safe environment for the supervisee to try out new methods, techniques, and responses to clients.

The essence of role playing is to make a situation outside of supervision real in the here-and-now—to switch from talking about problems with clients to experiencing them. For example, have the supervisee play the part of the client while the supervisor plays the supervisee. Stop partway through to process and then ask the supervisee to apply any awareness they have by trying out new behavior as the role play continues. However, the supervisor should understand that role playing can be a very powerful experience, and supervisees will need support before beginning and ample time for discussion afterwards (Feltham & Dryden, 1994). There are a number of role-playing techniques: mirroring, feeling with, doubling, soliloquy, spontaneity, being the protagonist, and role reversal (Corsini, 1966). Two of these with easy application to supervision are role reversal and doubling or soliloquy. Role reversal, whereby the supervisee exchanges roles with the client, can be used for any number of situations, to help the supervisee become unstuck with a client, to try out new behaviors, and to increase empathy and understanding. Using doubling or the soliloquy, where the supervisor speaks the unsaid thoughts of the supervisee as they participate in the role play, will give supervisors an excellent way to understand the supervisee's internal experience.

The empty chair technique popularized by Fritz Perls (1969) is also a wonderful means to explore emotionally charged situations with the supervisee (Haber, 1996). By asking the trainee to play both parts—client and counselor—and to switch back and forth between them helps the supervisee explore projections and blocks to understanding. Adding the technique of exaggeration, asking them as they play the two parts of client and counselor to exaggerate or do more of whatever they are doing, creates what Perls described as an "ah ha" experience (Perls, 1969).

Family sculpting or psychodrama can increase the supervisee's awareness of the impact of family-of-origin issues on their relationship with clients. Art therapy techniques, such as creating symbols and working in pictures or colors, can be used to enhance awareness of feeling responses to clients or supervision. Art therapy techniques could be combined with relaxation and guided visualization exercises to increase understanding and free up the supervisee's thinking about clients.

Supervisors are encouraged to become proficient in the use of these experiential techniques through reading, professional development workshops, conferences, and special certification programs.

EXPLORATION ➤ Supervision Methods and Techniques

To explore your familiarity with the methods and techniques mentioned in this chapter, please answer the following checklists. For each of the formats, methods, and techniques listed, indicate your level of experience: no experience, experience as a supervisee, use it now in supervision, and very comfortable with it.

Formats

Format	No experience	Experience as a supervisee	Use it now in supervision	Very comfortable
Individual				
Group				
Peer				
Team				

Methods and Techniques

Methods and techniques	No experience	Experience as a supervisee	Use it now in supervision	Very comfortable
Case consultation				
Live supervision				
Audio taping				
Videotaping				
Cotherapy				
Written material				
Case progress notes				
Simulated cases				
Demonstration				
Role playing				
Role reversal				
Family sculpting				
Psychodrama				
Gestalt empty chair				
Art therapy				
Visualization				

Review your knowledge and experience with the methods and techniques of supervision.

1. To practice skills for case consultation, write up one of your current cases using the sample format for a case consultation provided as Appendix B. Locate a group of peers either at your place of work or with your professional community. Practice giving a case presentation to this group. Ask for feedback on your presentation.

2. In order to improve your skills in the use of taping, particularly videotaping, it is suggested that supervisors make several practice tapes:

   a. Make a tape of a client session. Follow the instructions for taping included in Appendix C.

   b. Create your own sample release form.

   c. Review the tape twice, first by yourself and then with a colleague or fellow supervisor. Select one or two suggestions for review of the tape from the list of possible topics on p. 75.

   d. Practice using a rating sheet to rate the taped session. Use the sample evaluation checklist of basic skills of the supervisee in Appendix D, or create your own rating sheet.

   e. Write a summary of your session. Some suggested questions to respond to in the summary are:
      ➢ What happened in the session and how did it happen?
      ➢ What were your feelings and responses to the client?
      ➢ What were your hunches about the client?
      ➢ What were your plan of action, intervention strategies, and treatment goals?
      ➢ Did you identify any multicultural issues that affected the session?
      ➢ What did the client say or not say was the problem and how might this be important in the progress of therapy?
      ➢ What personal issues are you aware of that may affect working with this client?
      ➢ What were possible parallel process issues?

f. How did the review of the tape improve your work with the client? Give an example.

3. What are your experiences with live supervision? How would you describe these experiences? Were they positive or negative? Give an example.

4. Examine your current work setting. Imagine you wish to use live supervision. Describe what you would need to do to make that happen.

5. Was cotherapy used in your own supervision experience?

   a. How would you describe its use? What happened?

b. Do you feel comfortable using this cotherapy?

c. What problems do you see for yourself using this method?

.

d. What might you need to do to be successful using cotherapy as a supervisor? Describe specifically one or two behaviors you would need to try.

EXPLORATION ➤ Techniques of Supervision

1. To identify how familiar you are with the written techniques of supervision, rate yourself using the following scale. (Circle the appropriate number.)

   1 = no knowledge
   2 = some familiarity
   3 = method was used by your supervisor
   4 = have used this method yourself in supervision.

Record keeping	1	2	3	4
Progress notes	1	2	3	4
Process notes	1	2	3	4
Journaling	1	2	3	4
Verbatim	1	2	3	4
Structured questions for case presentations	1	2	3	4

Note your areas of weakness in any particular area. What do you need to do now to improve your knowledge?

2. To apply the information on modeling and demonstration, think of a situation with a current supervisee. Or, if necessary, imagine one. Think of a particular problem this supervisee may be having with clients, such as talking too much, interrupting clients to avoid feelings, or improper self-disclosure. Decide what skill needs to be demonstrated. Using role play, practice modeling and demonstrating this technique. Review the session to see what went well and what you need to do differently. If possible, videotape the role play to maximize learning.

3. Make a list of experiential and action techniques that you typically use with your clients.

a. Do you have any personal favorites? List them.

b. What kind of training do you have in the use of experiential techniques? Describe.

c. Think back to your own experience as a supervisee. Did your supervisor use action techniques? If yes, can you describe a specific experience and what happened as a result of that experience?

4. If you are now a supervisor, try applying one experiential action technique in your next supervision session.

a. What technique do you want to try?

b. How do you imagine this will help the supervisee?

c. What are possible drawbacks to using this technique with your supervisee?

➤ Chapter Highlights

- ➤ The effective supervisor must be flexible and be able to use and combine a number of different supervision formats, methods, and techniques.

- ➤ Supervisors need to plan ahead to structure the use of supervision methods and techniques in order to maximize learning.

- ➤ It is important to avoid relying on case consultation as the only method of supervision.

Suggested Readings

Bernard, J., & Goodyear, R. (1998). *Fundamentals of clinical supervision*. Boston: Allyn and Bacon. Chapter 5: Individual supervision; Chapter 6: Group supervision; Chapter 7: Live supervision; & Chapter 10: Managing clinical supervision.

Blatner, A. (1991b). *Imaginative interviews: A psychodramatic warm-up for developing role-playing skills. Journal of Group Psychotherapy, Psychodrama and Sociometry, 44*(3), 115–120.

Borders, L. D., & Leddick, G. (1987). *Handbook of counseling supervision*. Alexandria, VA: ACA Publications. Chapter 4: Choosing and implementing supervision interventions.

Bradley, L. (2000). *Counselor supervision*. Philadelphia: Accelerated Development. Chapter 9, Experiential supervision; & Chapter 10: Group supervision.

Corey, G. (1995). *Theory and practice of group counseling*. Pacific Grove, CA: Brooks/Cole.

Feltham, C., & Dryden, W. (1994). *Developing counselor supervision*. London: Sage. Chapter 2: Utilizing a variety of supervisory foci and methods.

Gendlin, E. T. (1996). *Focused-oriented psychotherapy: A manual of the experiential method*. New York: Guilford.

Haber, R. (1996). *Dimensions of psychotherapy supervision*. New York: Norton. Section II: Vehicles for supervision; & Chapter 7: Case management; Chapter 9: Consultation; & Chapter 10: Co-therapy.

Leveton, E. (1992). *A clinician's guide to psychodrama*. New York: Springer.

Liddle, H. A, Breunlin, D. C., & Schwartz, R. C. (Eds.). (1988). *Handbook of family therapy training and supervision*. New York: Guilford. Chapter 12: Cybernetics of videotape supervision by D. C. Breunlin, B. M. Karrer, B. M., D. E. McGuire, & R. A. Cimmarusti. Chapter 11: Muddles in live supervision by R. C. Schwartz, H. A. Liddle, & D. C. Breunlin.

Loganbill, C., & Stoltenberg, C. (1983). The case conceptualization format: A training device for practicum. *Counselor Education and Supervision, 22,* 235–242.

Perls, F. (1969). *Gestalt therapy verbatim*. Moab, UT: Real People Press.

Powell, D. J. (1993). *Clinical supervision in alcohol and drug abuse counseling: Principles, models, methods*. New York: Lexington Books. Chapter 12: Basic supervisory techniques; & Chapter 14: Innovative techniques in supervision.

Rosenthal, H. (Ed.). (1998). *Favorite counseling and therapy techniques*. Philadelphia: Accelerated Development.

Shulman, L. (1993). *Interactional supervision*. Washington, DC: NASW. Chapter 3: Preparatory and beginning skills in supervision.

Thompson, R.A. (1996). *Counseling techniques: Improving relationships with others, ourselves, our families and our environment*. Philadelphia: Accelerated Development.

Yalom, I. (1985). *The theory and practice of group psychotherapy*. New York: Basic Books.

5

WHAT IS THE ROLE OF THE RELATIONSHIP IN SUPERVISION?

For a number of years, interest has been growing in what are termed the nonspecific or common factors underlying change in all models and theories of psychotherapy (Goldfried & Newman, 1992). Assisted by the statistical technique of meta-analysis, a number of theorists have concluded that the therapeutic relationship itself is central to the therapeutic change process (Norcross and Goldfried, 1992; Norcross & Halgin, 1997). In other words, the specific methods or techniques used by practitioners are less important than the quality of their relationships with their clients. Some examples of the relationship factors found to be important to the change process include the feeling of being heard and understood, the offering of hope, the offering of feedback as a means to gain a new perspective on problems, and the opportunity to talk about problems in an accepting environment.

How to Form the Working Alliance

Just as in counseling and psychotherapy, the quality of the supervisory relationship is felt to be critical to the success of supervision (Barrow & Domingo, 1997; Bernard & Goodyear, 1998; Borders & Usher, 1992; Chung, Baskin & Case, 1998; Holloway, 1995; Kaiser, 1997; Ladany, Hill, Corbett, & Nutt, 1996; Lambert & Ogles, 1997; Stoltenberg et al., 1997;). The supervisor needs to recognize the importance of the development of skills to increase collaboration and the quality of the supervisory relationship. Bordin (1983) utilized the term "working alliance" to refer to this collaboration between the supervisor and supervisee. The working alliance is based on mutual agreement on the goals and tasks of supervision, and a strong bond of caring, trust, and respect. He listed the goals of the supervisory working alliance as follows:

> ➤ mastery of specific skills;
> ➤ enlarging one's understanding of clientel;
> ➤ enlarging awareness of process issues, which involves being alert to the how, what, when, and where of therapy sessions;
> ➤ increasing self-awareness, exploring the impact of self on the counseling process, and sensitizing the supervisee to his or her own feelings which may have an impact on the client;
> ➤ overcoming personal and intellectual obstacles that impede learning;
> ➤ deepening understanding of concepts and theory;
> ➤ provide a stimulous for research; stimulate questioning and observation;
> ➤ maintenance of standards of service;
> ➤ fostering awareness and observance of ethical guidelines.

A number of factors may affect the quality of the working alliance, including the supervisor's relationship skills, their ability to encourage collaboration with the supervisee as to the goals for supervision, their model and style of supervision, and their previous experience as a supervisor. Another factor that Bordin suggested might interfere with the working alliance is the anxiety and tension related to the "up–down" factor (hierarchical relationship) in supervision. Two specific factors, role conflict and role ambiguity, have been identified as particularly harmful to the working alliance. Certainly the supervisee's previous experiences in supervision and leftover material from those experiences should also be included as affecting the working alliance.

Role Conflict

Role conflict refers to the supervisee being asked to engage simultaneously in multiple roles that conflict or are inconsistent with the supervisee's personal values and judgments. Role conflict is particularly pervasive among therapist trainees who are typically graduate students and who may be called upon by their supervisor to act at times as a colleague or even as a client (Ladany & Friedlander, 1995). Post-degree supervisees also experience role conflict as they are typically seeking licensure in their work setting. Concerns about job performance, security, and promotion can influence communication, self-disclosure, and trust.

Given that role conflict refers to balancing the strains and demands of several different roles, it is important to gain a contextual understanding of the potential conflicts both the supervisor and supervisee may be experiencing. Shulman (1993), in his book *Interactional Supervision*, saw three interacting systems, supervisor, supervisee, and client, and suggested that all three must be taken into consideration. For example, supervisees may feel helpless and overwhelmed by the lack of resources or empowerment experienced by their clients as well as by the lack of resources (time, money, and staff) available to help. Both systems will have an impact on a supervisor's suggestions for intervention and the type or level of client care. These in turn will affect the motivation and professional development of the supervisee.

Role Ambiguity

Role ambiguity refers to the confusion that some supervisees experience as they are encouraged to explore their personal character and discuss their limitations while simultaneously being evaluated by a supervisor for their competencies and suitability for the profession. In addition, role ambiguity occurs because of the dissonance involved as supervisors respect the boundaries of supervision in order to avoid any dual relationship with the supervisee, yet have an acute awareness that it is necessary to address personal issues and their impact on the counseling process when difficulties arise.

When the issues of role conflict and role ambiguity are not addressed properly, the supervisee can develop anxiety and dissatisfaction with the working alliance. In fact, in a study by Ladany and Friedlander (1995), a supervisee's perceptions of role conflict and role ambiguity were significantly related to the quality of the working alliance. Role ambiguity is more common among beginning supervisees, whereas role conflict is typical for more advanced supervisees (Ladany & Friedlander, 1995). In general, supervisees perceived less role ambiguity and role conflict in working alliances that they characterized as strong and vice versa.

One way to minimize role conflict and role ambiguity is for the supervisor and supervisee to have a clear understanding of the goals of supervision, how these goals will be achieved, and how any problems and issues will be addressed as they arise. For example, in order to build the working alliance, the supervisor may wish to share with the supervisee the responsibility of setting goals, deciding how evaluation will occur, or selecting specific problems and issues to be presented during supervision sessions.

There are several instruments available to assess the working alliance. According to Ellis and Ladany (1997), the most valid and reliable measure is the Role Conflict and Role Ambiguity Inventory (RCRAI) developed by Olk and Friedlander (1992) which measures role difficulties in the supervisory relationship. Another assessment tool that is somewhat less valid for research but simple to administer by a practicing supervisor is the Supervisory Working Alliance Inventory (trainee and supervisor versions) developed by Efstation, Patton, & Kardash (1990). The Supervisory Working Alliance Inventory provides a general measure of the trainee's and supervisor's perceptions of the quality of the supervisory relationship and comprises three subscales: goals, tasks, and bond. Findings in general demonstrate that the quality of the working alliance is strongly related to perceived role conflict and role ambiguity. Samples of these instruments can be found in Appendix C of Bernard and Goodyear's (1998) *Fundamentals of Clinical Supervision*. It is suggested that the reader take the time to review and then use at least one or two of these instruments at some point in supervision.

What Is the Role of Anxiety in the Supervisory Relationship?

Anxiety is a natural response to supervision and may play a significant role in shaping the working alliance and the quality of the supervisory relationship. Supervisors need to consider its impact on the supervisory relationship and how to best work with it. Bernard and Goodyear (1998) point out that the supervisee may experience anxiety on two fronts: in their work with the client and in their work with the supervisor. A common term for this condition is performance anxiety. Bradley (2000) suggested two other categories of anxiety: approval anxiety and dominance anxiety. Approval anxiety is the desire to have others see one as competent. Dominance anxiety refers to the supervisee's response to the power and authority of the supervisor. Thus, the supervisee's level of anxiety could vary depending on setting, previous information they have received about the supervisor, their stage of development, their professional background, and their personality factors. For example, older adults changing fields or seeking licensure in a different area may experience supervision differently than someone just starting out.

Karen Horney (1950), a well-known psychodynamic theorist, presented one interesting theoretical model that may be helpful to supervisors in understanding and responding to anxiety in the supervisee. She described three positions individuals take to structure the unknown and handle anxiety: moving away, moving towards, and moving against. The reaction to "move toward" people may take the form of socially desired behavior such as compliance with others' wishes, agreement, or, in more extreme forms, acting helpless. The "moving away" reaction may take the form of acting distant or detached in order to avoid becoming hurt or abandoned. The last reaction, "moving against," may be observed in aggressive, dominating behavior like using arguing, criticizing, and disagreeing as a means to gain control of their anxiety.

Another model for understanding and responding to anxiety comes from family systems theory which describes three patterns for coping with anxiety: (a) triangulation: drawing another person into a relationship to cope with anxiety; (b) overfunctioning: acting overly responsible for another person; and underfunctioning; acting helpless and inadequate; and (c) pursuit and distancing: moving closer or moving away from a person as a result of anxiety (Getz & Protinsky, 1994). All three patterns are felt to be attributable to one's family of origin. Of these, overfunctioning and underfunctioning, are the most easily recognized patterns in supervision. As overfunctioners, trainees may take over the work of the client and work harder for change than the client does, while as underfunctioners, trainees may appear stuck and helpless. Supervisors can use this model to understand and explain the supervisee's reactions to supervision and then to form their own response to the situation.

Triangulation, the idea that when there is anxiety and conflict in a dyadic relationship, it is necessary to draw someone else into the relationship to help manage the anxiety, can be beneficial in explaining relationship problems in any system such as agency and school settings. For example, it could be understood that when a supervisee complains to the supervisor about others in the work setting, it is as a means for them to dilute feelings of helplessness and manage their anxiety. Lerner (1989) suggested that the amount of gossip in a system about another person's incompetence or craziness is an indicator of the amount of anxiety present in the system. To Lerner, gossip and complaining indicate a need to address relationship problems directly with the person or persons involved. In order to assess difficulties in a work setting, the supervisor might ask, "Whose problem is it" and "How am I going about solving this problem?"

In summary, to be effective as a supervisor, one must understand that anxiety is a natural response on the part of the supervisee to the process of supervision, particularly in the beginning stages, and that it can play a significant role in the development of the supervisory relationship. The supervisor needs to identify possible sources of anxiety for each supervisee, such as role conflict and role ambiguity, worry about competence, and the need for approval. Then the supervisor's responses can be tailored to each individual situation, depending on what is identified as the potential source of anxiety.

What Are the Relationship Skills Necessary to Be an Effective Supervisor?

Good interpersonal relationship skills are essential for effective supervision, both for building the working alliance with the supervisee and for the purpose of teaching and modeling. Continuing research in psychotherapy supports the importance of relationship factors in positive psychotherapy outcome (Bergin & Garfield, 1994). Carl Rogers (1951) described three conditions necessary for client change: genuineness, empathetic understanding, and positive regard. Carkhuff (1969), in his theory of helping, added three more conditions: respect, concreteness, and counselor self-disclosure. He termed them the facilitative condition of psychotherapy and designed scales to measure their presence in the counseling interview (See Carkhuff, 1969, for samples of these scales). To create such facilitative conditions, the supervisor needs to employ a variety of active listening techniques, including paraphrasing, reflecting feelings, empathetic responding, and to model genuineness, respect, concreteness, and empathetic understanding.

Borders et al. (1991) categorized two main types of intervention strategies necessary to be an effective supervisor: the supervision should be both supportive and challenging. Supportive responses are fundamental with beginners or in the formation stage of the working alliance, whereas challenging or confrontational responses are more useful in stage two or the intermediate stage of development (Fisher, 1989). A third category, collaborative skills, should be added to this list as essential for working with the more advanced supervisees.

Some examples of supportive interventions are: the use of active listening skills (such as attending, paraphrasing, summarizing, clarifying, reflection of feelings, perception checking, restatement, clarifying feelings or thoughts), encouragement, agreement, reinforcement, empathetic responding, self-disclosure, and open-ended questions (see Borders et al., 1991; Egan, 1998; Ivy, 1999; Shulman, 1993, for a detailed description of these skills). Additionally, solution-focused techniques, such as cheerleading, encouraging, and asking for success could also be included (Juhnke, 1996; O'Hanlon & Weiner-Davis, 1989; Thomas, 1992). As a cheerleader, the supervisor might say, "Wow, that was excellent," or to be encouraging, "How did you manage to . . . ? Can you give me another example?" Asking the miracle question ("If you had a magic wand to wave over this situation") and imagining successful solutions to problems ("Imagine this problem is solved; what would be different for you?") are also popular solution-focused techniques that will be helpful to support and encourage the supervisee.

Challenging interventions include both direct and indirect methods.

Direct methods include pointing out discrepancies (between verbal and nonverbal behavior or between one's stated goals and one's actions), giving specific corrective feedback on behavior, the demand for work, sandwiching, xyz theory, giving information, interpreting, and summarizing. Indirect methods include use of metaphors, self-disclosure and empathetic understanding, paradoxical interventions, agreeing (going with or honoring the resistance), and reframing.

Usually, beginning supervisors are much more comfortable with supportive interventions, shying away from being too confrontational with their supervisees because they believe this to be negative to the relationship. However supportive they want to be, though, supervisors must always keep in mind the potential for harm in *not* challenging the supervisee when his or her behavior is harmful to the welfare of the client (Mead, 1990). To be effective, supervisors must be able to confront or challenge their supervisee and give them corrective feedback in order to help them grow; they must also be able to handle the resistance of supervisees to evaluation, directions, suggestions, and goal setting (Borders et al., 1991). Shulman (1993) refers to this skill as the *demand for work*: the need to empathize and understand supervisees' anxiety, yet still challenge and push them to do more.

Challenging and giving corrective feedback can be a positive experience, helping supervisees to explore what they're saying or doing, to discover their own resources and personal strengths. However, how the supervisor challenges and gives feedback to the supervisee is interpreted as a personal style choice. Some supervisors and supervisees are more sensitive and uncomfortable with challenges, while others relish it. One common mistake made by supervisors is, in an effort to *not* sound critical or accusatory, to be too tentative and use too many disclaimers, so the real message is lost. Studies have shown that feedback that is specific to changeable behaviors, not vague or containing qualifiers, is more effective (Hulse-Killacky & Page, 1994).

Feedback is always more successful when given in the context of a positive working relationship. Sharing information and using self-disclosure and empathetic responding can also help one be both supportive and challenging. The more empathetic, the more likely a supervisee is to listen to feedback. Using empathetic responding and self-disclosure can defuse anxiety and facilitate openness. For example: "This is a problem most supervisees have. It was the hardest thing for me to learn. My supervisor suggested I try . . . " or, "I know I struggled with this when I first started out," or "It is still sometimes difficult for me to always know what to do."

Just as with clients, some challenging and confrontation may be necessary to stimulate growth, although constantly correcting the supervisee can be detrimental to building the working alliance. Supervisors should strive to use a moderate level of challenging and evaluative feedback, but not so much that it overwhelms the supervisee and creates nonproductive anxiety. Taping a supervision session and counting the number of interruptions and corrections will help beginning supervisors monitor this problem.

Feedback, whether positive or negative, should be specific, directly related to the learning goals of supervision and not global generalizations about the person. For example, it is more productive to say "At this point, you seem to have trouble engaging the client" rather than "I don't think you know what you are doing." When wanting to point out discrepancies between verbal and nonverbal behavior or between actions and intentions, stick to an example of specific observable behavior and use open-ended questions to stimulate thinking. For example, "I noticed that even though you told the client it was okay to cry in the session, when she began to do so, you asked a question and that cut her off. What do you think this is about? Have you noticed yourself doing this at other times?"

Powell (1993) suggested using sandwiching, or giving unfavorable feedback sandwiched in between positive comments: tell the supervisee specifically what they are doing right in the situation, then make your suggestion for change (keep it concise and manageable), then add a positive overall comment; for example, "I like how you did . . . ; I see you still struggle with . . . , and maybe you could try . . . next time. I see you are moving in the right direction" (p. 189). Use the word *and*, not *but*, when delivering praise. The word *but* negates all that comes before it while the use of *and* includes it.

Goleman (1995) described Haim Ginott's formula, the xyz formula, in which parents give feedback to their children to correct behavior without criticizing the person: "When you did x . . . it made me feel y . . . and I wish you would do z instead." Supervisors can combine this technique with empathetic responding: "I understand you were anxious then, but when you did x . . . the client seemed to respond y . . . and I'd rather you did z." Or supervisors may respond, "I know it is often difficult to know what to do, but when you say x . . . I feel y . . . and I wish you would do z."

Another technique that is helpful in both supporting and challenging the supervisee's thinking is the use of metaphors. Haley (1985) described a metaphor as any communication that can have two meanings, or in other words, taking a word or a phrase usually applied to one thing and using it for another (Webster New College Dictionary, 1999). Metaphors can be used with supervisees to help them gain understanding of themselves and their work with clients, to give feedback to them, to illustrate a point, and to create way to refer to difficulties in a less threatening way. While each supervisor needs to create personal metaphors, some popular possibilities are the sinking ship, life preservers, desert islands, birds or other animals, caves, doors, and stairs. See Hendrix (1992) or Haber (1996) for more suggestions.

How Does the Supervisor Work Collaboratively?

A third category of important interpersonal skills would be those skills that facilitate working collaboratively with the supervisee. One area of apparent agreement in the literature is the importance of working collaboratively with the intermediate or advanced supervisee. For example, Usher and Borders (1993), in a study of practicing counselors, found that respondents preferred a supervisor who is collegial and relationship oriented to one who is task oriented (p. 76). Teyber (1997) referred to this collegial relationship as a *collaborative alliance*, working together as partners on problems. Thus, the post-degree clinical supervisor needs to concentrate on developing interpersonal skills that enable a move from the role of teacher, expert, and evaluator into the role of consultant and colleague at the termination of training. What does this mean? It means that the supervisor works more as a consultant with the supervisee as he or she develops, trusting the level of knowledge, practice, and personal development of the supervisee; the supervisor can stop doing things *for the supervisee*. Instead, the supervisor can simply work *with* the supervisee. It also means that the supervisee will feel free to speak up about, comment on, and make contributions to the efforts of the supervisor.

There are a number of interpersonal skills necessary for establishing collaboration with the supervisee, including brainstorming, using process comments, probing, using solution-focused or problem-solving questions, empathetic responding, and self-disclosure, and asking open ended questions. Methods such as peer supervision, group supervision or cotherapy and applying techniques like peer rating forms or action techniques like role playing all provide the supervisor with means to work more collaboratively with the supervisee. Another way to work collaboratively is to co-supervise with a colleague who has a different style or approach and use that experience to encourage the supervisee's growth (Borders & Leddick, 1987).

Haber (1996) described the consultant role in supervision in more detail. He suggested that since supervisors have some distance from the client, they could take a different position on problems. To encourage collaboration, the supervisor uses open-ended questions—how, what, where, and when—to empower the supervisee. Perhaps some examples of consultant supervision would be helpful here to demonstrate what is meant:

➢ "Tell me how you experience the client's helplessness, (anger, frustration)."
➢ "Help me to understand how it is a problem for you that the mother is doing . . . "
➢ "When the client does that, what happens to you?"
➢ "What does it mean when the father does . . . ?"
➢ "You seem very protective of the son. Can you discuss why?"
➢ "What do you see this client wanting from therapy?"
➢ "How might the client's race or gender be affecting the family? The problem?"

Perhaps the best illustration of effective collaboration would be to draw a comparison between consultation in the expert mode and consultation in a shared-power mode. For example, the supervisor working in expert mode might state to this supervisee: "After reviewing the case, it seems to me that. . . . This is what I recommend you do. . . . " In a more collaborative mode, the focus of consultation shifts from problems solved by the expert to problems solved by the supervisee. For example, the supervisor, working as consultant, might ask the supervisee:

➢ How is this case (client) a problem for you?
➢ What do you want to do?
➢ What have you thought about doing?
➢ What have you already tried?
➢ Can you give me an example?
➢ What is the worst thing that could happen if you tried. . . . ?

Brainstorming and solution-focused questions that elicit the sharing of ideas also encourage collaboration. For example, "Let's brainstorm together; you throw out all of your ideas and then I will add mine." Or to help empower a supervisee who appears stuck with a client, ask questions such as, "What have you tried previously that worked?" or "Were there times when you did not have this problem? What is different now?" Another helpful line of questions would encourage the supervisee to take small steps ("Can you think of one thing to try with this person?"). Scaling questions—asking supervisees to rate on a scale of 1 to 10 how they feel they are doing with a particular goal or problem—can help objectify situations, demonstrate progress, and convey encouragement.

Perhaps, however, the most important skill necessary to promote growth and development in both the supervisee and the supervisory relationship is the use of process comments or observations about what is occurring between the supervisor and supervisee in the here and now. Process comments open up the relationship as a topic for discussion; they are essential to analyze parallel process, transference, countertransference, and relationship difficulties of all kinds. The effective supervisor needs to constantly ask, "How am I feeling or thinking about what the supervisee is doing now? What am I doing as a result of these thoughts?" Process comments challenge both supervisor and supervisee, provide a doorway to a more honest and open relationship, and can be used with any format or method, such as individual, group or live supervision, reviewing tapes, role playing, and exploring parallel process. (See Yalom, 1985, or Teyber, 1997, for further discussion of the use of process comments.)

EXPLORATION ➤ Building the Working Alliance

1. Bordin (1983) uses the term *working alliance* to describe the supervisory relationship.

   a. What does the term working alliance mean to you?

   b. Review the list of seven goals of the working alliance. Which ones are most important to you? Are there any you want to add or delete? Describe.

   c. What does your answer say about your focus in supervision?

2. The terms "role conflict" and "role ambiguity" are used to describe two potential problem areas in the working alliance.

   a. Describe some of the conflicts in role that you are now experiencing or have experienced in the past in your setting. (For example, do you often find yourself having to wear many hats, such as administrator, clinician, and supervisor?)

b. What positive or negative effects could these various roles have on your working alliance with your supervisee? Do you see any potential problems?

3. To help understand Bordin's concept of role ambiguity, think back to when you were starting out in the field.
   a. How comfortable do you remember being with your supervisor in discussing your limitations, weaknesses, and difficulties working with clients?

   b. Identify, if you can, anything your supervisor did or said that made you comfortable.

   c. Was there anything your supervisor said or did that made you uncomfortable?

4. Consider your work with clients now. Are you aware of any specific personal difficulties you are having with a particular type of client (e.g., clients who seem helpless and stuck, or angry clients) or client populations (e.g., gay, male, or sexually abused clients)?

    a. Have you ever discussed this with your supervisor or a colleague?

    b. If not, what is keeping you from doing so?

    c. How do you see this awareness possibly affecting your own supervisory style?

5. Using X's, rate on the chart below the degree of role conflict, role ambiguity, and impact on the working alliance that you experienced in the situations described above.

Role Conflict

High————————————————————————————————Low

Role Ambiguity

High————————————————————————————————Low

Working Alliance

Poor————————————————————————————————Good

EXPLORATION ➤ Anxiety in the Supervisory Relationship

1. A number of categories of possible anxiety for the supervisee have been outlined in this chapter, such as performance, approval, and dominance anxiety, as well as possible ways of responding to this anxiety, such as triangulation, overfunctioning or underfunctioning, and moving toward or away from people.

   a. Which of the three categories of anxiety—performance, approval, or dominance—do you think affects you the most?

   b. Horney (1950) described three patterns of responding to the unknown (moving toward, moving away, or moving against). Which is your dominant mode of responding to the anxiety generated by the unknown? Do you know? Can you think of an example? Describe.

   c. Overfunctioning and underfuctioning are two common patterns used by supervisees to cope with anxiety. Which one is more likely to be your style? Can you give an example?

2. Triangulation is a term used to refer to how anxiety can be handled in a system. Think about your work setting at this time. When problems arise,
   a. How do you typically respond?

   b. Do you talk directly to the person or do you talk to others about that person?

   c. How do others respond to difficulties?

   d. Do you see yourself being drawn into others' difficulties? Can you give some examples?

EXPLORATION ➤ Interpersonal Skills for Supervision

1. How would you rate yourself now on your knowledge of challenging and supportive intervention strategies? Use the chart below to rate yourself.

Intervention strategy	Not at all familiar with the strategy	Somewhat familiar with the strategy	Familiar with the strategy	Know a lot about the strategy	Consistently use the strategy
Paraphrasing					
Reflecting feelings					
Clarifying					
Active listening					
Agreeing					
Using reinforcement					
Using empathetic responding					
Using self-disclosure					
Asking open-ended questions					
Cheerleading					
Encouraging					
Miracle questions					
Asking for success					
Imagining successful solutions					
Pointing out discrepancies					
Giving corrective feedback					
Demanding work					
Sandwiching					
xyz					
Giving information					
Interpreting					
Summarizing					
Using metaphors					
Reframing					

2. Even though the research and literature in training and supervision points to the importance of challenging supervisees and giving "corrective feedback" to stimulate growth, many supervisors find this difficult.

    a. Think about how you personally feel about receiving corrective feedback. Do you experience this, no matter how well it's given, as criticism of yourself personally or of your overall competence? Can you give an example?

    b. Think about how you personally feel about giving corrective feedback to someone. Can you give an example?

    c. Do you associate the word challenge or confrontation with disagreements, criticism, and negative experiences? How comfortable are you with challenge in the supervisory relationship?

    d. Check your answers with a colleague or your supervisor. How do they perceive your comfort level with confrontation or challenging feedback?

3. What would the supervisee need to do for you to challenge them? Describe the circumstances.

4. Think of a recent situation in which you received critical feedback from a supervisor. Describe how it was done?

   a. How did you feel receiving this feedback?

   b. What do you wish the supervisor had done differently?

   c. Take this same situation and imagine you are the supervisor. Practice using sandwiching or the xyz formula to give the same critical feedback? If possible, do a role play and make a videotape of the session. Invite a colleague to play your supervisor and to help you review and critique your supervisory style.

5. Think about one of your clinical supervisors during your own training.
   a. Would you say this person used both support and challenge or did they emphasize one over the other?

   b. Do you wish they had challenged you more? Explain why or why not.

   c. Can you create a metaphor to describe that relationship? Explain it.

6. Review your answers. How do you see this information affecting your supervisory style?

7. To practice giving feedback, make a tape of a supervision session. If you do not have a current supervisee, invite a colleague to role-play the supervisee. Practice giving feedback to your supervisee during the session. Review the taped session and critique your feedback style.

   a. Was the feedback mostly positive or negative?

   b. Was the feedback tentative or concise?

   c. Was the feedback specific to the learning goals?

   d. What did you do well? What do you need to do differently?

EXPLORATION ➤ Working Collaboratively

1. At this time, what are your knowledge and skill levels, as well as comfort level, with the relationship skills for collaboration?

Relationship skills	Not at all familiar with these skills	Somewhat familiar with these skills	Familiar with these skills	Know a lot about these skills	Consistently use these skills
Brainstorming					
Process comments					
Probes					
Solution-focused questions					
Consultation skills					
Scaling questions					
Open-ended questions					
Empathetic responding					
Self-disclosure					
Examining parallel process					

2. How do you see the above answers affecting your supervision?

3. Think of a current client case and imagine you were working with a supervisee on this case. If you already are supervising, use a current case from supervision. Practice applying the suggestions for consultation to supervision. Ask a colleague to help you role-play the situation. If possible, videotape the practice session and review the tape afterwards.

➤ Conclusions

What conclusions might you draw from these exercises that may be helpful to you in working with your supervisee?

➤ Action Plan

What do you need to do as a result of these conclusions?

➤ Chapter Highlights

- ➤ The quality of the supervisory relationship is critical to successful supervision.

- ➤ Supervisors should recognize the importance of the therapeutic relationship as the agent of change and focus on methods and techniques to improve the supervisory relationship in the here and now.

- ➤ The working alliance between the supervisor and supervisee can be affected by anxiety, role conflict, and role ambiguity.

- ➤ Supervisors must be comfortable with challenging as well as supporting the supervisee.

- ➤ Supervisors must give challenging or corrective feedback in a climate of care and concern.

- ➤ Corrective feedback should be focused on behaviors that are specific and changeable, not on the person.

- ➤ Developing skills for collaboration is essential for post-degree supervision.

Suggested Readings

Bernard, J., & Goodyear, R. (1998). *Fundamentals of clinical supervision*. Boston: Allyn and Bacon. Chapter 4: The supervisory relationship: Process and issues. Section 2: Supervision as a two-person system—Supervisor and supervisee; & Section 3: Supervisee as a source of variance in the supervisory relationship.

Borders, L. D., & Leddick, G. (1987). *Handbook of counseling supervision*. Alexandria, VA: Association for Counselor Education and Supervision. Chapter 5: Supervisory relationship and process issues.

Borders, L. D., Bernard, J. M., Dye, H. A., Fong, M. L., Henderson, P., & Nance, D. W. (1991). Curriculum guide for training counseling supervisors: Rationale, development, and implementation. *Counselor Education and Supervision*, 31, 61–78.

Borgen, W. A., & Amundson, N. E. (1996). Strength challenge as process for supervision. *Counselor Education and Supervision*. 36, 159–169.

Bradley, L. (1989). *Counselor supervision*. Philadelphia: Accelerated Development. Chapter 2: The interpersonal relationship.

Cormier, S. & Hackney, H. (1999). *Counseling strategies and interventions*. (5th ed.). Boston: Allyn & Bacon.

Egan, G. (1998). *The skilled helper: A systematic approach to counseling*. Pacific Grove, CA: Brooks/Cole.

Ellis, M. V., & Ladany, N. (1997). Inferences concerning supervisees and clients in clinical supervision: an integrative review. In C. E. Watkins, Jr. (Ed.), *Handbook of Psychotherapy Supervision*. 447–507.

Feltham, C., & Dryden, W. (1994). *Developing counselor supervision*. London: Sage. Chapter 3: Fostering and using the supervisory relationship; & Chapter 5: Highlighting the supervisee's strengths and weaknesses.

Getz, H. G., & Protinsky, H. O. (1994). Training marriage and family counselors: A family-of-origin approach. *Counselor Education and Supervision*, 33, 183–190.

Haber, R. (1996). *Dimensions of psychotherapy supervision*. New York: Norton. Chapter 9: Consultation as a supervisory intervention.

Hendrix, D. H. (1992). Metaphors as nudges toward understanding in mental health counseling. *Journal of Mental Health Counseling*, 14(2), 234–242.

Horney, K. (1950). *Neurosis and human growth*. New York: Norton.

Ivey, A. (1999). *Intentional interviewing and counseling: Facilitating client development in a multicultural society*. (4th Ed.). Pacific Grove, CA: Brooks/Cole.

Juhnke, G.A. (1996). Solution-focused supervision: promoting supervisee skills and confidence through successful solutions. *Counselor Education and Supervision*, 36, 48–57.

Ladany, N., & Friedlander, M. L. (1995). The relationship between the supervisory working alliance and trainees' experience of role conflict and role ambiguity. *Counselor Education and Supervision*, 34, 220–231.

Lambert, M. J., & Ogles, B. M. (1997). The effectiveness of psychotherapy supervision. In C. E. Watkins, Jr. (Ed.), *Handbook of psychotherapy supervision*. New York: Wiley.

Lerner, H. G. (1989). *The dance of intimacy*. New York: Harper & Row.

O'Hanlon, W. H., & Weiner-Davis, M (1989). *In search of solutions: A new direction in psychotherapy*. New York: Norton.

Powell, D. J. (1993). *Clinical supervision in alcohol and drug abuse counseling: Principles, models, methods*. New York: Lexington Books. Chapter 8: The skills model; & Chapter 12: Basic supervisory techniques.

Shulman, L. (1993). *Interactional supervision*. Washington, DC: NASW. Chapter 3: Preparatory and beginning skills in supervision.

Teyber, E. (1997). *Interpersonal process in psychotherapy*. Pacific Grove, CA: Brooks/Cole. Chapter 2: Establishing a collaborative relationship.

Yalom, I. (1985). *The theory and practice of group psychotherapy*. New York: Basic Books.

6

HOW DOES THE SUPERVISOR SELECT METHODS AND TECHNIQUES TO HELP THE SUPERVISEE GROW AND DEVELOP?

The $64,000 question for all clinical supervisors is how to decide what method or technique to use with this particular supervisee at this particular time, with this particular client, in this particular situation to accomplish the dual goals of promoting the growth of the supervisee while providing quality care. With so many models of psychotherapy and so many available methods and techniques, how does the supervisor decide what to do? Just as with counseling and psychotherapy, there is no easy answer.

What does research tell us that might help answer this question? We still do not have the answer to the critical question of what supervision interventions by which supervisor will lead to what outcome for which supervisee (Avis & Sprunkle, 1990; Borders, 1989; Worthington, 1987). Empirical research is sparse to nonexistent for post-degree supervision (Borders, 1989; Magnuson & Wilcoxon, 1998). We know quite a bit about beginning supervisees in academic settings, but we do not know what supervisory interventions are needed to encourage growth to the higher stages of development, especially after graduation (Border, 1989; Russell & Petrie, 1994; Worthington, 1987).

One possible model to consider for this important task of selecting methods and techniques is from Loganbill et al. (1982), wherein five categories of intervention strategies were listed that facilitate the movement of the supervisee to a higher stage of growth: facilitative, prescriptive, conceptual, confrontive, and catalytic. Facilitative, or supportive, interventions reduce anxiety and provide a base of security for supervisees, thus promoting growth and risk taking. Prescriptive interventions, in which the supervisor gives the supervisee a specific plan of action, are primarily used early in supervision or when there is particular concern about client care (i.e., in a crisis situation). Conceptual interventions help the supervisee organize information and apply theory to practice. Conceptual interventions may facilitate the supervisee's movement to integrate learning in the more advanced stage of supervision. Confrontive and catalytic interventions address emotional aspects and are meant to promote self-awareness. Catalytic interventions include a broad category of responses such as questioning, probing, and process comments "designed to get things going" (p. 35). Prescriptive, conceptual, and facilitative interventions would be applied more in the beginning of supervision with a less experienced supervisee, while confrontive and catalytic interventions would be appropriate for the more experienced supervisee.

What Factors Should Be Considered in Selecting Methods and Techniques for Supervision?

It is recommended that supervisors consider a number of factors when selecting methods and techniques (Borders & Leddick, 1987; Liddle, Becker, & Diamond, 1997). These would include the developmental level of the supervisee, his or her learning style and prior experience with a variety of techniques, the supervisor's comfort level, experience as a supervisor, theoretical model, goals for supervisions, and the learning needs of the supervisee. Environmental factors such as availability of rooms and equipment, time, numbers of clients and budgeting, setting, populations served, ethical and legal concerns, regulations, and licensing requirements also should be considered when selecting methods and techniques.

Supervisors must be realistic about the role of environmental factors in supervision, but at the same time guard against engaging in patterns of negative thinking ("we don't have enough time, resources, money") that can drain positive energy and stifle creativity. To be effective, supervisors are therefore advised to examine environmental factors and any negative thinking about these factors and to apply problem-solving methods like brainstorming, or engage in consultation with peers, in order to alleviate any difficulties. Brainstorming requires the suspension of critical judgment while generating as many solutions to a problem as possible—the more fanciful and creative, the better.

For example, there is not enough time in the day for training. Create a seminar or workshop to give once a month or every 3 months for 1 to 3 hours, either inside or outside the workday. Provide CEU credit and invite other professionals to participate. If there is no special equipment, such as video cameras, borrow equipment from others. If your site does not have a room with a mirror, ask around the community for one to borrow. If there are problems with confidentiality or accessing populations, use simulated cases and borrow another staff member or supervisee to play the client. If stuck in the relationship with the supervisee, seek consultation. When there are problems with a dual relationship, trade supervisees across agencies or schools.

One of the key variables to consider when selecting methods and techniques is the supervisor's developmental level, areas of competence, knowledge, and ability. The supervisor must be able to assess his or her own level of skill and expertise in various methods and techniques of psychotherapy and supervision, know the benefits and drawbacks of applying these, and be flexible and adaptable in application. Some areas of expertise to consider are as follows: (Lists represent a compilation of topics from Borders et al. (1991), the certification requirements for the NBCC Approved Clinical Supervisor and for the AAMFT Approved Supervisor).

Counseling and Therapy Skills
➤ Knowledge of individual, group family and/or child counseling or therapy; communication and relationship skills;
➤ Conceptualization skills;
➤ Assessment or diagnositc skills;
➤ Knowledge and experience in the use of the methods and techniques of counseling or psychotherapy;
➤ Knowledge of a variety of intervention techniques for change;
➤ Written skills;
➤ Knowledge and application of ethical guidelines and standards in specific cases and situations;
➤ Crisis management;
➤ Knowledge and understanding of systems and the interaction between the individual, family, environmental factors and presenting problem(s);
➤ Awareness of the role of multicultural and contextual issues and ability to respond to those issues;
➤ Understanding of the role of developmental factors in client problems.

Supervision Skills
➤ Knowledge of the role and functions of clinical supervisors;

➤ Knowledge of the models, methods and techniques of clinical supervision; be able to articulate a personal model of supervision, structure supervision and to implement a variety of supervisory interventions such as group supervision;

➤ Understand the importance of the supervisory relationship and be able to facilitate this relationship

➤ Knowlege about the role of systems, cultural issues and environmental factors;

➤ Knowledge of legal and ethical issues unique to clinical supervision;

➤ Familiar with methods of evaluation of supervisee's competency and ability to apply them throughout supervision;

➤ Awareness of requirements and procedures required for licensure or certification.

A second critical variable in selecting methods and techniques includes the goals for supervision, the content areas deemed essential for professional competence, and the expectations for the level of competence in these areas for beginning or advanced supervisees. The supervisor must be able to identify expectations for competency in each content area at the beginning of supervision and at the end in order to set goals and plan for evaluation. The question to ask oneself is, "Are there some things I expect for the beginning supervisee to already know how to do and others I imagine will have to be gained through work experience?" For example, under the content area of professional ethics, the post-degree supervisor may expect the beginning supervisee to already have a knowledge base of ethical guidelines for the supervisee's discipline. However, learning to apply the guidelines to cases may be considered the heart of post-degree supervision. At the advanced level, when ready for licensure and independent practice, the supervisor might expect the supervisee to know the limits of his or her own professional expertise, be aware of what cases may be problematic, and be able to ask for help with these cases—all indications of professional judgment and demeanor. Establishing these expectations can then assist the supervisor in selecting the best methods and techniques to use to promote growth of the supervisee in each area. Readers are referred to an excellent 1998 article "Using Rubrics for Documentation of Clinical Work Supervision," by Hanna & Smith for a discussion and examples of this difficult task.

A third important variable to include in choosing methods and techniques of clinical supervision is the developmental level of the supervisory relationship itself. It is the premise of this workbook that the quality of the supervisory relationship is most crucial in effective supervision. As the relationship between the supervisor and supervisee also goes through developmental stages or phases, it is the developmental process of the supervisory relationship itself that will serve as a catalyst for the supervisee's personal and professional development and that will dictate the choice of methods and techniques for supervision. Thus, each of 3 variables—the supervisor, the supervisee, and the supervisory relationship—goes through its own developmental stages. The developmental level of the supervisor moderates the developmental level of the supervisee and the supervisory relationship. It is difficult for supervisors to encourage growth in their supervisees that goes beyond what they themselves can do. Since the quality of the supervisory relationship is most critical to the success of supervision, the supervisor must concentrate as much on their relationship skills as on the application of specific methods and techniques.

One quality required by effective supervisors is role flexibility, as they move from a hierarchical model of an unequal power base at the start of supervision to a more collegial one of an equal power base at termination. In the beginning, with any supervisee, no matter how skilled and experienced, the supervisor needs to get to know the person in order to collect a baseline of information on which a trusting, collaborative relationship can be built. During that time, it is often necessary for the supervisor to use the teaching role to provide some structure for setting goals and evaluation, and to explain his or her own model of working. This period of introduction can last anywhere from a week or two to several months, depending on a variety of factors. Live observation, demonstration, cotherapy, taping, and reviews of written work are all suggested supervision methods at this stage.

In the intermediate stage of the supervisory relationship, supervisors should move more into the counselor role, supporting supervisees to explore personal issues, examining parallel process and transference around such areas as personal power and competence, feelings, and personal style. A measure of conflict and anxiety surrounding these issues can be expected, but the supervisor should strive to be both supportive and challenging. In order to be most effective, supervisors may find it useful to combine methods and techniques, such as videotaping and IPR, case consultation and action techniques, solution-focused questions and parallel process, in order to help the supervisee move towards mutual goal setting and self-supervision.

At the final stage of the supervisory relationship, as the supervisee moves toward certification or licensure, the relationship should become more collegial. At this point, the supervisor will want to serve in a more consultative role, where the goals are created by the supervisee and some means are provided for self-supervision, including peer supervision, group supervision, or cotherapy.

The length of time spent in any development stage necessarily varies from supervisee to supervisee. It would be as much a mistake to remain in the expert mode throughout the relationship as to begin supervision assuming a collegial relationship while ignoring the evaluative and monitoring functions of supervision. The timing of the transition from expert to consultant to colleague depends on a number of factors. Supervisors must consider: (a) where the relationship stands or how much they know and trust the supervisee; (b) their assessment of the supervisee's skills, knowledge, and abilities; (c) their own skills and abilities and ideas about the supervision process; (d) the specific requirements and goals for supervision; and (e) the context and setting for supervision. For example, some settings and populations require the supervisee to be closely monitored and directed, as in hospitals and crisis units, while others require initiative, self-direction, and independent functioning, as in rural settings. Figure 6.1 illustrates this relationship.

		Supervisee		
		Within degree	Post-degree	Move toward licensure
Supervisor	Advanced supervisor Confirmation of identity and role	Lack of supervisor structure and goals; Supervisee anxiety about meeting expectations; Supervisee's need for structure; Insufficient monitoring; Lack of evaluation	Conflict between the needs of the supervisor and the needs and desires of the supervisee are not discussed	Collegial relationship; Use consultation to promote integration and self-supervision
	Intermediate-level supervisor Exploration	Conflict between supervisor's goals and desires and supervisee's needs and capabilities	Challenge supervisee; Conflict is present and resolved; Explore relationship issues; Confrontive; Catalytic	Explores; Challenges; Conflict is present and not resolved; Supervisor's lack of consultation skills
	Beginning supervisor Expert Structured	Learn skills; Immediate feedback; Structured learning; Demonstration model; Prescriptive; Facilitative	Conflict is present; Problems in relationship are ignored	Conflict is never resolved; No promotion of integration; No use of consultation skills
		Structure, support	Move to independence; Explore personal issues	Integration; Independence
		Goals set by supervisor	Mutual goal setting	Goals set by supervisee

FIGURE 6.1. Selecting methods and techniques: Interaction between the supervisor, supervisee, and the supervisory relationship

How Does the Supervisor Help the Supervisee Select Intervention Strategies for Working with Clients?

There is one model of psychotherapy, Prochaska's transtheoretical approach, that is highly applicable in helping supervisors conceptualize problems in order to help supervisees select methods and techniques to work with clients (Prochaska & Norcross, 1994). From work with addiction, Prochaska created a six-stage model to describe the cycle of change that occurs with any problem: Precontemplation, contemplation, preparation, action, maintenance, and termination (Prochaska & DiClemente, 1992; Prochaska & Norcross, 1994; Prochaska, Norcross, & DiClemente, 1994).

1. *Precontemplation.* The precontemplation stage is the period when a person may deny they have a problem or insist it is someone else's problem. Perpetrators ordered to counseling by the courts, adolescents brought in for therapy by parents, students referred to school counselors by teachers, and spouses brought in unwillingly for marital therapy are all examples of clients in the precontemplation stage of change. Yalom (1989) stated, "As long as one believes that one's problems are caused by some force or agency outside oneself, there is no leverage in therapy" (p. 8). Effective techniques for working with precontemplative clients are paradoxical, indirect, solution focused, and confrontational.

2. *Contemplation.* At this stage, clients may begin to be aware they do have a problem. They may have some idea of what needs to change but no real, solid commitment to take any action. For some people, this stage can take years or even last a lifetime. The presence of wishing, hoping, and waiting is an indication that the client is in the contemplation stage.

3. *Preparation.* While the assumption of responsibility for one's problems is crucial in psychotherapy, it only brings the person into the "vestibule of change, it is not synonymous with change" (Yalom, 1989, p. 9). Thus the preparation stage is like a bridge connecting contemplation and action. For some, the bridge between thinking about change and actually doing something is a very long bridge, full of cracks and holes, hanging over a mile-high canyon; for others, the bridge is short, wide, and easy to cross. Practitioners working with clients in the preparation stage need to help with the development of an individually tailored plan of action, going over the client's fears about change, and the ways that change may be sabotaged. Additionally, making the intended changes

public or joining support groups may also assist clients with the preparation stage (Prochaska, Norcross, & DiClemente, 1994).

4. *Action.* This stage is perhaps the most visible stage of change, and certainly the busiest. For example, most weight-loss programs are geared to support the action stage of change and to provide clients with many helpful, supportive suggestions. Prochaska, Norcross, and DiClemente (1994) estimated that less than 20% of individuals needing to make changes in their lives are at the action stage, yet over 90% of all behavioral programs are focused on that stage in the change cycle. Practitioners, however, must be careful that the investment for change is with the client and not with themselves. It is also easy to confuse action with change. The person may look as if they are actually changing, but stress, emotional upheavals, and lack of support can all undermine their ultimate success (Prochaska & DiClemente, 1992). Journals, checklists, regular reporting, rewards, and celebration of successes are all typical methods used in the action stage to help ensure that change is made.

5. *Maintenance.* This is not a static stage, and for some, it is more difficult to achieve than the action phase. Research by Prochaska and DiClemente (1992) has demonstrated that new behaviors must be repeated for a minimum of 6 months before the maintenance stage is achieved. The person must work to consolidate the change by consistently engaging in the new behavior over a long period of time. Support groups, group therapy, and periodic meetings with the therapist after the termination of formal therapy are all effective interventions for the maintenance stage.

6. *Termination.* At this stage, a person really feels finished with the problem. The changes are integrated into one's life, there is no need to invest any effort to maintain the new behavior, and there is no danger of any relapse to old behaviors.

In the transtheoretical approach, clients engage in therapy at any point in the change cycle. The practitioner must therefore use different methods and techniques to work with clients, depending on where they are in the cycle. Some psychotherapies, like client-centered or psychodynamic, focus on understanding and insight (the contemplation stage), while others, such as cognitive-behavioral and solution focused, are more action focused. Movement through the change cycle is not linear and it may take a client as many as three tries before successfully completing the cycle (Prochaska et al., 1994). The more specific the behavior change, and the more reasons the client has to make the change, the more likely they are to be successful.

When employing the transtheoretical approach in supervision, the supervisor will work as a consultant, providing the supervisee with a framework within which to conceptualize problems, form hypotheses, and select intervention strategies. Since the transtheoretical approach takes pressure off the action phase of psychotherapy, it frees both supervisor and supervisee to explore different possibilities for intervention. Typically, beginning mental health practitioners are too focused on the action stage, wanting and willing their respective clients to make changes in their lives. Only just starting their careers, these supervisees describe the "need to be helpful" as a core goal of their work. Only if the client is successful in making changes in their lives does the trainee feel successful. Beginning supervisors can experience similar thoughts. However, normalizing the idea of client's trying and failing to change, and thus giving validity to the precontemplation and contemplation stages of problem solving, can certainly stimulate creativity and prevent burnout. For example, school counselors and other overwhelmed mental health practitioners, by focusing on different ways they can be helpful to clients and redefining their role, can become re-energized.

Additionally, because of changes in the law, clients in the precontemplation stage are becoming a major part of many agencies' client base. The transtheoretical approach reminds all mental health practitioners that intervention strategies for clients involuntarily obligated to undergo therapy should necessarily involve working through resistance and toward increasing the client's ownership of their problems. The use of methods designed to bring about action with those still in the precontemplation stage is probably doomed to fail, as indicated by the poor success rate of counseling with perpetrators, victims of domestic violence, drug addicts, and drunk drivers.

EXPLORATION ➤ *Selection of Methods and Techniques for Supervision*

1. Loganbill et al. (1982) suggested five categories of intervention strategies designed to promote the supervisee's growth to higher stages: prescriptive, conceptual, supportive, confrontive, and catalytic. Think back to your own experience as a supervisee and select one or two supervisors to use for this exercise.

   a. Which of the five categories did the supervisor rely on most in supervision? Did he or she use all five? Describe and give examples.

   b. Did he or she change intervention strategies as you developed; for example, move from prescriptive to more confrontive? Describe.

   c. Can you identify examples of each one?

2. Think of a current supervisee or, if necessary, imagine a potential supervisee. How do you see yourself applying these five categories? Give an example of what to say or do for each category.

3. Make a map of your environment. First make a list of all the systems that have an impact on your professional life, such as work setting, professional goals, your health, government organizations and regulations, professional association, state and local laws, your religious and spiritual beliefs, and family. (Exercise adapted from Middleman & Rhodes, 1975).

   a. Rank-order them as to importance in your life now.

   b. Using circles to represent each system and lines to connect them, make a drawing or map to illustrate the relationships among these systems. Label the various parts of the drawing.

c. Examine the map as to any changes you would like to make. Draw dotted lines to represent the circles getting larger or smaller and dotted lines to represent any changes in the relationships among these systems. (Exercise adapted from Middleman & Rhodes, 1985.)

d. Explore negative thinking patterns about your changing environmental context. For example, "We don't have the time, money, and resources. We can't do this with this population, setting, and job description. My administrator won't let me." List which negative thinking patterns apply to you.

e. Apply problem-solving strategies such as brainstorming to answer these negative thoughts. Ask a colleague to help you do this.

EXPLORATION ➤ The Supervisor's Competence

1. Review the list of expected competencies for supervisors on pages 115-116.

   a. Rate yourself on your personal knowledge, skill and comfort in each of the areas.

Competency	No experience	Some experience and skill	Adequate skill	Very comfortable with my skills
Individual				
Group				
Family				
Child				
Adolescence				
Relationship skills				
Conceptualization skills				
Assessment or diagnostic skills				
Goal setting or treatment planning skills				
Variety of intervention techniques for change				
Written skills				
Ethical guidelines and standards in specific cases and situations				
Crisis management				
Systems and the interaction between individual, family, and environmental factors				
Role of multicultural issues and ability to respond to those issues				
Developmental factors				

Competency	No experience	Some experience and skill	Adequate skill	Very comfortable with my skills
Role and functions of clinical supervisors				
Models of supervision				
Methods and techniques of clinical supervision				
Personal model of supervision				
Variety of supervisory interventions				
Group supervision				
Role supervisory relationship				
Role of systems, cultural issues and environmental factors				
Legal and ethical issues unique to clinical supervision				
Methods of evaluation of supervisee's competency				
Requirements or procedures for licensure or certification				

2. In order to explore the impact of the stage of development of the supervisee on the selection of methods and techniques, answer the following questions.

   a. What does the beginning supervisee need and want from the supervisor? Give examples.

i. What techniques would you want to use with a beginning supervisee to meet those needs?

ii. What role or function would you want to emphasize?

iii. What relationship factors would be important to consider?

b. What does the intermediate supervisee need and want from the supervisor? Give examples.

i. What techniques would you want to use to meet those needs?

ii. What role or function would you want to emphasize?

iii. What relationship factors would be important to consider?

c. What does the advanced supervisee need and want from the supervisor? Give examples.

i. What techniques would you want to use with the advanced supervisee?

ii. What role or function would you want to emphasize?

iii. What relationship factors would be important to consider?

3. Review your answers and check to see whether your suggestions will facilitate learning in each component: knowledge, practice, and personal. Do you need to make any changes to your answers? Describe.

4. Establishing expectations for competency in each goal area has been identified as essential to the process of deciding what methods and techniques to use in supervision. Review your lists of goals and areas of competency from chapters 1 and 2.

a. Place them on the following chart.

b. In exploration question 2 of this section, you were asked to describe the differences in needs between beginning, intermediate, and advanced supervisees and what techniques you would want to use with supervisees at each developmental level. Take your answers, and fill in the following chart. Use the examples as a guide.

c. Retain this chart and your description of techniques for use in planning for evaluation. Chapter 9.

EXPECTATIONS				
Competency area	Beginning stage supervision	Intermediate stage of supervision	End of supervision	
Professional ethics	*Know the guidelines* Give a test; Have supervisees sign a statement that they have read the guidelines	*Apply to client cases* Case consultation; Videotaping	*Professional judgment and demeanor* Role-play situations with clients; Review case notes	**METHODS & TECHNIQUES**

EXPLORATION ➤ Helping Supervisees Select Intervention Strategies to Use With Clients

1. In order to practice using Prochaska's six-stage model of change, think of a new client.

   a. Where would you place this person (or persons) in the change cycle?

   b. What type of intervention strategy does this suggest?

   c. Think of another client with whom you are currently having troubles working. Describe the difficulties you are having.

   d. Now think through how you have been approaching this client. Where would you place this client in the change cycle?

e. Do you need to change your approach or your choice of intervention strategy? Describe specifically what changes you need to make.

f. Review your answers. Do you have any ideas on changing your approach or choice of intervention strategies that you could apply with other difficult clients?

g. Imagine that your supervisee is discussing a new case with you. How might you apply this learning in supervision?

What Are the Major Problems
in the Supervisory Relationship?

Though the overall goal in post-degree supervision is to work collaboratively with the supervisee, there are certain points in the relationship with some supervisees when the supervisor feels tension or discomfort. While conflict is normal and natural in any close relationship, especially as described in the intermediate developmental stage of supervision, it will likely still feel uncomfortable for the supervisor when tensions flare. In some instances, difficulties may indicate the existence of relationship issues and problems that extend far beyond that of supervision, and that indicate the need for the supervisee to engage in personal therapeutic work outside supervision. On the other hand, it may suggest that relationship problems are an expression of anxiety and require the supervisor to change supervision methods and techniques.

Psychodynamic theory of transference and countertransference could also be helpful for understanding and exploring relationship difficulties with supervisees. In self psychology (Kohut, 1971), a transference reaction is not just a distortion based on what was missed as a child, but represents what is needed now in relationships to make up for those deficits. In other words, supervisees may need for their supervisor to be different from their parents and to provide them something they did not receive in their own family of origin. For example, a supervisee who felt he could never win the approval of his father or mother may be highly needy of the supervisor's approval. In this instance, if the supervisor does not respond accordingly, the supervisee could overreact emotionally, feeling abandoned and hurt. Taking time out to examine such experiences can create understanding and promote the growth of the supervisory relationship.

It is hard to generalize about what types of relationship issues are most problematic for each supervisor. However, there are several categories of supervisee responses to supervision that can be described as generally problematic; including the highly dependent, helpless, or too agreeable supervisee, the closed and defensive supervisee, or the externalizing and oppositional supervisee. Each category can be the result of how the supervisee copes with anxiety. For example, beginning supervisees who lack practical experience with clients and who are just beginning their supervision may respond with these characteristic patterns of behavior as they attempt to manage their anxiety, such as appearing helpless and needing suggestions and reassurance, or defensive, uncooperative, and resistant to the supervisor's suggestions. It is easy for beginning supervisors, who are also anxious and unsure of themselves, to mistake the supervisee's genuine need for support and structure with psychological problems that go well beyond the supervisory relationship. For this reason, it is important to challenge the supervisee early on in the relationship concerning their perceived resistance and defensiveness, and to avoid jumping to the conclusion that all relationship difficulties are an indication of the supervisee's impairment.

It is also important for supervisors to examine their own patterns of responding to the supervisee's anxiety and how this may play a role in the supervisory relationship. Only after this self-examination can it be determined whether the supervisee really is stuck and unable to grow, or is simply lacking in experience and practice. Periodic consultation with other supervisors would help check perceptions and help with objectivity. Regardless of the causes of difficulties, the supervisor is expected to apply their relationship skills to improve the situation. This requires self-awareness, comfort with confrontation, and a willingness to tolerate anger and rejection in order to create a more open, collaborative relationship (Bradley, 2000).

In return, it is just as important for the supervisor to examine the possibility of the existence of countertransference whereby the supervisor might be responding to the supervisee from his or her own unresolved material, which can be very detrimental to the supervisee. For example, a clinical supervisor who has difficulty with anger and conflict could displace these feelings onto the supervisee or seek to have the supervisee act out anger for him or her. In other words, the supervisor's issues with expressing anger and fear of conflict become part of the supervisory relationship. To prevent countertransference reactions, supervisors need to continually reality-test their responses to each supervisee. Psychodynamic theory reminds supervisors, like supervisees, to be careful not to come to the mental health field as a means to resolve personal problems. In situations of serious dislike or continual negative responses to a supervisee, it is likely that some countertransference reaction is occurring. Ethically, it is not only necessary for the supervisor to seek immediate consultation and, if possible, referral of the supervisee to another supervisor, but to engage in their own personal psychotherapy to avoid any further damage to future supervisees.

How Does the Supervisor Apply Skills to Work With the Difficult Supervisee?

Any number of skills and techniques could be applied to work with difficult supervisees: analyzing parallel process, transference and countertransference, process comments, I-focus, asking for meaning, and indirect methods such as paradoxical interventions and reframing. Feltham and Dryden (1994) suggested that the supervisor's theoretical framework dramatically influences responses to the supervisee's anxiety and dependency. For example, a supervisor using the RET framework may want to challenge the underlying thought process of the supervisee (such as catastrophizing about mistakes, all-or-nothing thinking, generalizing, perfectionistic thinking). The person-centered supervisor may take a more nurturing stance. With psychodynamic supervision, anxiety would be analyzed as transference.

Perhaps the best method to assist supervisors to understand and work with difficulties in the supervisory relationship is to videotape a supervision session and then use IPR along with the parallel process model of supervision. Parallel process denotes the fact that problems the supervisee is having with clients will be reflected in the relationship with the supervisor. Using the parallel process model, supervisors could ask themselves:

➤ How does the supervisee's behavior affect me? Is this similar to or different from the impact the supervisee has on the client?
➤ How do I find myself reacting to the supervisee? His or her interpersonal style?
➤ How do I see this awareness affecting my relationship with the supervisee?
➤ What might I need to do to solve this problem?

The IPR model would be extremely helpful in introducing the topic of relationship difficulties with supervisees. For example, while reviewing a videotape of a supervision session with a supervisee, the supervisor might say, "I noticed that when I said that, you did . . ., and I am wondering what you were feeling and thinking right then. Was there something I did or said that made you anxious or angry?" or "You stated that you were feeling anxious when the client said or did x . . . Are you feeling that way now with me?" At the end of the review of the tape, inquire, "How did you find the reviewing of the tape with me? Was it helpful or not helpful? How could I improve?"

There are specific interpersonal skills and interventions that can be used with each one of the aforementioned categories of problematic responses by supervisees, externalization, helplessness, dependency, and defensiveness. The first category of responses, the externalization of blame or control by the supervisee, is a very common problem, particularly with beginning supervisees. When challenged about what they are doing, sometimes the supervisee finds it easier to externalize control. "The client wouldn't let me do . . . There wasn't enough time . . ., or this is what I was taught previously . . ., or my other supervisor told me to do it this way... or this client is just borderline or has no motivation to change."

Here, supervisors need to help their supervisees move from generalized thinking or feelings, ("There are some people you just can't help") to a more specific situational focus, "You are feeling stuck with this client; he or she is creating difficulties for you" (Shulman, 1993). Techniques such as moving from the general to the specific, asking open-ended questions, asking for examples or clarification, and summarizing are useful in this situation.

Another intervention suggestion is to create an internal focus, or "I-focus" (Teyber, 1997). He explains this as shifting from externalizing problems to focusing inward. One way to create an I-focus is to use process comments to bring the problem into the here and now, and to therefore help the supervisee move from complaining about others and wanting others to change, to looking at themselves. For example, the supervisor might ask, "When the client did that, what did you find yourself thinking?", "What did it mean to you when the person said that?", or "What was that like for you when the client said that?" (Teyber, 1997, p. 95).

Ivey (1999) described a technique of asking for and reflecting meaning that also could be used in this situation. Asking for meaning includes exploring the inner thoughts, beliefs, values, and motivations behind the behavior of the supervisee. Such questions as, "What does it mean to you to be . . . " or "As you look at this situation, what thoughts or beliefs underlie your actions? When the client said . . . how did you interpret that?" and "What personal values are important here in this interaction?" (Ivey, 1999, p. 237) will be useful to the supervisor asking for meaning. This technique can provide the supervisor with access to the deeper problems that are underlying supervisory relationship issues.

With overly anxious and dependent supervisees, the technique of "going with" or "honoring the resistance"—agreeing with the supervisee in order to resolve defensiveness and engage them in work—can be applied (Teyber, 1997; Mazza, 1988). Here, going with the resistance means abandoning the role of trying to push the supervisee to be more independent. For example, instead of exhorting and arguing, agree and sympathize with the supervisee's problem: "Yes, this is difficult, I'm not sure how you are going to solve it," or suggest the opposite: "I'm not sure you are ready to work independently."

In instances where supervisees respond defensively, rejecting directions or suggestions of the supervisor, paradoxical interventions are sometimes the most useful type of intervention strategy. Paradoxical interventions are influence techniques that block or interrupt a client's entrenched patterns of responding to situations, such as defensive or oppositional behavior (Watzlawick, Weakland, & Fisch, 1974). Three types of paradoxical interventions could be chosen to work with defensive or resistant supervisees: (a) prescribing the symptom: suggesting the supervisee do more of the thing that is causing problems ("I don't think you are really trying hard enough, you need to do more of . . . "); (b) restraining the supervisee from change ("It probably is not a good idea for you to change now; it is probably too soon to try that"), or (c) applying a position strategy ("I agree, your problems are too big to be solved. I probably can't help you"). For example, with supervisees who have trouble taking suggestions or accepting constructive criticism, the supervisor may say, "It probably won't work, but if you want to, you could try . . . " or "This probably is a crazy idea, but. . ."

Self-disclosure is another useful method for coping with defensive and anxious supervisees. Ladany & Lehrman-Waterman (1999) found a relationship between Supervisor self-disclosure and the strength of the supervisory working alliance and suggest the selective use of self-disclosure to repair problematic relationships. There are two kinds of self-disclosure: giving examples of similar problems from one's own training, as in the statement, "I know it was very difficult for me when my supervisor corrected me or gave me a suggestion . . . " or self-disclosing one's feelings in the here and now such as, "I am experiencing difficulty giving you feedback—what can I do? How do you want to hear this from me?" Teyber (1997) called this last technique *self-involving statements*: expressing here-and-now reactions to what the supervisee has just said or done. With the highly sensitive and perfectionistic supervisee who personalizes feedback, try combining self-disclosure and self-involving statements with a request for the supervisee to offer suggestions. Here, the supervisor might say: "I experience you as fragile, and feel unable to give you corrective feedback or suggestions without wounding you. How can I share my comments or suggestions without taking away your feeling of competency? Can you give me some specific suggestions?"

EXPLORATION ➤ Working With the Difficult Supervisee

1. How would you rate yourself now on your knowledge of relationship skills for working with the difficult supervisee? Use the chart below to rate yourself.

Intervention strategy	Not at all familiar with the strategy	Somewhat familiar with the strategy	Familiar with the strategy	Know a lot about the strategy	Consistently use the strategy
Agreeing					
Moving from the general to the specific					
Asking open-ended questions					
Asking for clarification					
Using self-disclosure					
Using self-involving statements					
Asking for meaning					
Using the "I" focus					
"Going with" or "honoring the resistance"					
Analyzing parallel process					
Using paradoxical interventions					
Reframing					

2. Imagine a difficult supervisee.

   a. Can you describe how this person would be difficult for you? In what ways?

b. Do you see any similarity between this situation and your relationship patterns in other situations? With family? Friends? At work?

3. Create a role-play scenario that revolves around a difficult supervisee. Choose any relationship difficulty, such as an overly pleasing supervisee or a defensive one. Ask a colleague to assist you in the role play. Make a practice tape of this role play. Apply one of the suggested techniques for challenging the supervisee: self-disclosure, I-focus, exploring meaning, or indirect methods.

4. Ask a colleague to play your supervisee. Using one of the suggested scenarios below, tape the session and practice reviewing the session afterwards using process questions.

   a. Initial contact, introductory session:

   ❏ Bad match between the goals of the supervisee and supervisor competencies.
   ❏ A colleague that wants you to "just sign off on the forms" for licensure ("You know me, so there is no need to be supervised really").
   ❏ Your supervisor assigns you the supervisee.

   b. Several sessions into supervision:

   ❏ You identify problems with the supervisory relationship
   ❏ You are having difficulties working with the supervisee.
   ❏ You identify personal issues that are interfering with the supervisee's work with their clients and professional development.

   c. Multicultural issues in the supervisory relationship:

   ❏ You and the supervisee are of different gender, race, ethnicity, sexual orientation, religion, etc.

5. To examine transference, review your own supervision experience.

  a. Make a list of your supervisors. Now ask yourself and record what you needed from each of them. (For example, the need to be needed, liked, powerful, competent, etc.)

  b. How badly did you need the approval of each of these supervisors? Was it more important with certain ones?

  c. Did you experience any of them as critical or disapproving?

  d. What about the need to be liked by your supervisor? (To be taken into the inner circle as a respected colleague? To be asked to colead, do cotherapy, or to copresent?)

e. Did you feel competitive toward any of your supervisors?

f. Did you feel competitive toward other supervisees for the supervisor's attention or approval? What did you do as a result? What are your thoughts or feelings as you recall this fact?

6. Think of a time when you reacted emotionally to something your supervisor did or said that surprised you.

a. Describe what the person did or said and then describe your reactions. Try to include your thoughts, feelings, and behaviors. Do you recall what this supervisor said or did that upset you? Describe.

b. Using the concept of transference, can you draw any parallels between your response in this situation and responses to your parents? Share this answer with a colleague or another supervisor.

c. Review your answer and think about how you reacted. Use the following list to guide your thinking. Did you feel the supervisor was:

- ❑ Too powerful and controlling (trying to persuade you or tell you what to do)?
- ❑ Too much like a friend and not acting authoritative enough?
- ❑ Too distant?
- ❑ Disapproving and critical?
- ❑ Nonsupportive?

Discuss.

d. Do you know how other supervisees experienced this person? Did you check out your feelings with any of them?

7. To explore countertransference, think about your current supervisor or administrator in your work environment.

a. Do you have some anger or resentment toward him or her or your work situation? How do you typically handle these feelings? (Complain to your peers? Your family? Keep it to yourself? Speak up in meetings and attempt to initiate change? Blow it off?) Describe.

b. How might these feelings or resentments get "transferred" to your supervisee?

c. What do you need to do about that?

➤ Chapter Highlights

> ➤ Effective supervisors should recognize the importance of the interaction among the supervisor, the supervisee, contextual issues, and the supervisory relationship.

> ➤ Supervisors should consider the developmental level of the supervisee, their own developmental level, and the developmental level of the relationship when selecting methods and techniques.

> ➤ Supervisors must be flexible, take a multimodal approach to supervision, and consider several sources of information to assess the skill level of the supervisee, including personality variables, learning style, and multicultural factors.

Suggested Readings

Bernard, J., & Goodyear, R. (1998). *Fundamentals of clinical supervision*. Boston: Allyn & Bacon. Chapter 3: The supervisory relationship: The influence of individual and developmental differences.

Borders, L. D., Bernard, J. M., Dye, H. A., Fong, M. L, Henderson, P., & Nance, D. W. (1991). Curriculum guide for training counseling supervisors: Rationale, development, and implementation. *Counselor Education and Supervision*, 31, 61–78.

Borders, L. D., & Leddick, G. (1987). *Handbook of counseling supervision*. Alexandria, VA: Association for Counselor Education and Supervision. Chapter 4: Choosing and implementing supervision interventions.

Bradley, L. (2000). *Counselor supervision*. Philadephia: Accelerated Development. Chapter 2: Games supervisees and supervisors play; Part III: Differential supervision activities; & Chapter 11: Supervision training: a model.

Feltham, C., & Dryden, W. (1994). *Developing counselor supervision*. London: Sage. Chapter 4: Using the developmental opportunities of supervision.

Kaiser, T. (1997). *Supervisory relationships: Exploring the human element*. Pacific Grove, CA: Brooks/Cole. Chapter 4: Shared meaning.

Liddle, H. A., Becker, D., & Diamond, G. (1997). Family therapy supervision. In C. E. Watkins Jr. (Ed.), *Handbook of psychotherapy supervision*. New York: Wiley.

Loganbill, C., Hardy, E., & Delworth, U. (1982). Supervision: A conceptual model. *The Counseling Psychologist, 10*(1), 3–42.

Mazza, J. (1988). Training strategic therapists: The use of indirect techniques. In Liddle, H., Breunlin, D. C. and Schwartz, R. C. *Handbook of family therapy training & supervision*. New York: Guilford.

Norcross, J. C., & Halgin, R. P. (1997). Integrative approaches to supervision. In C. E. Watkins Jr. (Ed.), *Handbook of psychotherapy supervision*. New York: Wiley.

Powell, D. J. (1993). *Clinical supervision in alcohol and drug abuse counseling: Principles, models, methods*. New York: Lexington Books. Chapter 12: Basic supervisory techniques; & Appendix A: Competencies of supervisors.

Prochaska, J. O., Norcross, J. C., & DiClemente, C. (1994). *Changing for good*. New York: William Morrow.

Shulman, L. (1993). *Interactional supervision*. Washington, DC: NASW. Part II: Supervision and the phases of work.

Stoltenberg, C. D., McNeill, B. W., & Delworth, U. (1997). *IDM supervision: An integrated development model for supervising counselors and therapists*. San Francisco: Jossey-Bass. Chapter 8: Supervision across settings.

Teyber, E. (1997). *Interpersonal process in psychotherapy*. Pacific Grove, CA: Brooks/Cole. Chapter 3: Honoring the client's resistance; Chapter 4: An internal focus for change; & Chapter 5: Responding to conflicted emotions.

Watzlawick, P., Weakland, J. H., & Fisch, R. (1974). *Change: Principles of problem formation and problem resolution*. New York: Norton.

7

WHAT ARE THE ETHICAL AND LEGAL ISSUES IN CLINCAL SUPERVISION?

There are two main areas of ethical concern for clinical supervisors: the supervisory relationship and the supervisee's actions with clients. Clinical supervision is a three-tiered relationship with a dual purpose to promote the development of the supervisee and to monitor the quality of client care. This dual purpose can contribute to role conflict for the supervisor and a plethora of ethical dilemmas. Contextual issues, such as setting, budget and manpower, licensing rules, and legal codes, only add to the supervisor's difficulties when making ethical decisions. Hence, "doing the right thing" is not always as easy as it seems, and ethical choices can become very complicated for the clinical supervisor.

What Are the Ethical Issues in the Supervisory Relationship?

Both supervisor and supervisee need to understand the main ethical issues and concerns in supervision. First and foremost would be problems resulting from dual relationships. Because dual relationship issues are so pervasive in post-degree supervision, supervisors are required to pay special attention to the role they play in the supervisee's training.

Sherry (1991) suggested three other factors that can have great ethical impact: (1) the power differential, (2) the therapy-like quality of the relationship, and (3) the conflicting roles of supervisor and supervisee (especially with regard to performance evaluation). These elements, common to each supervisory experience, can make the relationship particularly vulnerable to ethical confusion and misconduct. A final ethical issue is the need for competent supervisors and supervisees.

What Are Dual Relationships in Supervision?

Before beginning supervision, it is important for the supervisor to examine the type and number and the nature of the potential dual relationships one might have with a supervisee, remembering that the ethical standard of "do no harm" should prevail. A dual relationship exists whenever a practitioner has an additional relationship of some kind outside of their primary professional relationship, in this case, as clinical supervisor. In actuality, however, dual relationship issues permeate the post-degree supervisory process (Navin, Beamish, & Johanson, 1992). Licensure supervision may be offered to a new employee as part of their employment contract and their administrator, who is also their boss, appointed clinical supervisor. In rural settings, small communities, school districts, churches or agencies, situations often arise in which the supervisor is a co-worker or professional colleague. In some cases, experienced practitioners, seeking a new certification or a state license, may approach a colleague, who is also a friend, for supervision. Thus, clinical supervisors are continually challenged to evaluate the potential that harm may come from such dual relationships, and to decide whether such relationships are unavoidable. Perhaps, because they are so prevalent, it is more practical to discuss how to manage dual relationships in post-degree supervision and limit their harm, rather than attempting to avoid them completely.

What Constitutes a Harmful Dual Relationship?

Supervisors must clearly understand what constitutes a dual relationship and they must be able to weigh its potential for harm. There are several questions that should be asked:

➤ What could go wrong (i.e., loss of a friend or peer, loss of reputation, loss of license, potential malpractice suit)?
➤ What is the potential worst-case scenario should something go wrong?
➤ What could be done to avoid any potential harm?

> What are the available alternatives?
> What is the best plan?

But first we need to ask: What is a harmful dual relationship? It should be obvious to all practitioners that any kind of sexual relationship with a supervisee would be exploitative and harmful to the supervisory relationship. It should also be obvious that attempting to supervise a relative, an employer, or a close personal friend would be unethical. Friendship may impair judgment and the ability to objectively evaluate the supervisee, and can affect actions and choices of intervention strategies with clients. However, it is less clear how other types of collegial friendship can create ethical problems in supervision. One problem occurs when clinical supervision leads to the development of a close personal relationship with the supervisee, in which case it can be hard to set limits and boundaries. For example, part of the process of professional development often requires the attendance of both supervisor and supervisee at professional lunches, workshops, or conferences. How do supervisors draw appropriate boundaries in these situations? Is there any potential for harm if they don't? Another ethical problem for clinical supervisors can develop when the supervisee is also their employee. What is the potential for harm to result from this dual relationship? For example, how will this relationship affect factors such as openness, feedback, evaluation, and client intervention?

Regardless of the circumstances, Herlihy and Corey (1992) wrote that, "as in any professional relationship, it is essential the supervisory relationship be grounded on a clear contract" (p. 117). They suggested that proper boundaries should be agreed upon during the initial stage of contracting with a supervisee and should be clarified continuously throughout the relationship to avoid exploitation and impaired objectivity and judgment.

How Does the Hierarchical Nature of the Supervisory Relationship Create Ethical Concerns?

Perhaps most ethical dilemmas are the result of the hierarchical nature of the supervisory relationship and unequal power sharing between the supervisor and the supervisee. Because of their subordinate position, supervisees have limited power to protect themselves from potential abuses of power that can result in exploitation or even severe harm. This is particularly true for postgraduate supervises who require licensure or certification to advance professionally. For post-degree supervisors not prepared to handle the responsibility, the unequal power can lead to exploitation of the supervisee, poor objectivity, diminished consent, and role conflict (Disney & Stephens, 1994). The ACA ethical guidelines for supervisors state clearly that the supervisee should be made aware that a differential in power exists and of the impact this differential may have. Appendix E reprints the American Counseling Association's guidelines for supervisors. Supervisors from other disciplines such as social work, psychology, and marriage and family should refer to their own ethical standards for guidance in this matter.

What Is the Problem With the Therapy-Like Quality of the Supervisory Relationship?

Often, the therapy-like nature of clinical supervision makes it difficult to delineate boundaries and to set limits. The supervisor may find it difficult to avoid becoming a supervisee's therapist, and thus engaging in a dual relationship. Many supervisors continually struggle with the problem of how to explore personal issues within supervision without crossing established boundaries. Kaiser (1992) suggests that personal issues necessarily arise in the supervisory relationship, just as they do in counseling and therapy. One could argue that it would be unethical for the supervisor not to adopt a therapist role with the supervisee when it is recognized that personal issues are interfering with client care (Russell & Petrie, 1994). However, there will likely be a difference in each supervisor's view of how these personal issues should be addressed, to what extent, and at what point in supervision. The supervisor should be aware that their knowledge of a supervisee's personal issues might have a detrimental effect on performance evaluation, their choice of methods and techniques, and on the supervisory relationship in general. For more discussion on this important topic, see chapter 10.

How Do the Conflicting Roles of the Supervisee and Supervisor Create Ethical Dilemmas?

The conflicting roles of both supervisor and supervisee can also contribute to ethical dilemmas (see chapter 5 on the working alliance). Misunderstanding the role and function of the supervisor, particularly with respect to responsibility for both client care and evaluation of the supervisee, can contribute to ethical confusion. The supervisor is ethically bound to give a fair and honest evaluation of the supervisee's competency and qualification for licensing or certification. This important role may have an impact on the nature of the relationship and be particularly problematic because of dual relationship issues discussed in the previous section.

As supervision progresses over time, the supervisor will likely shift in role from evaluator to colleague and, for many, to friend, making it hard to accurately evaluate the supervisee. However, until formal supervision is terminated, evaluation is still an aspect of the relationship, and the supervisor will be still held responsible for the actions of the supervisee. Without clear role definition, there can be difficulties and misunderstandings.

Role conflict and issues of evaluation also create ethical dilemmas for the supervisee. The supervisee is ethically bound to inform the supervisor of any areas of weakness, gaps in learning, personal limitations, or other potential problem areas. In order to monitor the quality of client care, supervisees need to give supervisors details of their cases and to notify them of any problem cases and possible mistakes. Such disclosure is requisite, even at the risk of a negative evaluation by the supervisor. In situations in which the supervisor is also the employer and the supervisee's job is on the line, however, the ownership of mistakes can become more problematic for the supervisee.

Another area of potential misunderstanding for supervisors and supervisees can arise over the limits to confidentiality of evaluative information. The method of evaluation chosen by the supervisor can affect the supervisee's privacy in several ways. For instance, supervisors may seek consultation from another professional concerning problems they are having with supervisees. Additionally, the supervisor will be passing on an evaluation of the supervisee's competency to licensing boards, program administrators, or potential employers. Though such disclosure is the necessary result of supervision, this fact can have a direct effect on the supervisee's professional status and career. Therefore, it is recommended that supervisors discuss the limits to confidentiality with their supervisee before commencing supervision, and that these limitations be incorporated into the supervision contract.

How Is the Supervisor's Competency an Ethical Concern?

Stoltenberg and Delworth (1987) discussed another area of ethical concern in supervision; the competency of the supervisor. Ethical supervisors need to be competent and knowledgeable in order to protect client care and further the supervisee's development. Thus, the supervisor must be a competent model of ethical decision making for the supervisee. Current ethical standards indicate the need for supervisors to periodically evaluate their own competence in order to avoid harm to supervisees and clients. Supervisors also need to examine their own biases and limitations and how these factors might affect their clinical judgment and intervention strategies. Sherry (1991) advised supervisors to periodically review their training goals, methods, and techniques, to seek additional training in supervision or in areas of professional weakness, and to update their knowledge of current ethical issues.

Supervisors should consider obtaining either periodic consultation of their work or ongoing supervision in order to protect the client, the supervisee, and the mental health profession as a whole. Additionally, ethical supervisors also need to offer a means for their supervisees to evaluate them. Appendix K provides a sample evaluation form for this purpose.

What Can the Supervisor Do to Avoid Ethical Misconduct?

1. Seek specialized training in supervision.
   - ➤ Keep knowledge of supervision issues current.
   - ➤ Read or attend workshops on a regular basis.
   - ➤ Join a professional organization that publishes current information on ethics and other content areas.
2. Avoid dual relationships whenever possible in order to reduce risk of harm.
   - ➤ Refer the supervisee to another supervisor if a dual relationship exists. If this is not possible, seek personal supervision to maintain objectivity.
   - ➤ Use informed consent and keep discussion open with regard to the supervisee's pitfalls and problems.
   - ➤ Be aware of the therapy-like nature of supervision. Limit supervisee's processing of personal issues to those that affect client care.
   - ➤ Refer supervisee to an outside therapist if concerned about the impact of the supervisee's personal issues on clients.
3. Avail oneself of consultation to help with ethical dilemmas.
   - ➤ Develop a network of respected experts to use for consultation.
   - ➤ Create a peer network of other supervisors in the community.
   - ➤ Meet regularly to discuss cases.
4. Utilize written informed consent. Delineate roles, methods of evaluation, issues of confidentiality, areas of expertise and knowledge, availability, methods of feedback, and recourse available to the supervisee should problems arise. See Appendix M for a sample supervision consent form.
5. Document supervisory activities by keeping a journal or log.

EXPLORATION ➤ Ethical Issues in Supervision

1. Think back to your experience as a supervisee. Describe below any ethical problems you had with your supervisor related to:

   a. Misuse of power

   b. Dual relationships

   c. Role conflict (concern about evaluation)

   d. Competency

2. If you have had previous experience as a supervisor, answer the following:

   a. Have you had an experience supervising someone with whom you had some kind of a personal relationship?

   b. What kind of a relationship did you have with this person (e.g., colleague, friend, relative of someone of influence)?

   c. How did you see this outside relationship affecting your supervisory relationship?

   d. Did you see any potential for harm?

   e. Did you decide to work with this person or not? Why?

f. If you decided to work with this person, did anything harmful actually occur?

g. Looking back now, what do you wish you had done?

3. Can you think of a current situation in which you might be asked to supervise someone with whom you have some kind of a personal relationship?

  a. What kind of relationship do you have with the person (e.g., colleague, friend, relative of someone of influence)? Describe.

  b. What areas for potential harm do you see should you decide to proceed with supervision?

c. Is there anything you can do to protect yourself and the supervisee from harm if you do proceed?

d. There are three areas of potential harm in supervision resulting from dual relationships: evaluation of the supervisee's competence, choice of intervention strategies, and confrontation of weaknesses. How do you see your outside relationship with this supervisee affecting the supervisory relationship in these three areas? Describe.

e. If a colleague came to you for consultation with a similar problem with dual relationships, how would you tell him or her to proceed?

4. Fill out the following questionnaire about dual relationships in supervision. Reflect on your responses and then answer the questions about dual relationships with supervisees as accurately as possible.

Attitudes About Dual Relationships with Supervisees
(courtesy of Barbara Herlihy, Ph.D., University of New Orleans)

Is it ethical to:	Never ethical	Rarely ethical	Unsure	Usually ethical	Always ethical
1. Barter with a supervisee for goods or services?					
2. Provide supervision to a friend?					
3. Accept a gift from a supervisee if the gift is worth less than $10?					
4. Accept a gift from a supervisee if the gift is worth more than $50?					
5. Invite a supervisee to a personal party or social event?					
6. Go out to eat with a supervisee after a session?					
7. Accept a supervisee's invitation to a special occasion?					
8. Become friends with a supervisee after termination?					
9. Engage in sexual activity with a supervisee after termination?					

a. Do you think outside relationships of any kind are potentially harmful to the supervisory relationship? Describe.

b. Based on the continuum below, how strong are your attitudes about dual relationships in supervision?

Avoid at all costs   Depends on the situation   Not really a concern
1   5   10

c. How do you see your work situation and environmental context affecting your answers? Describe.

d. Is there anything else you are aware of as you review your answers?

5. What does the term "practice within areas of competence" mean to you?

   a. What specific criteria would you use to define "competence" (i.e., years of formal training in an area, number of clients seen, attending a workshop on a topic, reading a book or articles)?

   b. In which areas do you consider yourself "competent"? What criteria did you apply to arrive at this answer?

6. Review the list of supervisor competencies on pp. 115–116 as well as your answers to the exploration questions on pp. 125–126 related to knowledge, skills, and personal comfort with each area of competency.

    a. In what areas do you feel most competent?

    b. In what areas do you feel you need more training?

What Are the Ethical and Legal Issues in Supervision Relating to Client Care?

Another area of concern in supervision is the relationship among the behavior of the supervisor, that of the supervisee, the profession of counseling and therapy, and the public's trust (Sherry, 1991). Though psychotherapy as a practice is traditionally taught through supervision and the supervisor's role in helping the supervisee to develop professionally is widely recognized, the bottom line, both ethically and legally, is that the supervisor is held solely responsible for the supervisee's actions and the quality of client care. The supervisor must understand the importance of this responsibility and must possess a thorough knowledge of both ethical codes and legal guidelines affecting client care in order to appropriately guide the supervisee's actions.

Sheer numbers of clients, problems of staffing and funding, school and agency mandates, types of service provided, and populations all influence ethical decision making in the supervisory relationship. For example, some ethical guidelines for supervisors require that they monitor the complete care of each client, even stating that the supervisor should sit in on the first one or two sessions the supervisee has with a new client. These guidelines may work effectively in academic settings, where graduate students can be assigned a small number of cases in practicum or internship. However, with many post-degree practitioners seeking licensure in schools or agencies, caseloads may number 60 or more, making such requirements impractical. In school settings, the counselor may be responsible for an entire grade or a school.

Thus, there are continuing ethical dilemmas as to how to monitor supervisees. One solution is for the supervisor to emphasize different ethical concerns depending on the setting, the population served, the supervisee's level of ability and experience, and the types of activities assigned to the supervisee. For example, ethical concerns in a school setting may largely lie in areas of crisis intervention and issues of confidentiality. In an agency, these may be risk management and boundary setting, while in private practice they may be clinical judgment, intervention strategies, and personal issues as they relate to client care. Early on in supervision, the supervisor may want to use methods and techniques such as taping to closely monitor the supervisee's activities, later relying more heavily on selected case presentations as supervision progresses. Regardless, both ethically and legally, the overriding principle of *do no harm* to the client must prevail. When making decisions, supervisors should be aware that in the end, they will be held responsible for the supervisee's overall actions with clients. This responsibility is referred to as *vicarious liability*.

Vicarious Liability: What Does It Mean and How Does It Affect the Supervisor's Actions?

Vicarious liability is a legal term used to describe the full responsibility of the supervisor for the actions of the supervisee with respect to client care. It is important for all supervisors to understand the definition of vicarious liability and its limits. A brief synopsis will be given here, but complete information about vicarious liability should be obtained from a legal expert with specialization in mental health law.

According to Disney and Stephens (1994), the courts look at five factors in assessing the extent of vicarious liability in supervision:

> ➤ the supervisor's power to control the supervisee (did the act take place as part of the supervisee's assigned role with clients?);
> ➤ the supervisee's duty to perform the act (was the supervisee obliged, for example, to report abuse?);
> ➤ time, place, and purpose of the act (did the act take place in the work setting as part of service delivery?);
> ➤ supervisee's motivation in committing the act;
> ➤ whether the supervisor could have anticipated the supervisee doing this particular act.

In determining vicarious liability, the court will examine both the supervisee's actions and the supervisor's role in that action. Overall, it is not likely that the supervisor will be held accountable for actions of the supervisee that take place outside of the work setting and the supervisee's defined role in that setting. Additionally, documentation of the supervisor's actions concerning problems with the supervisee, such as seeking consultation, will also be important. Appelbaum and Gutheil (1991) stated that, for counselors and therapists, documentation and consultation are the two pillars of malpractice prevention. This certainly holds true for supervisors as well. Finally, in determining vicarious liability, the courts will require documentation of demonstrated expertise in supervision on the part of the supervisor, such as certification, coursework, or training.

What Are the Areas of Vulnerability for the Supervisor With Vicarious Liability?

1. The client is not informed of the supervisee's status as a trainee.
2. The supervisee fails to identify client problems, such as potential for suicide or a medical condition, and thus gives the supervisor incomplete information.

3. The supervisor does not discuss cases thoroughly enough to pick up that the supervisee provided incomplete information, so protective action is not taken nor is a referral made.
4. Because the supervisor does not discuss cases thoroughly, or read progress notes or have other means available to check the supervisee's work, he or she is unaware that the supervisee's diagnosis or conceptualization of the severity of the client's problem is faulty.
5. The supervisee has too many clients for the supervisor to ethically monitor.
6. The supervisee withholds information from the supervisor that might be damaging to evaluation, particularly in cases of boundary violations such as social or sexual intimacy; because the supervisor does not sufficiently monitor all cases, this fact is not discovered.
7. The supervisee mistakenly breaches confidentiality because the supervisor has not thoroughly explained limits of confidentiality or is not available in a crisis situation.
8. The supervisee does not follow the recommendations of the supervisor but reports that he or she has done so; this action is allowed because the supervisor does not request a report from the supervisee as to the success or failure of recommended actions.

How Can Supervisors Protect Themselves?

1. Be able to demonstrate competency in supervision; attend workshops and obtain certification or credentials.
2. Be knowledgeable concerning current ethical codes and legal standards.
3. Document all activities in supervision.
4. Choose competent supervisees; check their level of knowledge.
5. Manage as much as possible, especially in the beginning of supervision, the number and type of clients seen by the supervisee.
6. Take time to make certain that the supervisee is well informed about ethical codes, laws, and agency or school policies.
7. Periodically review the supervisee's record keeping and documentation skills.
8. Read, approve, and cosign any communication, reports, or paperwork that the supervisee sends outside the office.
9. Be available for emergencies, and be sure to create a crisis management plan and identify steps to be taken in an emergency.

10. In crisis situations or where legal action is possible (such as threats of suicide, child abuse, or custody battles), document all suggested actions and intervention strategies given to the supervisee and request a response back from the supervisee as to how they followed through on all suggestions.
11. If you are uncertain how to proceed, utilize outside consultation and document all suggestions.
12. In summary, be knowledgeable, be available, and use consultation, documentation, and informed consent.

(List adapted from Hess, 1980.)

What Are the Main Supervisee Mistakes With Clients?

There are four main areas of vulnerability for the supervisor in terms of the supervisee's actions with client care: (a) communication, (b) confidentiality, (c) dual relationships, and (d) boundaries.

The Problem of Communication

Clients and third party payors must be informed of the supervisee's position as a nonlicensed trainee. It is unethical to bill insurers for work done by the supervisee without clearly indicating his or her licensure status. It is also unethical not to inform the clients fully of the supervisee's position, role, and licensure. Therefore, it is particularly important to discuss with clients how supervision will affect the limits of confidentiality. The purpose of each method, technique, and approach used in supervision, such as taping, behind-the-mirror teams, group supervision, and formal case presentations, should be explained to clients and a signed release obtained. If clients are uncomfortable, an effort must be made to thoroughly discuss their objections and concerns before proceeding. If their anxiety is not relieved, then other arrangements need to be made.

Typical common problems encountered by supervisees in the area of confidentiality and communication are as follows: the use of phones, especially cell phones, in public venues; ignorance about how to contact and leave messages for clients with answering machines, voice mail and caller ID; sending client data by fax; lack of protection of client data and computer files; mishandling files and tapes, such as leaving them in cars or briefcases; and informal discussions in bathrooms, hallways, and lunchrooms. (For a more detailed discussion, see *Prudent Practice: A Guide for Managing Malpractice Risk* by Houston-Vega, Nuehring, & Daguio, 1997.)

The Problems of Client Confidentiality

It is the supervisor's responsibility to clearly explain the limits of client confidentiality and the possible ramifications of breaking confidentiality with the supervisee. The supervisor must also help the supervisee to identify high-risk clients whose confidentiality may be breached.

In many instances, the supervisee recognizes the need to break client confidentiality in order to comply with state or local laws, but might question its impact on the relationship with the client and whether the breach is really necessary. The question then becomes not simply in which instances should the supervisee break confidentiality, but to what extent it will be broken—are there ways to comply with the law and still protect the welfare of the client? There are other instances in which legal guidelines and ethical codes are in conflict, such as in the case of HIV clients or cases in which there has been threatened harm. The supervisor must help the supervisee to weigh harm to the client against the protection of other interests such as the welfare of other members in the family and the community (Haber, 1996). Supervisors may wish to approach the issue of confidentiality as a therapy issue first and foremost and as a legal issue secondarily. Thus, supervisees can be encouraged to think through the ethical issues related to practice and the legal parameters guiding that practice. The following questions can be used to guide discussion with the supervisee on the breaking of client confidentiality:

> If client information is disclosed, who must know the information? Is there some way to limit the amount of privacy lost by the client?
> How important is this breach of confidentially to the safety and welfare of the client?
> How important is the information in helping government, agencies of the government (e.g., police, Child Protective Services), or other private interests (e.g., employers, insurers, and HMOs) do their job?

The Problem of Dual Relationships With Clients

The supervisor should not assume that the supervisee understands completely what constitutes a dual relationship and how it may be harmful. Just because it should be common knowledge to all mental health practitioners at this time that one does not have sex with clients, supervisors still need to clearly define exactly what is meant by "another personal relationship" and to continue this discussion on dual relationships throughout supervision. Some typical mistakes that supervisees make are: trying to work with someone they know as a client because the person approaches them; getting involved with clients in some way outside the office, such as lunch or dinner meetings; starting to do business with a client or member of their family; or becoming socially or sexually intimate with clients.

The Problem of Boundary Setting With Clients

Understanding issues like setting boundaries with clients, practicing within one's areas of competency, and using consultation and referrals can also be problematic for supervisees. Beginners, in their eagerness to be helpful, frequently overstep roles and boundaries. Some mistakes, such as taking over the work of the client or trying to do everything for them may not be truly harmful. However, going beyond one's competency and training, such as giving legal or medical advice, discounting the seriousness of the situation, and ignoring the client's need for referral, can be a serious and dangerous error. Supervisors should familiarize themselves with the supervisee's philosophy of helping, idea of responsibility and their role as a helper, gaps in knowledge or experience, and personal limitations that may affect client care.

Summary

Ethical codes, while providing the supervisor with a road map to guide decision making, cannot provide a guarantee that mistakes will not be made or malpractice claims filed as a result of some action on the part of the supervisee. Ethical codes can help one look beyond the immediate to the possible realm of consequences for choices made (Haber, 1996). In the words of Barbara Herlihy (1994), "Supervisors need to be knowledgeable, prepared to justify their actions, use documentation and consultation, and then go forward and sin bravely." Both supervisor and supervisee can be sued for what they do and what they do not do. However, if supervisors follow ethical guidelines, they can reduce risk and protect both the client and the supervisee from harm.

EXPLORATION ➤

1. Fill out the *Ethics At-Risk Test for Therapists* (Appendix F). Review your answers. Did you locate an area or areas of ethical vulnerability? Describe.

2. There are three main areas of ethical concern with supervisees: confidentiality and communication, dual relationships, and boundary issues. You should be familiar with the main problems in each area.

   a. On a scale of 1 to 10, with 1 being least and 10 being most, rate how knowledgeable you feel about the following by circling the appropriate number.

   Crisis intervention

   1   2   3   4   5   6   7   8   9   10

   Problems of high-risk clients

   1   2   3   4   5   6   7   8   9   10

   Duty to warn

   1   2   3   4   5   6   7   8   9   10

   Limits of confidentiality

   1   2   3   4   5   6   7   8   9   10

   b. Have you read and studied the current ethical guidelines for your license or credential? For that of your supervisee if he or she is in another discipline?

c. Are you familiar with state and local mental health laws?

d. Describe the steps you need to take now to become thoroughly grounded in knowledge of professional ethical codes and current laws.

3. The use of consultation is continually emphasized for effective supervisors.

a. Do you have a consultation network at this time?

b. If so, describe it: Who is in that network? Does it contain an expert in ethics? Legal issues? A respected member of your profession or expert in the field? Who do you need to add?

c. What is your peer network of other supervisors? How often do you consult them?

4. Can you think of any examples when, as a supervisee, you were required to break confidentiality? If yes, describe:

    a. Describe an example in which the choice to break confidentiality was clear-cut.

       ➤ What happened?

       ➤ What steps did you take to ensure client welfare?

       ➤ What did you learn as a result of this experience?

    b. Describe an example in which the choice to break confidentiality was not so clear.

       ➤ What happened?

➢ What steps did you take to ensure client welfare?

➢ What did you learn as a result of this experience?

5. What was the main difference between the two?

6. What role did your job and setting play in your decision making?

7. Some kinds of dual relationships, such as having sex with a client, are harmful to clients and must be avoided. However, the harm of other kinds of dual relationships may not be so clear, and practitioners vary on how they perceive them. Fill out the questionnaire below and reflect on your answers.

Attitudes About Dual Relationships with Clients
(courtesy of Barbara Herlihy, Ph.D., University of New Orleans)

Is it ethical to:	Never ethical	Rarely ethical	Unsure	Usually ethical	Always ethical
1. Barter with a client for goods or services?					
2. Provide therapy to a friend?					
3. Accept a gift from a client if the gift is worth less than $10?					
4. Accept a gift from a client if the gift is worth more than $50?					
5. Invite a client to a personal party or social event?					
6. Go out to eat with a client after a session?					
7. Accept a client's invitation to a special occasion?					
8. Become friends with a client after termination?					
9. Engage in sexual activity with a client after termination?					

a. Which categories do you feel strongly about?

b. Which are not so definite?

c. How do you see your answers affecting your approach to supervision?

8. Can you think of an example in your own experience as a supervisee in which dual relationship issues with a client were a problem? Describe.

a. How was it a problem?

b. How did the supervisor handle this situation?

c. What role did you take?

d. Did any harm occur to the client or to you as a result of this dual relationship? How was this relationship harmful?

e. If this same situation occurred with your supervisee, what would you do?

9. Can you think of an example from your experiences as a supervisee where you overstepped boundaries?

a. Describe the situation.

b. Did any harm occur?

c. What action did your supervisor take?

d. If, as a supervisor, you faced the same situation, what would you want to do?

➤ Conclusions

What conclusions might you draw from these exercises that may be helpful to you in working with your supervisee?

➤ Action Plan

What do you need to do as a result of these conclusions?

➤ Chapter Highlights

- ➤ Ethical supervisors should be knowledgeable about legal and ethical codes.
- ➤ Supervisors should remember that the primary ethical and legal responsibility of the supervisor is to the client and the client's welfare.

➤ Whenever possible, supervisors should avoid dual relationships with their supervisees.

➤ It is the responsibility of the supervisor to know the four main problem areas in supervisees–client relationships: communication, confidentiality, boundary setting, and dual relationships.

➤ Supervisors should be aware of the fact that documentation and consultation are the two pillars of malpractice prevention.

Suggested Readings

Ethical guidelines for each of the major disciplines, which can be obtained from the major professional organization. See Appendix G for a list of national professional organizations and contact information.

Bernard, J., & Goodyear, R. (1998). *Fundamentals of clinical supervision.* Boston: Allyn and Bacon. Chapter 9: Ethical and legal considerations.

Borders, L. D., & Leddick, G. (1987). *Handbook of Counseling Supervision.* Alexandria, VA: Association for Counselor Education and Supervision. Chapter 7: Ethical and legal considerations for supervisors.

Bradley, L. (2000). *Counselor supervision.* Philadelphia: Accelerated Development. Chapter 10: Ethical principles in supervision.

Corey, G., & Herlihy, B. (1996). *ACA ethical standards casebook* (5th ed.). Alexandria, VA: American Counseling Association.

Disney, M. J., & Stephens, A. M. (1994). Legal issues in clinical supervision. In Remley, T. P. (Ed.). *ACA Legal Series.* Alexandria, VA: American Counseling Association.

Feltham, C., & Dryden, W. (1994). *Developing counselor supervision.* London: Sage. Chapter 4: Protecting the client and counselor.

Haber, R. (1996). *Dimensions of psychotherapy supervision.* New York: Norton. Chapter 5: Ethical supervision.

Herlihy, B., & Corey, G. (1992). *Dual relationships in counseling.* Alexandria, VA: American Counseling Association. Part II: Issues in counselor preparation; & Chapter 5: Supervision.

Houston-Vega, M. K., Nuehring, E. M., & Daguio, E. R. (1997). *Prudent practice: A guide for managing malpractice risk.* Washington, DC: NASW Press. Chapter 2: Primary principles of malpractice prevention; Chapter 7: Vicarious liability; & Appendix A: NASW Code of Ethics.

Kaiser, T. (1997). *Supervisory relationships: Exploring the human element.* Pacific Grove, CA: Brook/Cole. Chapter 2: Power and authority; & Chapter 3: Dual relationships in supervision.

Knapp, S. & Vandercreek, L. (1997). *Ethical and legal aspects of clinical supervision.* In C. E. Watkins (Ed.), *Handbook of psychotherapy supervision.* New York: Wiley.

Powell, D. J. (1993). *Clinical supervision in alcohol and drug abuse counseling: Principles, models, methods.* New York: Lexington Books. Chapter 15: Ethical and legal concerns.

Sherry, P. (1991). Ethical issues in the conduct of supervision. *The Counseling Psychologist, 19*(4), 566–584.

Stoltenberg, C. D., McNeill, B. W., & Delworth, U. (1997). *IDM supervision: An integrated development model for supervising counselors and therapists.* San Francisco, CA: Jossey-Bass. Chapter 10: Ethics and legal issues.

8

WHAT IS THE ROLE OF MULTICULTURAL ISSUES IN SUPERVISION?

"Culture is like air. It is all around us and we are immersed in it whether we notice it or not."

—Haber, 1996, p. 56

In the mental health field, there is increasing attention being paid to the role of multicultural issues in the helping profession. As a profession, as well as a society, we are moving from a "let's not talk about multicultural differences for fear it will create problems or offend someone" attitude to a belief that we need to talk about them. The term *multicultural* is a multidimensional concept that includes not only minority groups (cross-cultural) but also gender, age, religion, socioeconomic status, sexual orientation, and disabilities (Leong & Wagner, 1994). Some professionals such as Patterson (1996) see the term multicultural as so generic and broad in nature that all counseling is by nature multicultural, and in turn, that multiculturalism is basic to all helping. Thus, it is unnecessary to single it out as a distinct issue in the counseling relationship. Others, however, have argued that mental health professionals need to pay attention to differences, to name and categorize them, in order to open a conversation about how these differences may affect the therapeutic relationship (McGoldrick, 1998; McGoldrick & Green, 1998). Promoting an interest in multiculturalism is viewed as healthy because it creates a dialogue in counseling and psychotherapy about the role of diversity in society, it increases tolerance and respect for differences, and it points to how multicultural variation enriches everyone's lives (Fowers & Richardson, 1996).

There are two crucial questions for the supervisor to consider regarding multicultural differences. First, how do multicultural differences affect the supervisory relationship and what should the supervisor do to respond to these differences? Second, do these same multicultural issues affect client care, and if they do, how, and how should the supervisor respond?

How Do Multicultural Issues Affect Supervision?

Until recently, the majority of training programs for mental health professionals were offered in predominantly White institutions where students and faculty were mostly White, and the techniques and theories taught were created by White Euro/American males. During the 1980s, due to the women's movement, this limited environment expanded as recognition of gender's role in counseling and psychotherapy grew. Then, in the 1990s, the focus on group differences grew to include multiculturalism. Because multicultural awareness is largely a recent phenomenon, older established practitioners, particularly those in a supervisory position, may have no formal coursework or training in the area of multicultural differences, although they might have much practical first-hand experience. Given the fact that ethical guidelines require supervisors to be sensitive and responsive to issues such as gender, ethnicity, religion, and age in the supervisory relationship, supervisors will need to increase their knowledge and understanding of this important area.

There are two important areas in which multicultural differences will play an important role in supervision: first in building trust and the working alliance, and second, in evaluation of the supervisee's competency and ability (Ladany, Brittan-Powell, & Pannu, 1997; Lopez, 1997). Effective supervisors should consider that multicultural differences affect attitude toward, as well as interactions with, supervisees, and it is their responsibility to prevent these biases from negatively affecting the supervisory relationship. For example, as in society as a whole, gender differences do exist in supervision, and gender stereotyping is still very much a reality (Rigazio-DiGilio, Anderson, & Kunkler, 1995). Consequently, the supervisor must explore with the supervisee the ways gender differences are affecting the supervisory relationship. Another easily overlooked multicultural difference in post-degree supervision is the fact that mental health professionals of different disciplines might be asked to supervise someone with an entirely different background, training, and theoretical approach to practice, which can lead to conflict and relationship problems.

Feltham and Dryden (1994) indicated that, because unique issues of power and choice exist in supervision, greater problems might arise with supervisees as a result of multicultural differences than with clients. The supervisee may have had little or no choice in choosing a supervisor and therefore might feel powerless to challenge the supervisor concerning any biases the supervisor may have and vice versa. Supervisees are frequently assigned and supervisors told to supervise them, regardless of potential problems and discomfort.

Therefore, to be an effective supervisor, it is important to identify one's beliefs and underlying attitudes toward those who are of a different race, gender, or ethnicity. It is the supervisor's responsibility to work toward resolving negative beliefs, attitudes, and biases about multicultural differences in order to provide effective supervision and to promote quality client care (Buhrke, 1989).

It is not enough, however, for supervisors to be aware of, and sensitive to, how beliefs and attitudes about differences in people might affect their relationship with the supervisee. The effective supervisor must be able to respond to these differences. Multicultural differences can become "obstacles to the ultimate goal of helping the client unless addressed" (Feltham & Dryden, 1994, p. 53). Because supervisors are responsible for the climate and conditions for learning in supervision, it is their responsibility to open discussions on cultural differences with their supervisees. These conversations should take place early in supervision to prevent any serious damage to the relationship. In fact, the discussion about multicultural differences can be an important part of a supervisee's personal and professional growth and should be continued throughout supervision, not just in the beginning of the relationship (Bernard & Goodyear, 1998).

Effective supervisors must also understand the role multicultural differences play in evaluation of the supervisee's competence. Variables such as assertiveness, expression of feelings, sense of time, respect, and ability to function independently all have a cultural component. To prevent bias, supervisors must employ a variety of methods to evaluate the supervisee, seek suggestions from their supervisee for improvement in communication and understanding, and watch for generalizations and labeling (Wong, 1996). For example, supervisors should be cautious when applying labels such as afraid, resistant, or dependent to their evaluation of the supervisee.

EXPLORATION ➤ Multicultural Awareness in Supervision

1. Please answer these questions to increase your awareness about your own multicultural biases:

   a. What did you learn as a child growing up about people who were different from you? Describe.

   b. How important was cultural or ethnic identity to your family? To you?

   c. Was there a time when you felt you experienced prejudice or were treated unfairly because of your cultural or ethnic identity? How about your gender? Age? Socioeconomic class?

d. List in the table below at least three or more characteristics or qualities of people from the demographic groups. Try to be as honest as you can. Please keep this list for later referral. Add other groups to the list if desired.

Demographic group	Characteristics
Male	
Female	
African American	
Asian	
American Indian	
Hispanic	
Gay or lesbian	
Jewish	
Moslem	
Christian (Catholic/Protestant)	
Poor	
On welfare	
Old	
Young	
Disabled	

2. Think back on your own supervision experience.

a. The concept of multiculturalism involves people who are different in age, gender, race, or ethnicity from you. Apply this concept to your own experience. Make a list of your supervisors. Write under or next to each supervisor's name how each one was different from you in age, gender, race, religion, and in other ways.

b. Did you have a different degree or training background from the supervisor?

3. Review your answers to question 2.

   a. Did any of these differences influence your experience in supervision? For example, levels of trust, expectations, or evaluation of your competency? Describe.

   b. Did any of these differences create conflict? If so, how was it addressed?

   c. Concerning these differences, is there anything you wish you had done differently?

   d. Is there anything you wish your supervisor(s) had done differently?

4. To improve awareness and responsiveness to differences in gender, race, or ethnicity, take the answers given to the previous three exploration questions and create a personal checklist of biases. Place the checklist in your supervision file and periodically refer to it when reviewing tapes, evaluating cases, or assessing a supervisee's overall competence and abilities.

5. Think of a current or potential supervisee. If you are not currently supervising, use a colleague for your example.

   a. Write a paragraph evaluating your supervisee's skill, professionalism, and professional judgment. Also include a brief statement about how you feel about working about with this person.

   b. List multicultural differences that exist between you and this supervisee.

   c. Now review your answer to Question 1, part d in this section where you discussed generalizations and labels concerning different cultural groups. Compare your list of charcteristics and evaluate your answer to possible bias.

   d. Ask a colleague or another supervisor to review your description for hidden bias.

How Do Multicultural Differences Affect Client Care?

At this time, most national professional organizations in the mental health field, including the American Psychological Association, American Counseling Association, the American Association of Marriage Family Therapy, and the National Association of Social Workers, have published guidelines or standards that urge practitioners to be aware of and sensitive to the role of multicultural issues in client care. As supervisees move from the relative shelter of academic training programs into actual practice in schools, public agencies, and hospitals, they are more likely to come into contact with culturally different populations. These differences in culture and life experience can affect the practitioner's point of view, interpretation, and understanding of client problems, as well as his or her choice of intervention strategies (Kaiser, 1997; Lopez, 1997).

Arredondo et al. (1996) recommended that effective multicultural counselors should be aware of their own cultural values, of their clients' personal world views, and of culturally appropriate intervention strategies. Thus, it is the supervisor's job to challenge the supervisee's attitudes and beliefs about multicultural differences throughout the supervisory experience. Effective supervisors need to appreciate the impact of multicultural issues in client care and know when and where they play important roles in the clients' problems. The supervisor must challenge supervisees about the impact their attitudes have on their conceptualization of client problems and choice of intervention. The main question to be asked is: "Given the fact that the client is _____, how can I best help him or her solve the presenting problem(s)?"

The supervisor needs to help supervisees to explore and understand their personal values and beliefs about multicultural differences, their biases, stereotypes, and prejudices. One hypothesis that has been advanced is that investigating attitudes and beliefs on controversial topics such as racism, homophobia, ethnicity, sexism, and ageism, increases counseling competence (Torres Rivera, 1996). Confronting differences in any relationship is crucial to building trust and opening communication. When evaluating cases or reviewing tapes, written reports, forms, and process notes, the supervisor should help the supervisee to identify significant multicultural issues such as race, gender, and age that may affect the perception of the client's problems and hence the intervention strategies (Lopez, 1997).

The impact of beliefs and attitudes about multicultural differences may become more and more important as supervisees gain experience (Hilton, Russell, & Salmi, 1995). Carney & Kahn (1984) detailed specific learning tasks for each level of the trainee's professional development. Their model emphasized the importance of both challenging and supporting the supervisee in an exploration of the role of ethnicity and cultural differences in therapy, throughout the supervision process. The stages they described are:

> ➤ Stage 1: Encouraging awareness of attitudes.
> ➤ Stage 2: Expanding knowledge through reading and experiences.
> ➤ Stage 3: Beginning to recognize the impact of behavior on clients.
> ➤ Stage 4: Formulating a new identity as a counselor or therapist as a result of this awareness.
> ➤ Stage Five: Taking action to promote social change and cultural pluralism.

If, after exploring the beliefs and attitudes held by your supervisee about cultural differences, some biases are discovered that will be detrimental to client care, supervisors should suggest that the supervisee participate in therapy and should attempt to limit referral of these clients until some positive resolution of the problem occurs. If negative attitudes or beliefs, such as racial prejudice, homophobia, or religious animosity, are really entrenched and interfere with care of clients, the supervisor should propose work in other, less sensitive, environments or, in extreme cases, should deny licensure.

What Are the Techniques for Introducing Multicultural Issues in Supervision?

Training of mental health practitioners should include critical self-examination of values, biases, and perspectives on other cultures, religions, and human behavior (Sue & Sue, 1990). Several techniques for doing this are listed now.

Exercise 1. To introduce the issue of culture into supervision (or client care), you might what to say the following: "I'm thinking about the fact that you are Black and I am White (or male and female, etc.). What impact do you think this will have on our relationship? Do you have any concerns about that? Do you see any problems? I realize that I don't have a lot of experience working with _____. What do you want me to know? What things do you want me to be sensitive toward? How would you like to handle communication, especially when you feel I don't understand?"

Exercise 2. A second technique to increase awareness of how cultural issues affect work with clients is to make culture the "identified patient" (Haber, 1996, p. 58). For example, while reviewing a case with your supervisee, you might use the following questions to help the supervisee become more sensitive (adapted from D. A. Cook, 1994, p. 138).

> At what point did you notice the client's race (gender, ethnicity, etc.)?
> What thoughts or feelings did you have about that person's race (gender, ethnicity)?
> What did you do as a result?
> How do you imagine the client was thinking or feeling about you as a result of your race (gender, ethnicity, etc.)? What did the client do or say that led you to believe this?

Exercise 3. A third technique to increase awareness of and sensitivity to multicultural issues is to make a cultural genogram (Hardy & Laszloffy, 1995). The genogram is a popular technique used by therapists to explore family patterns and the impact of family issues on a client's current problems. The purpose of a cultural genogram is to make the supervisee more conversant with his or her cultural identities and also to highlight culturally linked issues that may impede effectiveness with clients (Hardy & Laszloffy, 1995). In this exercise, supervisees are asked to define their culture of origin, identify issues of pride and shame related to this culture, and then use a series of questions to explore the impact of their family of origin on their work with clients. For example, this exercise would be particularly useful for a gay or lesbian supervisee to explore issues such as family acceptance, shame and guilt, and other factors that might have an impact on client care (Buhrke, 1989).

In closing, professional guidelines and standards ask supervisors to be sensitive and aware of multicultural issues, but these guidelines are less clear on exactly how to include multicultural issues in supervision. One unanswered question remains: How central are cultural issues such as gender and race to effective supervision (Rigazio-DiGilio et al., 1995)? Do they override all other aspects of the supervisory relationship or are cultural differences just one component? For example, the supervisor must acknowledge group differences, such as race or gender, but be aware that people within any group can vary with respect to values, attitudes, and beliefs. It is wrong to assume that just because the supervisee is Black or Hispanic, he or she are more culturally sensitive and better able to relate to Black or Hispanic clients?

Manaster and Lyons (1994) cautioned the following: "It is as big a mistake to counsel someone according to a group classification as it is to counsel someone without regard to their group identity" (p. 47). Sometimes it is easy to overestimate or underestimate the role of culture in supervision. It is the job of the supervisor to explore both possibilities.

Leong and Wagner (1994) indicated that the mental health profession has barely scratched the surface regarding the importance of cross-cultural issues in supervision. More research is certainly needed to understand fully how multicultural issues affect the supervisory relationship, and to know what techniques are needed to promote awareness, increase knowledge, and develop cross-cultural skills.

After reading this chapter, it is hoped that all supervisors will open a conversation on the topic of multicultural differences not only with their supervisees, but also within their work environment and the larger community, in an effort to work toward making all environments more multiculturally accepting (Lopez, 1997; McGoldrick, 1998; Peterson, 1991; Sue & Sue, 1990).

EXPLORATION ➤ Techniques for Multicultural Awareness in Supervision

1. Did you ever have a conversation like the one described in Exercise 1 with a supervisor?

   a. If so, describe what happened.

   b. If not, do you think it would have made a difference in your relationship?

2. Have you ever had such a conversation with a client?

   a. Describe an example.

   b. How do you see this conversation affecting your conceptualization of this client's problems or suggested intervention strategies?

3. Exercise 2 suggests making culture the "identified patient" (Haber, 1996). Apply the questions listed in Exercise 2 to one of your current client cases.

    a. What did you discover about your multicultural sensitivity?

    b. How did you respond to or feel about your discovery?

    c. Is there anything you wish you had done differently? Describe.

    d. How might you apply this learning to supervision? To your own practice?

4. Exercise 3 describes how making a cultural genogram can increase sensitivity to and awareness of multicultural issues. Create a cultural genogram of your family Instructions for constructing a genogram are included in chapter 10 and a sample genogram is provided as Appendix L. In preparing the cultural genogram, go back three generations if possible (adapted from Hardy & Laszloffy, 1995, pp. 229–232).

   a. Define your own culture of origin. How do you typically describe yourself and your family to others?

   b. Select a color to show each country of origin in your genogram (Irish, Swedish, American Indian, African, etc.). Identify intercultural marriages. Use (~) to denote them on the genogram.

   c. Identify major organizing principles and issues of pride and/or shame associated with these origins. Some possible topics are education, wealth, social responsibility, status, importance of the family name, closeness, and approach to problem solving. Then, write a short paragraph describing these organizing principles. For example, "Our family is Irish Catholic, settled in Boston, mostly uneducated until arrival in the United States, then became wealthy business owners. Proud of our heritage and accomplishments. Education, class status are important in our family. Independence is a family virtue. It is important to save face at all cost, and never to let anyone outside the family know our problems."

d. Select symbols or other methods, such as hatched lines, to denote these pride and/or shame issues and mark them on the genogram.

5. After completing your genogram, find a partner to process information and learning from the exercise. Create a list of questions to help process the information in the genogram. This processing could be done first in writing (journaling) and then verbally. Remember that the goal of this exercise is to increase the supervisee's awareness of issues that might affect your response to supervisees and clients. Some sample questions are included here (adapted from Hardy & Laszloffy, 1995).

a. Look at the color code used in the genogram.

  ➤ Do you see in your family a high degree of homogeneity (indicated by few colors) or a high degree of multiculturalism?
  ➤ Would you say race, religion, ethnicity, class, or religion play significant roles in your family identity? Describe the roles they play.

  ➤ What do you see as the organizing principles of your cultural background? Refer to the example in part c of Question 4 in this section.

b. Study the symbols in the genogram.

  ❏ Is culture mostly a source of pride or shame in your family?
  ❏ Is there a disproportionate number of either pride or shame issues relating to culture?

❏ What prejudices or stereotypes do others have about your cultural background?

❏ How do these affect you?

❏ How are issues of gender regarded in your family? For example, are boys more prized than girls? Are there different expectations for boys and girls?

❏ Sexual orientation?

❏ Age? Education? Wealth?

6. How do you think the information gained from the cultural genogram will help you work more effectively with the following:

a. Your clients: Are there any particular client populations about whom you will have difficulties being objective? Describe.

b. Your supervisee(s): How might your cultural biases, such as pride or shame issues, interfere with objectivity regarding a supervisee's competency? Are there particular supervisees you know now about whose abilities it will be difficult for you to remain objective?

c. Your organization or institution of employment?

d. Other areas of your life?

e. How do you see these answers altering your actions?

7. Repeat the cultural genogram exercise with your supervisee and process the information gained from the genogram. If you do not now have a supervisee, ask a colleague to participate.

➤ Conclusions

What conclusions might you draw from reviewing the material and completing the exploration exercises in this chapter that will help you to be more effective as a supervisor?

➤ Action Plan

What do you need to do as a result of these conclusions? Be as specific as possible.

➤ Chapter Highlights

➤ Multicultural issues impact the supervisory relationship, particularly trust, the working alliance, and evaluation.

➤ It is not only important for supervisors to be aware and sensitive to differences; they must also be able to respond to these differences.

➤ It is the supervisor's responsibility to bring up multicultural issues early in the supervisory relationship to improve the working alliance.

➤ Supervisors must challenge their supervisees to include the role of multicultural differences in their conceptualization of client problems and in their selection of intervention strategies.

Suggested Readings

Bernard, J., & Goodyear, R. (1998). *Fundamentals of clinical supervision.* Boston: Allyn and Bacon. Chapter 3: The supervisory relationship & the influence of individual and developmental differences.

Haber, R. (1996). *Dimensions of psychotherapy supervision.* New York: Norton. Chapter 3: Diversity in the supervisory relationship.

Hardy, K. V., & Laszloffy, T. A. (1995). The cultural genogram: Key to training culturally competent family therapists. *Journal of Marital and Family Therapy, 21*(3), 227–237.

Kaiser, T. (1997). *Supervisory Relationships: Exploring the human element.* Pacific Grove, CA: Brooks/Cole. Chapter 4: Shared meaning; & Chapter 5: Trust.

Leong, F. T., & Wagner, N. (1994). Cross-cultural counseling supervision: What do we know? What do we need to know? *Counselor Education and Supervision, 34,* 117–131.

Liddle, H. A., Breunlin, D. C., & Schwartz, R. C. (1988). *Handbook of family therapy training & supervision.* New York: Guilford. Chapter 21: Learning to think culturally.

Lopez, S. R. (1997). Cultural competence in psychotherapy: A guide for clinicians and their supervisors. In C. E. Watkins (Ed.), *Handbook of psychotherapy supervision.* New York: Wiley, 570–588.

McGoldrick, M., Giordano, J., & Pearce, J. (1996). *Ethnicity and family therapy.* New York: Guilford.

Powell, D. J. (1993). *Clinical supervision in alcohol and drug abuse counseling: Principles, models, methods.* New York: Lexington Books. Chapter 16: Special issues in supervision.

Sodowsky, T., Gurkin, & Wise (1994). Development of the Multicultural Counseling Inventory: A self-report measure of multicultural competencies. *Journal of Counseling Psychology, 41*(2), 37–148.

Sue, D. W., Ivey, A. E., & Pederson, P. (1996). *A theory of multicultural counseling and therapy.* Pacific Grove, CA: Brooks/Cole.

Walters, M., Carter, B., Papp, P., & Silverstein, O. (1988). *The invisible web: Gender patterns in family relationships.* New York: Guilford.

WHAT IS THE ROLE OF ADMINISTRATIVE TASKS IN SUPERVISION?

9

In today's world, administrative tasks are an essential component of clinical supervision. Bernard and Goodyear (1998) stated that the purpose of administrative tasks is both to prevent burnout of the supervisee and to structure the supervisory process. Good administrative skills play a large role in improving the quality of the supervisory relationship and help to reduce role conflict and role ambiguity. Time management is an example of one such administrative skill; the ability to set priorities and to keep them is a critical tool for all mental health practitioners. Time management is an administrative task that should be both modeled and taught by the supervisor. For example, scheduling time for supervision can require a conscious effort on the part of busy practitioners, but because accessibility and consistency are important characteristics of an effective supervisor, priority should always be given to this difficult task.

What Should Good Record Keeping Include?

Good record keeping is another important administrative task. Supervisors should model good record-keeping practices in order to teach these skills to their supervisees. Careful documentation is an important cornerstone of practice. Should problems occur with the supervisee or, in the worst case scenario, a malpractice suit be filed, documentation will be vital. Complete supervision records should include the following:

> ➤ a copy of the requirements for the supervisee's licensing or certification;
> ➤ the supervisee's vita, summarizing background and experience;
> ➤ a copy of the informed consent and supervision contract;
> ➤ a log of supervision sessions, dates, and time, including canceled or missed sessions; (See Appendix H for a sample log of supervision hours.)
> ➤ A summary of each session, including notation of cases discussed, concerns of the supervisee, significant problems, intervention suggestions, and recommendation for follow-up. Supervisors may want to include written samples of the supervisee's record-keeping practices as part of this file as well as all evaluations of the supervisee and documentation of any difficulties experienced with the supervisee that you think had direct impact on client care.

What Is the Role of Evaluation in Supervision?

In supervision, evaluation is a crucial administrative task. However, it is perhaps the most overlooked component of supervision because of three main problems: (a) confusion about the evaluative role of the supervisor, (b) lack of skill, and (c) anxiety related to this component. However, evaluation affects all aspects of the supervisory relationship and thus cannot be ignored. Even late in the supervisee's training, the evaluative function is always present to some degree. It can be strongly emphasized with beginners and de-emphasized with the more advanced supervisee.

The goal of evaluation in clinical supervision is not just to review prior performance, but to shape goals for future learning. Shulman (1993) called it *formative evaluation*, and viewed it as an ongoing process throughout the course of supervision, while Holloway (1995) described evaluation as the foundational element of supervision. Supervisors must be able to define their expectations and goals at the beginning of the supervision experience and, at the end, to measure the supervisee's progress toward these goals and to define what represents successful completion of those goals. Additionally, supervisors should recognize the wisdom of developmental models that stress the importance for intermediate and advanced supervisees of actively participating in setting goals and designing evaluation. Therefore, it is suggested that the post-degree supervisor take time, even at the beginning of supervision, to work collaboratively to establish supervision goals. For instance, give the supervisee a goal-setting sheet to fill out and then go over the answers together.

There are numerous evaluation models available, including behavioral, cognitive, psychodynamic, or growth models (such as IPR or client-centered). Each one of these models applies its particular concepts and techniques to evaluation methods. Behavioral models focus on skills and utilize checklists, practice, and positive reinforcement. For example, behavioral checklists would list descriptions of specific skills required by the supervisee and then ask the supervisor to note the number of times a supervisee performs a particular skill as a means to demonstrate competence in a content area (Hanna & Smith, 1998). Cognitive models would evaluate the use of distorted or irrational thinking, client-centered models would focus on relationship skills, and psychodynamic models would examine transference and countertransference. Regardless of the supervisor's primary theoretical orientation, it would be very helpful to locate some sample performance appraisal instruments in order to develop better evaluation skills. An excellent example from the field of counseling is the *Scoring Rubric for Clinical Supervision*, created by Mary Ann Hanna, and available by contacting her at MHanna37@aol.com or (540) 831-5214.

Bradley's idea of dividing the content areas of supervision into three components, knowledge, practice, and personal, can serve as a simple and straightforward way to approach evaluation. The knowledge component includes evaluation of the supervisee's knowledge of theory, ethics, the law, intervention strategies, multicultural issues, and agency policies. The practice component examines the supervisee's skills and abilities, such as conceptualization and application of a variety of methods and techniques to client problems. The personal component includes evaluating the ethical and professional behavior of the supervisee, including personal characteristics that may assist with or impede client care. Thus, the supervisor must create a multifaceted plan considering not just the content areas but what kind of evaluation method would be needed for each component. For example, evaluation of the knowledge component might come through written assignments, readings, and discussion of application of the material to particular cases, while practice may be assessed through taping and live observation. The personal component is the most difficult to evaluate objectively, as it is most likely to be influenced by one's personal issues and biases. See Figure 9.1 for a sample checklist.

One easily overlooked area of evaluation is the supervisee's evaluation of the supervisor. Both ethically and in terms of creating an effective working alliance, it is necessary to also provide the supervisee with means to give evaluative feedback. Just as evaluation of the supervisee should take place several times during supervision, so should the evaluation of the supervisor. Supervisors should use this feedback to make changes in the supervisory process, methods and techniques, and goals and expectations. A sample form for the supervisee to use to evaluate the supervisor is included in this workbook (Appendix K). Other samples may be found in Appendix C of Bernard and Goodyear (1998).

(Competencies)	Poor	Below average	Average	Above average	Excellent
Knowledge					
Has knowledge of theory and intervention strategies					
Has knowledge of assessment and diagnosis					
Is understanding of cultural and ethnic issues					
Has knowledge of resources in community					
Has knowledge of current ethical guidelines and legal issues					
Practice					
Demonstrates mastery of intervention techniques					
Is timely and thorough in documentation					
Able to develop rapport					
Able to conceptualize problem					
Can respond to multicultural issues					
Able to formulate treatment goals					
Personal					
Demonstrates ethical behavior					
Demonstrates use of good judgment and counseling skills					
Is interpersonally competent					
Is able to identify own strengths and weaknesses					
Is able to accept and learn from feedback					
Is an asset to the profession					

FIGURE 9.1. Sample Checklist

What Can the Supervisor Do to Reduce Anxiety About Evaluation?

Giving and receiving evaluation can be anxiety producing for both supervisor and supervisee. It is easy for experienced practitioners to forget how it feels to be critically evaluated. Hopefully, with the correct techniques, the experience of evaluation can change from a fearfully avoided activity to a more positive experience. Bradley (2000) suggested that the supervisor should strive to create an environment where the evaluative function creates positive motivation, not anxiety, in the supervisee. Both the supervisor and supervisee should ask themselves: "Am I becoming the best professional possible at this time?" and should not be anxious about discovering the answer. Some ways to reduce anxiety about evaluation are:

➤ Clearly establish the goals for supervision.
➤ Have the supervisee give input into the setting of these goals.
➤ Have the supervisee perform some of the evaluative functions (i.e., self-evaluation).
➤ Set a specific time aside for evaluation feedback and include it in the supervision schedule.
➤ Prepare for the session.
➤ Focus on behavior, not personality, when giving feedback.
➤ Look for things that can be changed and give the supervisee specific suggestions for improvement.

If there are problems with a supervisee and a negative final evaluation is probable, it is imperative that supervisors have clearly defined the criteria for success, used a variety of different methods for evaluation, sought out consultation with others, and documented what steps were taken to correct the situation. In these situations, Shulman (1993) recommended that supervisors seek outside consultation for three possible reasons: to help with their objectivity, to protect the supervisee from possible bias, and to process any feelings of guilt that may be present because of failure to teach the supervisee the skills required or to actively promote their success.

In summary, to be effective, evaluation should include the following:

➤ identification of the crucial competencies that the supervisee needs to acquire;
➤ description of what would be required to be competent in each area;
➤ identification of changed expectations as to levels of competency in each of these areas as the supervisee gains in experience;
➤ establishment of clear and proper evaluation methods (Holloway, 1995).

EXPLORATION ➤ Administrative Tasks in Supervision

1. Think about the different administrative tasks discussed: time management, planning and scheduling, documentation, record keeping, and evaluation.

   a. What are your strengths in each of these areas? Describe.

   b. In what area(s) do you feel you need to improve?

   c. What would you say overall about your administrative abilities?

2. Review your own supervision experience.

   a. Did any of your supervisors model good administrative skills? Give one or two examples.

b. Did you receive training in each area, such as planning and scheduling, documentation, record keeping? Describe how these skills were taught.

c. Are there any administrative skills you wish had been taught? Give an example.

EXPLORATION ➤ Evaluation in Supervision

1. Before beginning to choose methods for evaluation, it is best to review one's personal issues associated with this task, because the more uncomfortable one is with being evaluated, the more likely one is to avoid evaluating others. Think back to your first experience in supervision while in graduate school.

    a. How was evaluation handled?

    b. What feelings do you associate with that experience?

2. Think about your experience with evaluation in post-degree supervision.

    a. Can you describe a situation in which evaluation was handled well?

    b. Can you describe a situation in which evaluation was handled badly?

3. Can you recall a specific piece of evaluative feedback you received during your training that stands out for you now? Was it supportive or challenging?

4. How do you feel about the process of evaluation in general? Do you desire feedback and feel challenged by it? Do you experience feedback as criticism?

5. When being evaluated, what would you need and want from a supervisor? Be specific.

   a. How do you prefer conflicts to be handled?

b. How do you feel about using feedback sheets and questionnaires?

6. It has been recommended that supervisees evaluate their supervisors.

   a. How do you feel about being evaluated by your supervisee?

   b. How would you like that to go?

   c. What is the one criticism you would not want to hear of your supervisory style?

EXPLORATION ➤ Planning for Evaluation

1. Take a minute now to review the suggestions given in the chapter for improving the evaluation experience. Imagine you are planning to evaluate your supervisee.

    a. What would you want to be sure to do?

    b. Can you create an implementation plan? Describe.

2. An important point made by supervision experts is that you should tie your goals for supervision to evaluation, and that these goals should be specific and realistic.

    a. Refer back to the table you created in the "Exploration section" of chapter 6 (p. 130) and review your list of competencies and expectations for supervision. Then, in order to evaluate the supervisee, create your own evaluation form.

b. Write next to each goal area one or two specific indicators of successful completion of that goal. For assistance with this task, refer to the sample evaluation forms provided as Appendices I and J.

c. Are your goals realistic for a beginner? For a more advanced supervisee?

d. Are they realistic for you in your current setting? Time? Resources?

3. Take a minute to reflect on a current supervisee or a potential supervisee.

a. Is your current or potential supervisee just beginning, or in the more advanced stage of supervision?

b. Imagine you are planning to evaluate this particular supervisee in your stated goal areas. What would you want to be sure to do?

c. Are there any areas of conflict or difficulty with your supervisee that might influence your evaluation?

d. Are these differences in:
- ➤ Theoretical orientation?
- ➤ Style?
- ➤ Personality?
- ➤ Gender?
- ➤ Race or ethnicity?

e. Describe these areas of difficulty and how you plan to handle them. What methods do you plan to use to remain objective?

4. It is important to evaluate the supervisee at several different points during the contracted period for supervision. Imagine it is halfway through the supervision year and you are having difficulties with a supervisee.

    a. How would you want to proceed?

    b. What would you want to say and do? Describe your actions.

5. When faced with giving a negative final evaluation of a supervisee,

    a. What steps would you need to be sure to take?

    b. Whom would you seek out for consultation?

➢ Conclusions

What conclusions might you draw from reviewing the material in this chapter and completing the exploration exercises that will help you to be a more effective supervisor?

➢ Action Plan

What do you need to do as a result of these conclusions?

➢ Chapter Highlights

➢ Administrative tasks are an essential component of effective supervision

➢ Administrative tasks structure and document the supervisory process, reduce anxiety and conflict, and prevent burnout.

➢ The effective supervisor understands the importance of evaluation as a supervisory function.

➢ It is important to include several means of evaluating the competence of the supervisee to ensure objectivity.

➢ In order to build the working alliance, supervisors should include the supervisee in setting goals and selecting methods of evaluation.

➢ Effective supervisors provide methods and means for the supervisee to evaluate their own performance.

Suggested Readings

Bernard, J., & Goodyear, R. (1998). *Fundamentals of clinical supervision.* Boston: Allyn and Bacon. Chapter 8: Evaluation; Chapter 10. Managing clinical supervision; & Appendix C.

Borders, L. D., & Leddick, G. (1987). *Handbook of counseling supervision.* Alexandria, VA: Association for Counselor Education and Supervision. Chapters 6: Evaluation of the supervisee; & Chapter 8: Evaluation of the supervisor.

Bradley, L. (2000). *Counselor supervision.* Philadelphia: Accelerated Development. Chapter 11: Supervision training: A model, & evaluation.

Holloway, E. (1995). *Clinical supervision: A systems approach.* Thousand Oaks, CA: Sage. Chapter 2: Tasks and functions of supervision.

Houston-Vega, M. K., Nuehring, E. M., & Daguio, E. R. (1997). *Prudent practice: A guide for managing malpractice risk.* Washington, DC: NASW Press.

Powell, D. J. (1993). *Clinical supervision in alcohol and drug abuse counseling: Principles, models, methods.* New York: Lexington Books. Chapter 13: Evaluation and feedback; p. 224; & Appendices E, F, & H.

Shulman, L. (1993). *Interactional supervision.* Washington, DC: NASW Press. Chapter 7: Evaluation function of supervision.

10

WHAT IS THE ROLE OF PERSONAL DEVELOPMENT IN SUPERVISION?

One important aspect of supervision is personal development. To be effective, counselors and psychotherapists must be comfortable with themselves and with intimacy, and they must understand the role of anxiety and conflict in relationships and have a genuine respect for individual differences. It is clear that a supervisee's personal issues can affect client care. It is the ethical responsibility of the supervisor to assist the supervisee in uncovering these problem areas and to protect the client from any resulting harmful experiences. Ethical guidelines support the idea that it would be unethical no*t to challenge supervisees about issues that may interfere with quality care.*

How Does the Supervisor Assist With the Personal Development of the Supervisee?

One of the oldest and best known means to encourage introspection by supervisees is the requirement of a personal journal. A supervision journal can serve as a private venue for exploring emotions, successes, and failures without fear of censorship, as well as means to track events, make sense of incidents and experiences, and organize and integrate understanding. For many, writing in a journal is itself therapeutic, as it provides a forum for exploring worries, fears, and mistakes without threat of judgment or ridicule. Particular questions or exercises can be assigned by the supervisor to help structure the experience and to increase learning; then supervisees could be invited to share any insights they have had that could potentially affect their work with clients.

Other effective methods that will provide a rich source of information for personal development are the use of the parallel process model of supervision, IPR, the psychodynamic concepts of transference and countertransference, and experiential methods such as role playing, psychodrama, gestalt empty chair, and the assignment of self-awareness exercises.

What Is the Difference Between Psychotherapy and Supervision?

One of the inherent struggles in facilitating personal development is understanding and respecting the difference between personal counseling or psychotherapy and supervision. Both are interpersonal relationships, but they are distinctly different in their nature and purpose. As described earlier, the primary purpose of supervision is to monitor client care and facilitate the training of new professionals. What can be confusing, perhaps, is that although supervision may require the exploration of personal issues, the purpose of this exploration is much different. In supervision, the focus for discussion is how the supervisee's personal issues and problems can affect client care, the conceptualization of client problems, the counseling process itself, and the accomplishment of client goals. In counseling or psychotherapy, on the other hand, the focus of exploration is the roots, causes, and feelings associated with personal issues for the purpose of understanding and change in one's personal life and relationships.

It is essential to explore with supervisees their limitations as they relate to delivering service to clients, but the supervisor must understand that to go beyond this context may constitute a dual relationship and become an ethical pitfall. Supervisors should limit their "therapist role" to exploring and clarifying personal problems that are creating barriers to the supervisee's work with clients (Russell & Petrie, 1994; Whiston & Emerson, 1989). In other words, when discussing personal issues with the supervisee, the processing of these difficulties must remain anchored solely to the relationship between the supervisee and the client (Russell & Petrie, 1994).

To accomplish this difficult task of maintaining boundaries and to keep the focus on training, the supervisor must move to the consultant role. The following series of process questions are offered as a sample guideline:

➤ What is the client doing to push your buttons?
➤ What is it about the client's behavior that brings about these responses?

- ➤ Does anything remind you of another person or situation?
- ➤ Is there anything happening in your life right now that may be contributing to this situation?
- ➤ How do you see this awareness affecting your relationship to this client?
- ➤ What might you want to do differently with the client to solve this problem?

To best address the impact of personal issues on therapeutic effectiveness, the supervisor might need to require the supervisee to tape their client sessions or to participate in live supervision. In some cases, the supervisor should also consider personal consultation with another professional in order to maintain their objectivity. If, after reviewing tapes or sitting in on sessions, personal problems continue to limit the supervisee's professional competence with clients, then referral to another professional for psychotherapy may be necessary. However, in such extreme cases, it is important to avoid creating any dual relationships when making this referral. For example, referral for therapy should not be made to a co-worker, professor, or administrator who may have another relationship with the supervisee.

What Are Some of the Issues That Limit Personal Development?

There are any number of personal issues that can limit the development of the supervisee: discomfort with intimacy, closeness, or expression of feelings, anxiety generated by certain problems; negative thinking patterns, perfectionism, the need to be liked, the need to be helpful, and patterns of under- or overfunctioning.

The primary area that limits personal development is the supervisee's ingrained patterns of responding to anxiety. Yalom (1980) said, "The capacity to tolerate uncertainty is a prerequisite for the profession" (p. 13). Effective counselors and psychotherapists must be able to understand and be comfortable with anxiety as a part of life and of most relationships. To identify these patterns, supervisors could use gestalt exercises, role playing, or family sculpting, or assign self-awareness exercises like the family genogram or Adler's Lifestyle Inventory, and apply the information gained to the supervisee's relationship difficulties with both clients and themselves.

An analogous area that should be discussed early in supervision is the role of the supervisee's family history in his or her responses to the client's expression of feelings. For instance, the supervisee's own history of losses, parents' prohibitions about expression of feelings, role as family caretaker or peacemaker—all can limit the supervisee's comfort level with strong affect. Teyber (1997) hypothesized that dominant modes of responding to life situations, such as anger or sadness, are learned through experiences in one's family of origin and usually mask deeper feelings of pain, hurt, or shame. He termed this pattern of responding the *affective constellation*, a sequence of interrelated feelings such as anger, sadness, and guilt, which repeatedly recur throughout one's lifetime. Helping the supervisee uncover their affective constellations and dominant mode of responding to life events can facilitate the processing of transference issues and an understanding of their resistance or defensiveness. Role playing, family sculpting, journaling, and Adler's Lifestyle Inventory could be used to this purpose. Other patterns of responding to clients such as under- and overfunctioning, the need to be helpful, and the need to be liked, could be included in this exploration.

A third personal issue for supervisors to explore with the supervisee is the tendency toward perfectionistic thinking and resulting feelings of guilt and self-doubt when the ideal is not met. Two examples of guilt-producing perfectionistic thinking would be: "One can never do enough," or "One can never do it right," which is often the underlying issue in the supervisee's response to challenging or corrective feedback and patterns of overfunctioning with clients. Before endeavoring to help others, supervisees must be able to accept their own failures and mistakes, and to believe that even though they are not perfect, they are also not failures.

For most people, the roots of perfectionistic thinking are in their religious upbringing and how their parents and other important adults responded to them during their childhood (Kushner, 1996). Since guilt, self-doubt, and demands for perfectionism underlie so many client therapeutic problems, supervisees must confront their own demons of perfectionism before venturing to help others. Self-exploration exercises such as the family genogram, Adler's Lifestyle Inventory, or the inclusion of self-report inventories of cognitive distortions could be suggested to facilitate discussion.

EXPLORATION ➤ Personal Issues in Supervision

1. In your own experience in supervision, how was the exploration of personal issues handled?

   a. Can you think of an example when this was handled well? Describe it.

   b. Can you think of an example when this was handled badly?

   c. What do you notice when you compare the two situations?

d. How might you use this information with your own supervisees?

2. Ethically, whenever supervisee's personal issues interfere with client care and cannot be resolved during supervision, supervisors are required to refer supervisees to an outside psychotherapist in order to avoid a dual relationship.

   a. To whom in your professional community would you refer an impaired supervisee?

   b. How would you go about making a referral to this person? What factors would you need to consider?

3. In order to understand the existence of the *affective constellation*, can you identify one or two times when you have reacted emotionally in a current situation? Describe them.

a. What was your primary feeling response in these situations? Was it anger or sadness or guilt?

b. Now ask yourself: If I wasn't feeling angry, hurt or guilty, what else would I be feeling? Can you identify any underlying feelings of hurt or shame?

c. How do you see your answers to this question affecting your work with clients?

d. How might you apply this learning in supervision?

4. Demands for perfection can be a significant part of performance anxiety and/or transference reactions in supervisees, especially in the beginning of the relationship. To process your own perfectionistic thinking, do the following exercises:

   a. Make a list of 10 things you *want to do*, ten things you *should do*, and 10 things you *have to do*. These can be anything, not just professional. Compare and contrast the lists. Do you see any patterns?

Things I want to do	Things I should do	Things I have to do

b. Can you take each one of your *shoulds* and *have tos* and make them *want tos*? What happens to you when you do this? What are your thoughts? Your feelings? Please note under *shoulds* and *have tos* the presence of any generalizations and negative thinking patterns that might occur.

c. Now take each listed *should* and *have to* and add the word *because* after each one; then finish the sentence. For example, "I should do this or I have to do that because if I don't, some one will be mad or I will disappoint someone" instead of "I want to do this because it would make me (or others) feel good." Note the existence of the need to please others or receive approval from others as a reason for doing something.

d. Fritz Perls (1969) stated that underneath guilt, there is unexpressed resentment. To explore this possibility, after each *should* or *have to*, make a list of resentments. For example: "I should do . . . but I feel angry that I have to please you," or "I should do . . . but I resent the fact that whatever I do, it won't be good enough."

e. When you recognize these resentments, do you notice yourself speaking to anyone in particular? Are you talking to your mother or father? Both parents? A teacher or supervisor?

5. Two guilt-producing generalizations that underscore most perfectionistic thinking are:

➤ I can never do enough or I am never good enough—"Why didn't you do this?"
➤ I can never do it right—"How come you didn't get an A?"

a. Which one of these is your personal favorite?

b. Can you give an example of one of these generalizations from your own thinking? For example, "I feel guilty that I let you down or disappointed you. I should have done more or I should have done it differently."

c. Take the above material and describe in a short paragraph how you see these patterns affecting:

➤ Client care

➢ Your supervision

6. Do you see any problems as a supervisor implementing the concepts outlined in this section?

How Can Self-Awareness Exercises Be Utilized in Supervision?

Self-awareness exercises, such as the family genogram, can be very useful in supervision for the purpose of increasing the supervisee's awareness and understanding of important background experiences and the application of this information to problems and difficulties with clients. Some helpful exercises appropriate for supervision are the family genogram to understand family patterns and the role of culture, the lifeline to examine the impact of significant events, people, and feelings, and Adler's Lifestyle Inventory to examine relationships within the family. It is suggested that supervisors complete each of these exercises and discuss them with a colleague before using them with supervisees. Certainly, both supervisor and supervisee would be advised to seek personal psychotherapy if entrenched problematic patterns of responding are uncovered that could interfere with the quality of client care.

To increase effectiveness, a series of processing questions should always be included with each exercise to guide exploration of the relationship between personal issues and client care. For example, the supervisee could be asked to make a genogram of his or her family and answer a series of written questions to help identify family patterns of coping with anxiety, anger, loss, or conflict and how these patterns might present themselves while working with clients. Afterwards, the material could be further processed in supervision by applying it to particular cases. In this way, processing the relationship between personal history and family patterns and the effect of these patterns on work with clients becomes a training issue. A typical scenario might go as follows. In a particular setting, supervisees are to work extensively with victims of violence and sexual trauma. After observing their work, the supervisor begins to suspect the presence of some personal history that is affecting how they are interacting with the clients. The genogram reveals that the supervisee has a history of trauma. The supervisor's role is to help the supervisee examine how this history may be limiting their effectiveness with clients. If it is determined that the roots of the supervisee's problems with clients goes much deeper than can be resolved through supervision, then it is up to the supervisor to evaluate the severity of the problem and what to recommend.

Exercise 1: The Family Genogram. The goal of this exercise is to apply a systems approach to understanding the historical context and relationship patterns of one's family, and to identify coincidences, concurrent events, and the resulting "flow of anxiety" (McGoldrick & Gerson, 1985, p. 6). It is assumed that past relationship patterns affect current personal and family functioning. Thus, generational issues and patterns of conflict, distancing, boundary setting, and triangulation can be explored using the genogram. In supervision, genograms can provide an excellent source of information for the purpose of exploring transference reactions, parallel process, patterns of responding to anxiety, and other relationship difficulties with the supervisee (see Kuehl, 1995, for a more complete discussion of the uses of genograms in supervision).

1. Use a large piece of paper to make your genogram. Go back three generations. Use shapes and colors as symbols to represent family members. See Appendix L for a sample genogram.

2. After completing the genogram, go back through it and look at the roles and relationships in your family of origin. Can you identify patterns in your family like unfinished business, healthy or problematic triangles, or areas of conflict and anxiety (Haber, 1996)? One very important area to examine is the role of multicultural issues such as ethnicity, race, gender, and socioeconomic status in your family of origin.

3. Next, examine this information in light of your own work with clients and then apply it to supervision. In order to facilitate the processing and integration of material with your supervisee, you could use any number of action techniques, such as role playing, psychodrama, the empty chair, or family sculpting. Keep in mind that the goal of this processing is to connect family history and relationship patterns to the supervisee's current functioning with clients and in the supervisory relationship.

Following are a list of potential processing topics and questions that can be used with the genogram to explore the supervisee's own relationship patterns.

1. Explore the genogram thinking about how closeness was handled in your family. What were typical patterns of responding to conflict? Anxiety? Triangulation, underfunctioning or overfunctioning, distancing or pursuit? How was anger handled? Between your parents? Between your parents and their parents? Between you and your parents? Between you and your siblings? Friends?

2. Another area to explore is separation, loss, and abandonment. What does the genogram tell you about the role of loss in your family? What types of losses occurred? How were losses handled? What happened to family members as a result of these losses? What happened to needs for safety and security? How were these losses shared and processed?

3. Other possible topics could be:

   ➤ How was success and failure seen in your family?

   ➤ How was sadness and hurt expressed?

   ➤ What happened when people (you) made mistakes?

   ➤ What was the role of religion? Race or ethnicity? Gender roles and stereotypes?

➤ What was it like to grow up in your family?

➤ Other questions?

Using the information learned from the above genogram, answer the following questions:

1. How might family patterns of coping with events and feelings get in the way of client care?

2. How might these patterns affect supervision and parallel process issues in supervision?

3. How might these patterns contribute to areas of conflict with the supervisee (transference and countertransference issues)?

Exercise 2: The Lifeline. The goal of this exercise is to identify significant events in one's life, to explore affective patterns and loss history, and to place oneself in the larger context of history and society in order to understand the roots of significant beliefs and values. It is best to do this exercise in one sitting if at all possible. Choose a quiet place. Take a blank sheet of paper, the bigger the better. Draw a line across the middle of the page and write birth at one end of the line and death on the other. Using dots, note each major event in your life on the line. For those events that seem neutral, place the dot directly on the line. Put dots below the line to represent sad events, and put dots above the line to represent positive or happy events. Use the amount of space between the line and the dot to represent the intensity of the impact of that event. Simply follow your stream of consciousness to guide what to put on your lifeline. Next, extend the line out after your current age; hypothesize events until your death and the age you will die.

Sample Lifeline

- Wedding

- First day of school

Birth _____ Current age _____ Death

- Break-up with first boyfriend

- Death of spouse

After completing your lifeline, answer the following questions:

1. What does the line say about you?

2. What do you notice about your life? Do you notice any clear patterns?

3. What strengths do you see in yourself?

4. Are there any important events that are not on the line? Do you have any idea why you left them off?

5. What thoughts and feelings do you have as you do this exercise? Is there anything you may want to explore more?

6. What did it feel like to hypothesize about your future and your death?

7. If you showed this line to someone, what do think they would see?

8. Write a brief summary of your thoughts and awarenesses.

9. Take the lifeline and date all the dots. What ages were you at the time of these events?

10. How do developmental issues play a part in the line?

11. Study the dates and ask yourself: What was happening in society at this time? What historical events were taking place? What was the cultural milieu?

12. How might these factors be important in your development? For example, wars, economic depression, and the economic needs of your family might have influenced your occupation, education, age of marriage, etc. Be sure to include regional and religious influences, the role of discrimination, and other social issues as you think about your lifeline. Write a brief summary below.

13. Discuss the impact of your lifeline on your approach to counseling and psychotherapy, your choice of population or problems to work with, and your theoretical model.

14. How might your life experiences affect client care? For example, discuss in your answer areas of difficulty, anxiety, and frustration working with clients, sensitivity to client problems, multicultural issues, blocks to expressing feelings, expectations for coping with life's problems, and your values and beliefs about life.

15. Do you see any issues such as significant loss, trauma, intense or unresolved anger, sadness, or hurt that would suggest you should seek personal counseling to resolve them in order to improve client care? Write a brief summary here.

16. Answer the same questions on the impact of your lifeline in terms of supervision. How do you see your lifeline affecting supervision and the supervisory relationship? Write a brief summary.

Exercise 3: Lifestyle Inventory. The Lifestyle Inventory was created by Alfred Adler as an assessment tool for clients (Sweeney, 1998). The purpose of filling out the questionnaire is to explore one's family constellation and early recollections in order to identify beliefs about oneself, strengths and weaknesses, and personal characteristics. The Lifestyle Inventory can be expanded to include other family-of-origin material. Supervisors should first fill out the questionnaire, highlighting any answers they feel are relevant to supervision, and then have supervisees do the same. For example, how do the answers affect the supervisory relationship? Evaluation? Expectations? Style of relating? (The complete Lifestyle Inventory can be found in Sweeney, 1998.)

1. Make a list of your siblings from oldest to youngest. What was your relationship like with each of your siblings? Explore in particular issues of anger, hurt, rejection, and caretaking. How was your relationship with your siblings overall?

2. Rate yourself and your siblings with regard to characteristics such as achievement, social skills, responsibility, getting along with others, and independence. Add other attributes to this list.

3. What was your role in your family?

4. Describe what it was like to grow up in your family. What stands out for you?

5. What were your parents' expectations of you when growing up? Have you met them? Exceeded them?

6. If your mother, father, sisters, or brothers were here to describe you, what would they say? Would they all say the same things?

7. What were the most important values in your family? Which ones did you acquire yourself? For example, beliefs about gender and gender roles? About other races?

8. Is there anything in particular that you dreamed of doing when you were a child? Have you done it?

9. What is one thing you really don't like about yourself?

10. What is one thing you particularly do like about yourself?

11. Look at differences and similarities of family members and at family roles and relationships. Who was the identified "responsible" parent? Child? Who was the irresponsible or incompetent one?

12. What was your role in the family? Were you the peacemaker in your family? Was it your job to make everyone feel better or were you the problem child, the difficult one?

13. Did you have to work to be seen or heard? Did you have to do something to receive attention?

Summarize your answers to the above questions and apply your answers to your experiences in supervision. Combine this exercise with your genogram and Lifestyle Inventory and write a brief summary of the overall awareness you have gained as it relates to your ability to supervise. Include a discussion of your strengths as well as weaknesses.

What Is the Role of Stress in Personal Development?

An increasing amount of attention is being paid today to the importance of taking care of the caregiver. It is widely recognized that those in the helping profession are at risk for exhaustion and burnout caused by the stressful aspects of therapeutic work; those working with victims in crisis and trauma are at an even greater risk. *Compassion fatigue* is the term Charles Figley (1995) coined to describe situations in which therapists themselves are traumatized by a sense of helplessness and confusion as a result of traumatic events. Compassion fatigue is different from burnout. Burnout is usually associated with a reduced sense of accomplishment and job effectiveness. This typically occurs when mental heath workers and counselors feel caught between the needs of their clients and the structures and policies of the organization in which they work. Symptoms of burnout include fatigue, irritability, loss of interest in work, withdrawal, defensiveness, and feelings of helplessness, guilt and depression. Compassion fatigue, on the other hand, is more directly related to the exact nature of the client's problems, such as sexual assault, murder, family violence, or the destruction of assumptions about the world, and the extreme difficulty of finding meaning in these traumatic events.

One contributing factor to compassion fatigue with beginning supervisees is their first-hand experience with trauma in their own lives. Caretakers who have themselves been victims can find personal feelings and memories triggered as they work with their clients. Symptoms of compassion fatigue include feeling overwhelmed by the events of the client's experience, finding it difficult to stop thinking about work, making exceptions to your rules about clients, doing extra things for clients, or feeling betrayed and abandoned or victimized (Figley, 1995). If the supervisor suspects that a supervisee is experiencing compassion fatigue, he or she may need to reinforce two aspects of training: helping the supervisee set boundaries with clients, and being available to process the supervisee's feelings and experiences and to offer support. Supervisors might wish to make use of the Compassion Fatigue Self-Test for Psychotherapists (Figley, 1995). It is recommended for both supervisor and supervisee alike, particularly when working with situations involving trauma, violence, or natural disasters. For a copy of the test, please contact Dr. Charles R. Figley, Psychosocial Stress Research Program, Florida State University.

EXPLORATION ➤ Burnout and Compassion Fatigue in Supervision

1. Answer the following questions to evaluate your potential for burnout.

   a. Are you satisfied with your effectiveness on the job?

   b. Do you have a sense of accomplishment about the work that you do?

   c. Do you feel helpless at work, stuck between the needs of your client population and the structures and policies of your organization or agency?

   d. On a scale of 1 to 1- (1 = low and 10 = high), how would you rate your sense of satisfaction with the work that you do?

   e. Rate yourself on a scale of 1 to 10 (1 = low and 10 = high), on satisfaction with year work environment.

2. Refer to the list of symptoms of burnout below. Rate yourself on each according to the scale that follows.

a *Physical Symptoms*: Exhaustion, fatigue, sleep difficulties, headaches, upset stomach, colds.

Never	Occasionally	Frequently	Continually
1	2	3	4

b. *Emotional Symptoms*: Irritability, anxiety, depression, guilt, sense of helplessness.

Never	Occasionally	Frequently	Continually
1	2	3	4

c. *Behavioral Symptoms*: Callousness, defensiveness, pessimism, aggressiveness, substance abuse.

Never	Occasionally	Frequently	Continually
1	2	3	4

d. *Work-Related Symptoms*: Poor work performance, absenteeism, tardiness, wanting to quit, poor concentration.

Never	Occasionally	Frequently	Continually
1	2	3	4

e. *Interpersonal Symptoms*: Withdrawal, intellectualizing, perfunctory communication, dehumanizing.

Never	Occasionally	Frequently	Continually
1	2	3	4

3. To evaluate your level of compassion fatigue, ask yourself the following questions. (Taken from the Compassion Fatigue Self-Test for Psychotherapists, Figley, 1995, p. 13–14).

a. How often do you lose sleep over a client's traumatic experiences?

Rarely/never	At times	Not sure	Often	Very often
1	2	3	4	5

b. How often do you feel a sense of hopelessness associated with working with clients?

Rarely/never	At times	Not sure	Often	Very often
1	2	3	4	5

c. How often do you feel weak, tired, and run down as a result of your work as a therapist?

Rarely/never	At times	Not sure	Often	Very often
1	2	3	4	5

4. How do you and your supervisee take care of yourselves; how do you relax, rest, and deal with stressful circumstances? Some issues to consider are the use of drugs and alcohol; diet and exercise; the existence of supportive relationships with others; and activities outside of work, including hobbies, recreation, and involvement with groups such as religious organizations or clubs. The following questions can be used to help you identify your own self-care strategies as well as those of your supervisee.

   a. List 10 things you do to relax and reduce stress.

   b. What is the role of alcohol or drugs in stress reduction? Do you use either of them regularly?

   c. What do you like to do for fun? Do you take time out on a daily or weekly basis to do this? If not, why?

d. Do you do some form of physical exercise regularly? How does this help with stress?

e. Do you have relationships outside of work that offer support? List them below. How often do you seek support from those listed?

f. Review your answers. What do you need to do differently to cope with stress and increase your self-care?

g. Choose one possible change out of the above list and make a specific action plan to implement this change. Give a date and specific description of the change you will make. Share your plan with a colleague.

➤ Conclusions

What conclusions might you draw from these exercises that may be helpful to you in working with your supervisee?

➤ Action Plan

What do you need to do as a result of these conclusions?

➤ Chapter Highlights

- ➤ Personal development is an important area of supervision.

- ➤ Personal issues, when not identified, can impede the quality of client care.

- ➤ The supervisor's role is to help the supervisee identify areas of personal difficulty and suggest means for resolution of these difficulties.

- ➤ Self-awareness exercises can be included in supervision to facilitate exploration of these personal issues.

- ➤ Effective supervisors are careful to avoid a dual relationship with their supervisees by limiting exploration of personal issues to their impact on client care.

Suggested Readings

Bloomfield, H. (1983). *Making peace with your parents.* New York: Ballentine Books.

Burns, D. D. (1999). *The feeling good handbook: Using the new mood therapy in everyday life.* New York: William Morrow.

Feltham, C., & Dryden, W. (1994). *Developing counselor supervision.* London: Sage. Chapter 6: Protecting the client and counselor.

Figley, C. R. (Ed.). (1995). *Compassion fatigue: Coping with secondary traumatic stress disorder in those who treat the traumatized.* New York: Brunner/Mazel Publishers.

Haber, R. (1996). *Dimensions of psychotherapy supervision.* New York: Norton. Chapter 1: Genogram in family therapy.

Kaiser, T. (1997). *Supervisory relationships: Exploring the human element.* Pacific Grove, CA: Brooks/Cole. Chapter 3: Power and authority.

Kuehl, Bruce P. (1995). The solution-orientated genogram: A collaborative approach. *Journal of Marital and Family Therapy, 21*(3), 239–250.

Kushner, H. S. (1996). *How good do we have to be? A new understanding of guilt and forgiveness.* Boston: Little, Brown and Company.

Lerner, H. (1985). *The dance of anger.* New York: Harper & Row.

Lerner, H. (1989). *The dance of intimacy.* New York: Harper & Row.

Powell, D. J. (1993). *Clinical supervision in alcohol and drug abuse counseling: Principles, models, methods.* New York: Lexington Books. Chapter 16: Special issues in supervision; & Appendix J.

Shulman, L. (1993). *Interactional supervision.* Washington, DC: NASW Press. Chapter 9: Helping staff cope with trauma.

Sweeney, T.J. (1998). *Adlerian counseling: A practitioner's approach* (4th ed.). Philadelphia: Accelerated Development.

Weiner-Davis, M. (1995). *Fire your shrink: Do-it-yourself strategies for changing your life and everyone in it.* New York: Simon & Schuster.

Williamson, D. (1991). *The intimacy paradox.* New York: Guilford.

Yalom, I. D. (1989). *Love's executioner and other tales of psychotherapy.* New York: Basic Books.

11

HOW DOES
A SUPERVISOR
PLAN FOR
THE FIRST SESSION?

Preparing for the first session with supervisees is a very important part of successful supervision; the clearer supervisors are as to their goals, expectations, and needs, the more likely they are to establish an effective working alliance with supervisees. Therefore, there are several required tasks: to review one's preparation for the supervisor role, to make a series of choices regarding supervision, and to then plan for the first meeting with the supervisee.

What Is My Preparation for the Supervisory Role?

In preparing for their new role, beginning supervisors may feel that they have little or no experience in such a role. Fortunately, this assumption is not true. Although formal training for the supervisory role may be limited, there are many personal and professional experiences and skills and much knowledge that supervisors may draw upon as they get started. Borders and Leddick (1987) suggested that new supervisors engage in a qualitative self-assessment of skills and knowledge related to supervision by creating a supervision resume. An exercise is included in "exploration section" of this chapter to assist supervisors in taking stock of their preparation for the supervisory role.

What Choices Do I Need to Make Before Beginning to Supervise?

It is understood that in the field, particularly in schools, agencies, and hospital settings, an administrator may appoint a practitioner to be a clinical supervisor as part of his or her job duties. Supervisors may feel they have neither a choice in accepting this role nor in selecting their supervisees. However, even appointed supervisors can *make choices* as to how they *approach* the role in spite of such limitations. For example, in an effort to prevent problematic situations from arising, appointed supervisors can identify what difficulties and conflicts may arise for them, particularly dual relationship issues, and then establish a preventive plan for resolving them. Thus, before beginning to supervise, there are a number of choices that should be made in order to ensure success as a supervisor:

1. Goals of supervision: What are the goals? How will time together be best spent to meet these goals?
2. Supervisory style: Will a collaborative, autocratic, consultative, or expert approach be most effective with this individual?
3. Format: Which format, individual or group, will bring the best results?
4. Methods and techniques: Which methods and techniques will maximize learning?
5. Evaluation: What is the best plan?
6. Environmental factors: How will the environment influence supervision?
7. Multicultural issues: What will their impact be on supervision?
8. Ethical concerns: How will issues of safety, power, and control be addressed?

Taking time to ponder these choices will provide supervisors with an overall road map to follow in supervision.

What Paperwork Is Required?

As in all areas of mental health practice, there is substantial paperwork involved in supervision. Before beginning supervision, it is very important to review a copy of whatever supervision and licensing requirements are involved, as well as the final evaluation form. Because of the threat of vicarious liability, it is recommended that both supervisor and supervisee carry personal malpractice insurance over and above any insurance provided by their institution. Supervisors should also obtain a copy of their supervisees' resumes of previous training and experience; supervisees should be provided with similar material from their supervisors.

A file should be created for each supervisee that will include the following: a copy of the license or certification requirements of the supervisee along with his or her temporary license if required, a copy of the supervisor's certification as an approved supervisor; a copy of malpractice insurance; and a resume of background training and experience. Most of this material can be obtained prior to the first meeting in order to facilitate communication and understanding.

The supervisor should also have on hand a written informed consent form. McCarthy et al. (1995) recommended the use of such agreement in supervision. They suggested that this agreement include the following information:

- ➤ the purpose of the form;
- ➤ professional disclosure of your background and experience;
- ➤ practical issues such as time, location, and cost of supervision;
- ➤ short description of the supervision process and its purpose;
- ➤ discussion of what type of record keeping will be required;
- ➤ description of evaluation methods;
- ➤ review of the legal and ethical issues that apply to supervision;
- ➤ statement of agreement to be signed by both supervisor and supervisee.

In addition, many states require a written supervision contract before supervision can begin. A supervision contract is very useful in delineating roles, relationships, and requirements for supervision. A generic contract form should include a statement of intent; an outline of responsibilities and requirements, such as length, time, and fees; and a description of the format for supervision. See Appendices M and N for a sample consent form and a generic supervision contract. Supervisors should, however, check with their state licensing board for exact requirements and a contract form. Many experienced supervisors also require their supervisees to read the appropriate legal and ethical codes and attach a signed statement of understanding and agreement to the supervision contract before beginning the supervision process.

Another important piece of paperwork to include is a resume of the supervisee's background and experience. Since post-degree licensure candidates can come from a variety of backgrounds, the supervisor needs to take time to go over the supervisee's training and experiences. It is important not to confuse experience with knowledge and capability, so the supervisor must establish ways to assess the supervisee's basic skills and knowledge as they relate to the goals of supervision. There are a number of effective methods for reviewing the supervisee's basic skills, their knowledge base, and their relevant work experience. For example, the supervisor could ask to review transcripts of the supervisee's course work in their graduate program and supporting documentation such as course outlines, syllabi, or catalog descriptions of course content. Another method is to ask the supervisee to provide a synopsis of his or her training experience in a graduate program, outlining course by course what material was covered. Also, a resume of work experience with a description of skills and knowledge should be obtained from the more experienced supervisee or from one who is unfamiliar. As suggested in chapter 4, on techniques, some additional material could be requested from potential supervisees including samples of note taking, record keeping or charting, or sample audio- or videotapes; alternatively, the supervisor could schedule a live observation session before contracting for supervision.

Another effective method is to ask new supervisees to supply in writing a short summary of the following topics:

- ➤ their education, particularly their knowledge of theories and techniques;
- ➤ their own theoretical model and philosophy of working with clients;
- ➤ their practical experience in internships, field settings, and other work-related arenas;
- ➤ the types of clients they have seen and their supervision experience with these clients;
- ➤ their special skills with particular populations and methods;
- ➤ their knowledge of current ethical codes and writings;
- ➤ their knowledge of their own strengths and weaknesses;
- ➤ their goals and expectations for supervision.

This type of document will provide supervisors with a means to gather necessary information and to review the writing and conceptual abilities of the supervisee. In all likelihood, supervisees will benefit from the exercise because they will have the opportunity to confront these important issues before supervision begins.

How Do I Structure the First Session With a Potential Supervisee?

The first meeting with a new supervisee should include a discussion of the basic ground rules, overall expectations, goals, structure and methods, review of record keeping, evaluation, crisis management, issues related to setting and population served, meeting time, location, and accessibility, as well as procedures to resolve any disagreements that should arise. As this is an extensive list of topics, several sessions may be needed to establish rapport and cover the needed content. For example, the introductory session may extend for 1½ hours and be preceded by an exchange of written information. Another entire session may need to be devoted to a review of the code of ethics, particularly as it relates to confidentiality, record keeping and documentation, dual relationships, and boundary setting with clients. The focus of this introductory session will vary for each supervision setting; on-site supervisors may want to stress organizational issues, whereas those off-site may need to thoroughly discuss procedures for handling crises and communication. With a colleague or coworker, it is important to discuss expectations and to review potential areas of conflict or harm, because of the risk of dual relationship problems. If the supervisee is unknown, more emphasis may be placed on gathering background information. Part of this introductory session may be done by phone or in writing.

Because the first meeting with a supervisee is so important and there is so much material to be covered, it is extremely beneficial to create an outline of important topics and issues of concern. For example, some supervisors might feel discomfort at reviewing the background and experience of a known colleague who is also a supervisee in order to make a supervision plan. They may be uncomfortable with exploring their supervisee's deficits in skills or knowledge, so there may be a tendency to ignore or skip over certain topics. Unfortunately, though, it is easy to confuse experience with knowledge or professional ability, which could prove harmful at a later date. Therefore, creating an outline of introductory information to be obtained from any and all supervisees, regardless of experience, and topics to be covered in the first session, may be useful to avoid difficulties and overcome any anxiety felt by beginning supervisors.

To assist supervisors, the following outline is offered as a suggested format for the first session:

I. Initial contact with the potential supervisee (by phone or in person)
   A. Topics to discuss
      1. Expectations
      2. Tentative goals for supervision
      3. Time, location, fees, if any
   B. Issues
      1. Is this a good match?
      2. What difficulties might occur?
      3. Do I have any choice as to working with this supervisee?

C. Tasks
    1. Information to obtain from supervisee
        a. Background and experience
        b Documents
            • Resume and transcripts
            • Copy of license or license forms
            • Other documents required by the licensing board (supervision contract, evaluation forms, log of hours)
            • Copy of malpractice insurance
    2. Information to provide supervisee
        a. Your background and experience, expertise, skills
        b. Copy of informed consent
        c. Copy of supervision contract outlining terms and expectations
        d. Copy of certification as supervisor
        e. Copy of ethical code(s)

II. First session
  A. Topics to discuss
    1. Goals for supervision
    2. Administrative details (logging, record keeping, and evaluation)
    3. Crisis management strategies
    4. Ethical issues as they relate to supervision (discussion of vicarious liability, negligence, and confidentiality)
  B. Issues
    1. Establish working alliance
    2. Explore areas of difficulty and procedures to resolve them
  C. Tasks
    1. Sign informed consent and supervision contract
    2. Provide necessary forms to supervisee (evaluation forms, logs, and sample record keeping)

EXPLORATION ➤ Preparation for the Role of Supervisor

Create a supervision resume

In order to identify your sources of preparation for the supervisory role, and your knowledge, skills, and strengths relevant to the function of supervisor, use the following example as a guide to create a supervision resume (adapted and expanded from Bernard & Goodyear, 1998; Borders & Leddick, 1987; Powell, 1993).

1. Experience as a supervisee. If you had multiple settings and supervisors, list the information for each one. If it has been a long time since you were in training, you may want to simply summarize this part of your supervision resume.

   a. List setting, population, tasks, and length of time as a trainee.

   b. List your experiences with individual, group, couple, and family therapy.

   c. List your supervisor's style, techniques, activities and theoretical model(s), for example, use of individual or group supervision, case presentations, live or review of tapes, cotherapy, examination of written work.

d. Note the method of evaluation used by the supervisor.

e. List any training you have done with particular client problems and populations.

f. List any training you have done in cross-cultural populations, working with differences (i.e., race, ethnicity, gender, age, religion).

g. List your experience with peer supervision and consultation.

h. List your experience in personal therapy.

i. List your overall experience in training; include the the positives and the negatives.

j. Summarize your strengths.

2. Work background and experience

    a. What is your job experience. For example, do you have experience as a counselor or therapist, teacher, administrator, case manager, consultant, trainer, or researcher?

    b. What is your experience with particular methods and populations. For example, do you have experience with groups, individual, family, couples, children, and adolescents?

c. What is your specialized training with particular problems or populations. For example, with sexual abuse, crisis, post-traumatic stress disorder, learning disabilities, and testing?

d. What is your experience working with multicultural populations and their issues?

3. Training in supervision

a. Do you have any formal training in supervision?

b. What are your informal experiences as a supervisor. For example, do you have experience as a parent, coach, or president of an organization?

c. Summarize your supervision training experience.

4. Major strengths (clinical and personal) as a counselor or therapist. List them.

After you have made your list, rank-order the characteristics according to their importance to you as a supervisor.

EXPLORATION ➢ *Choices to Make as a Supervisor*

There are a number of choices that a beginning supervisor needs to make before beginning to supervise. Review the list on p. 240, go back through the workbook, and review your reflections on each of these topics. Then take some time to condense your thoughts and make an outline on a separate sheet. Keep the outline to use as a guide for the first session.

EXPLORATION ➤ Planning for the First Session

1. Before you begin, what are the pros and cons of being a supervisor? Do you want to do it?

2. Take a minute to review your reflections on your background, knowledge, and skills. What do you think are your overall strengths and skills as a supervisor?

3. What information would you like to have about your potential supervisee before you agree to a supervision contract? Be as specific as possible. Put this in outline form on a separate sheet of paper and place it in your supervision file for later use.

Is There a Comprehensive Model of Supervision Available?

The mental health field has not been able to develop a comprehensive model of supervision (Haber, 1996; Powell, 1993; White & Russell, 1995). Competencies required of effective practitioners vary greatly from discipline to discipline. Differences abound regarding models of change, conceptualization of problems, intervention methods, and skills required in each particular setting (e.g., schools vs. mental health agencies vs. private practice). For example, a survey of AAMFT supervisors generated 771 variables that influence supervision and are important to supervisory outcome (White & Russell, 1995). While developmental models of supervision are currently receiving a great deal of interest and enthusiasm, there is little empirical support outside of academic settings for these models and their assumptions (Borders, 1989; Magnuson & Wilcoxon, 1998; Watkins, 1997). Thus, the question still remains for post-degree supervision: "Which skills and techniques will help the supervisee work most effectively with the problems of a specific case in his or her general caseload?" (Haber, 1996, p. 78)

How Do I Create a Supervision Model for Myself?

What is needed in order to create such a model is a system for organizing information into which all the important variables can be factored. Such variables include the supervisor's own skill level and model of change, environmental factors, ethical and legal concerns, multicultural issues, the supervisee's skills and abilities, the developmental level of both the supervisee and the supervisor, the developmental stage of the supervisory relationship, and the needs of the client. Powell (1993) suggested the use of a four-level pyramid to guide supervisors' thinking. The bottom layer of the pyramid is the philosophical foundation, or one's underlying viewpoint on change. The next level is the descriptive dimension, or the practices of the supervisor, which follows from the philosophy of change. The third level is the developmental level: the training, experience, knowledge, and skill of the supervisee and supervisor. The cap of the pyramid represents the contextual factors, characteristics of the client, counselor, supervisor, and setting that affect supervision. Beginning supervisors might find this pyramid image helpful in creating their own comprehensive models of supervision.

Another important variable to consider when creating one's own model of clinical supervision is the developmental stage of the supervisory relationship. It is also necessary to consider the interaction among all developmental factors—the developmental levels of the supervisee and supervisor and of the supervisory relationship—and the environment. For example, the supervisory relationship itself must be placed in an environmental context that both constrains and supports the development of the supervisor and supervisee. Environmental factors, such as the setting, rules and regulations, population served, service provided, and state laws and licensing regulations, all serve as critical moderating factors in the development of the supervisory relationship, the supervisor, the supervisee (Powell, 1993; Shulman, 1993). In summary, a comprehensive model of supervision must go beyond a simple list of variables to recognize the interaction among these variables.

There are 10 steps to follow in building a comprehensive model of supervision, and each step requires that several important questions be answered. The material to complete the steps and answer these significant questions is contained in each chapter of this workbook. To facilitate the task of building a personal model of supervision, readers should refer back to their answers to the exploration questions at the end of each chapter.

Step 1: Identify personal philosophy of change that guides practice.

Question: How do people change? What factors should be considered?

Answer: Refer to the exploration questions in chapter 3.

Step 2: Identify goals for supervision.

Question: Which competencies must an effective and ethical practitioner possess in a particular discipline and setting?

Answer: Refer to the exploration questions in chapters 1 and 6.

Step 3: Define specific content areas for supervision, and describe what supervisees must know and be able to demonstrate in each content area.

Question: What are supervisees expected to know to be competent professionals?

Answer: Refer to the exploration questions in chapters 2, 6, and 9.

Step 4: Identify expectations for supervisees in each content area depending on developmental level.

Question: What are the expectations for supervisees at the beginning and at the end of their supervision experience?

Answer: Refer to the exploration questions in chapters 6 and 9.

Step 5: Assess developmental level of the supervisee.

Question: What is the developmental level of the supervisee? What are his or her skills and abilities? Does he or she possess a different level of knowledge, experience, and expertise in each content area?

Answer: Refer to the exploration questions in chapters 6 and 11.

Step 6: Identify the development level of the supervisor, as well as his or her skill level and expertise in the various techniques and methods of supervision.

Question: What are the supervisor's skills and abilities? Is the supervisor just beginning to supervise or does he or she have considerable expertise in the field?

Answer: Refer to the exploration questions in chapters 6 and 11.

Step 7: Identify preferred style of supervision.

Question: How do multicultural issues, personality factors, and learning style preferences influence supervisory style?

Answer: Refer to the exploration questions in chapters 2 and 8.

Step 8: Identify environmental and contextual factors that influence supervision: ethical and legal issues, multicultural issues, needs of clients, resources available.

Question: What are the environmental constraints and supports that will influence supervision?

Answer: Refer to the "Exploration" sections of chapters 6, 7, and 8.

Step 9: Identify the stage of development of the supervisory relationship.

Question: What is the stage of development of the supervisory relationship? Is it just beginning, well developed, or close to termination?

Answer: Refer to the exploration questions in chapters 3 and 6.

Step 10: Identify relationship skills, roles, methods, and techniques necessary to help the supervisee grow and develop.

Question: How should supervisors proceed? What relationship factors should be considered?

Answer: Refer to the exploration questions in chapters 4, 5, 6, and 10.

In conclusion, before beginning, clinical supervisors must take time to consider the important questions and choices facing them and the necessity of building their own models of supervision. They must understand that the goals for supervision are different in nature and purpose from counseling and psychotherapy and that they need to develop different skills and abilities than a counselor or psychotherapist needs. Additionally, supervisors must be aware of the ethical mandate that holds them responsible to protect clients while promoting the growth and development of the supervisee. For post-degree clinical supervisors, this task becomes more onerous as they serve as the final gatekeepers between the mental health profession and the public. In order to accomplish the two tasks, supervisors must take a multimodal approach to supervision—to be flexible in balancing their own needs and those of the supervisee. They must develop relationship skills to support, challenge, and collaborate with supervisees in order to build an effective working alliance. Most importantly, clinical supervisors must value supervision and commit themselves to continuous training and ongoing consultation or supervision of their own work as a supervisor in order to be most effective.

EXPLORATION ➤ Building Your Own Model of Supervision

Using the material generated by answering the questions listed in the 10 steps, can you now build your own model? Put it on a separate sheet to include in your supervision file.

➤ Conclusions

What conclusions might you draw from these exercises that would be helpful to you in working with your supervisee?

➤ Action Plan

What do you need to do as a result of these conclusions?

➤ Chapter Highlights

- ➤ The clearer the supervisor is with the supervisee about goals and expectations, the more likely the supervisor is to create an effective working alliance with the supervisee.

- ➤ Planning for the first session with the supervisee is essential to effective supervision.

- ➤ Background information and requirements for supervision should be obtained before proceeding.

- ➤ Creating a consistent outline to follow for the first meeting with all supervisees helps prevent later difficulties.

- ➤ Supervisors must build their own personal models of supervision.

➤ Supervisors must take in to account a host of different factors such as their own developmental level, the developmental level of the supervisee, the developmental level of the supervisory relationship, and important environmental factors that both constrain and support supervision.

➤ In order to be effective, supervisors should value supervision and seek additional training.

Suggested Readings

Borders, L. D., Bernard, J.M., Dye, H.A., Fong, M.L., Henderson, P., & Nance, D. W. (1991). Curriculum guide for training counseling supervisors: Rationale, development, and implementation. *Counselor Education and Supervision, 31,* 61–78.

Borders, L. D., & Leddick, G. (1987). *Handbook of counseling supervision.* Alexandria, VA: Association of Counsleor Education and Supervision. Chapter 1: Assessing supervisor knowledge and skills; & Chapter 2: Initial supervisory sessions: Working contract and assessment of the supervisee.

Bradley, L. (2000). *Counselor supervision.* Philadelphia: Accelerated Development. Chapter 9: Advocacy in counseling supervision; & Chapter 11: Supervisory training: A model.

Feltham, C., & Dryden, W. (1994). *Developing counselor supervision.* London: Sage. Chapter 4: Using the developmental opportunities of supervision

Haber, R. (1996). *Dimensions of psychotherapy supervision.* New York: Norton. Chapter 1: My professional journey.

Liddle, H. A., Becker, D., & Diamond, G. M. (1997). Family therapy supervision. In C. E. Watkins, Jr. (Ed.), *Handbook of psychotherapy supervision* (pp. 400–420). New York: Wiley.

Powell, D. J. (1993). *Clinical supervision in alcohol and drug abuse counseling: Principles, models, methods.* New York: Lexington Books. Chapter 11: Establishing a supervision contract; Chapter 16: Special issues in supervision; Chapter 5; Building a model of clinical supervision; Appendix C: Assessing one's preparation as a clinical supervisor; & Appendix D: Determining readiness to be a supervisor.

Stoltenberg, C. D., McNeill, B. W., & Delworth, U. (1997). *IDM supervision: An integrated development model for supervising counselors and therapists.* San Francisco, CA: Jossey-Bass.

Watkins, C. E., Jr. (1997). Some concluding thoughts about psychotherapy supervision. In C. E. Watkins, Jr. (Ed.), *Handbook of psychotherapy supervision.* New York: Wiley, 603–616.

White, M., & Russell, C. (1995). The essential elements of supervisory systems: A modified study. *Journal of Marital and Family Therapy, 21*(1), 33–53.

Sample Group Leadership Skills Evaluation

	Not observed	Not effective	Effective	Very effective
Uses communication skills				
Attends to nonverbal behavior				
Uses open-ended questions to facilitate group functioning				
Uses time effectively to open group				
Uses time effectively to close group				
Uses structured exercises effectively to accomplish goals				
Encourages participation				
Handles conflict in the group				
Maintains order and focus on tasks				
Initiates activities to accomplish group goals				
Uses process comments to increase group effectiveness				
Uses modeling to teach desired skills				
Demonstrates use of problem-solving skills				
Gives periodic feedback to the group				
Gives periodic feedback to individual members				
Uses leadership skills to promote group cohesion				
Understands stages of group development				
Manages difficult members and counterproductive behavior				
Creates safe environment, confidentiality, boundaries, rules				
Models appropriate self-disclosure				

Sample Case Consultation Format

Name of the presenter:

Date: Session number:

Identifying data about the client:

Presenting problem:

Short summary of the session:

Important history or environmental factors (especially multicultural issues):

Tentative assessment or problem conceptualization (diagnosis):

Plan of action and goals for therapy (treatment plan):

Intervention strategies:

Concerns or problems surrounding this case (ethical concerns, relationship issues, etc.):

Instructions for Audio and Videotaping

1. *Use quality equipment.* Make sure of the sound quality, volume and clarity. It is best to use equipment with separate clip on microphones unless one is in an actual sound studio with a boom microphone. Clip-on microphones are inexpensive and easy to obtain.

2. *Buy good-quality tapes*; it is not necessary to buy the top of the line, but avoid the bargain basement kind. Better tapes give better sound and picture and can be reused.

3. *Placement of equipment matters.* Use a tripod for the video camera. Check angle of camera, seating, volume, and stability of picture. To reduce anxiety, place equipment out of direct view. For example, place the tape recorder out of immediate view but within reach, such as on a side table between chairs. With video camera, place at an angle, not directly facing the client. If there is a TV monitor with the video camera, turn it off while taping, as it can be distracting to watch oneself.

4. *Check background sound and volume.* Choose a quiet, private place to do this, both to protect confidentiality and to improve tape quality. Do not use an open space, an office with windows facing the street, or anywhere that is subject to interruption. Loud air-conditioning fans, ringing phones and pagers, street noise, and office conversations all disrupt the quality of taping. Turn off pagers, cell phones, and other potential sources of noise to avoid interruption.

5. *Know how to use the equipment.* Use it in a dry run. Be sure to check the volume background noise level, placement of chairs, video camera angles, and picture quality before you begin. If the supervisee is especially anxious or unfamiliar with the equipment, have him or her make a practice tape.

6. *Protect the confidentiality of the supervisee and the client.* Choose a private, controlled space for taping. Protect the tapes: Keep them in a locked cabinet and don't include identifying data on the outside of the tape. When finished with supervision, erase the tape completely before reusing. Do not just tape over the previous session.

7. *Process with the supervisee any anxiety and concern generated by taping.* Three areas of potential anxiety are technical aspects (equipment and room availability), concern for the client (confidentiality), and the effect of taping on the session (critical evaluation of performance by the supervisor).

8. *Explain taping, its goals and purpose, to the client* at least one session before proceeding. Review with the client any concerns about confidentiality. Remember that the more comfortable and enthusiastic you and your supervisee are with the value of taping, the more comfortable the client will be. Sometimes just reassuring the client that the tape can be turned off at any point if the client is really uncomfortable increases a sense of control and reduces anxiety. Usually after the first few minutes of taping, both client and therapist forget its presence and this option is

rarely used. If the client appears resistant, a decision should be made as to the appropriateness of using this particular method of supervision in this situation.

9. *Get a written release from the client.* Be sure release includes a description of the purpose of the tape, limits of confidentiality, identity(s) of those viewing the tape, and assurance of erasure of tape afterwards. If the tape is to be used in group supervision or a staffing seminar, the client should be informed of that fact.

10. *Before beginning the actual session, check the equipment* by making a short practice tape covering background material on the client. Then, rewind the tape and play it to check sound, volume, camera angle, and picture. When satisfied, begin the actual session.

Generic Rating Sheet & Evaluation Form
Supervisee's Basic Skills & Techniques

Date: _____ Supervisee: _____

Supervisor: _____

Videotape _____ Audiotape _____

Direct observation _____ Case Presentation _____

	Not observed	Not effective	Effective	Very effective
Established rapport				
Reflected feelings				
Used open-ended questions				
Used silence				
Kept focus				
Explored problem(s)				
Clarified problem(s)				
Paraphrased				
Summarized				
Challenged client				
Reframed problem(s)				
Provided interpretation				
Demonstrated ethical behavior				
Was multiculturally responsive				

Comments:

_____ _____
Signature of Supervisor   Date

_____ _____
Signature of Supervisee   Date

Ethical Guidelines for Clinical Supervisors

The following is the Association for Counselor Education's code of ethics specific to clinical supervision.

Association for Counseling Education and Supervision
(Adopted: March, 1993)[1]

Preamble

The Association for Counselor Education and Supervision (ACES) is composed of people engaged in the professional preparation of counselors and people responsible for the ongoing supervision of counselors. ACES is a founding division of the American Counseling Association (ACA) and as such adheres to ACA's current ethical standards (AACD, 1988) and to general codes of competence adopted throughout the mental health community.

ACES believes that counselor educators and counseling supervisors in universities and in applied counseling settings, including the range of education and mental health delivery systems, carry responsibilities unique to their job roles. Such responsibilities may include administrative supervision, clinical supervision, or both. Administrative supervision refers to those supervisory activities which increase the efficiency of the delivery of counseling services; whereas, clinical supervision includes the supportive and educative activities of the supervisor designed to improve the application of counseling theory and technique directly to clients.

Counselor educators and counseling supervisors encounter situations which challenge the help given by general ethical standards of the profession at large. These situations require more specific guidelines that provide appropriate guidance in everyday practice.

The Ethical Guidelines for Counseling Supervisors are intended to assist professionals by helping them:

1. observe ethical and legal protection of clients' and supervisees' rights;
2. meet the training and professional development needs of supervisees in ways consistent with clients' welfare and programmatic requirements; and
3. establish policies, procedures, and standards for implementing programs.

The specification of ethical guidelines enables ACES members to focus on and to clarify the ethical nature of responsibilities held in common. Such guidelines should be reviewed formally every five years, or more often if needed, to meet the needs of ACES members for guidance.

The Ethical Guidelines for Counselor Educators and Counseling Supervisors are meant to help ACES members in conducting supervision. ACES is not currently in a position to hear complaints about alleged noncompliance with these guidelines. Any complaints about the ethical behavior of any ACA member should be measured against the ACA Ethical Standards and a complaint lodged with ACA in accordance with their procedures for doing so.

One overriding assumption underlying this document is that supervision should be ongoing throughout a counselor's career and not stop when a particular level of education, certification, or membership in a professional organization is attained.

[1]From Supervision Interest Network, Association for Counselor Education and Supervision. (1993, Summer). ACES ethical guidelines for counseling supervisors. *ACES Spectrum,* 53(4), 5–8. Copyright © 1993 by the Association for Counselor Education and Supervision. Reprinted by permission.

Definitions of Terms:

Applied Counseling Settings—Public or Private organization of counselors such as community mental health centers, hospitals, schools, and group or individual private practice settings.

Supervisees—Counselors-in-training in university programs at any level who work with clients in applied settings as part of their university training program, and counselors who have completed their formal education and are employed in an applied counseling setting.

Supervisors—Counselors who have been designated within their university or agency to directly oversee the professional clinical work of counselors. Supervisors also may be persons who offer supervision to counselors seeking state licensure and so provide supervision outside of the administrative aegis of an applied counseling setting.

1. Client Welfare and Rights

1.01 The primary obligation of supervisors is to train counselors so that they respect the integrity and promote the welfare of their clients. Supervisors should have supervisees inform clients that they are being supervised and that observation and/or recordings of the session may be reviewed by the supervisor.

1.02 Supervisors who are licensed counselors and are conducting supervision to aid a supervisee to become licensed should instruct the supervisee not to communicate or in any way convey to the supervisee's clients or to other parties that the supervisee is himself/herself licensed.

1.03 Supervisors should make supervisees aware of clients' rights, including protecting clients' right to privacy and confidentiality in the counseling relationship and the information resulting from it. Clients also should be informed that their right to privacy and confidentiality will not be violated by the supervisory relationship.

1.04 Records of the counseling relationship, including interview notes, test data, correspondence, the electronic storage of these documents, and audio and videotape recordings, are considered to be confidential professional information. Supervisors should see that these materials are used in counseling, research, and training and supervision of counselors with the full knowledge of the client and that permission to use these materials is granted by the applied counseling setting offering service to the client. This professional information is to be used for the full protection of the client. Written consent from the client (or legal guardian, . if a minor) should be secured prior to the use of such information for instructional, supervisory, and/or research purposes. Policies of the applied counseling setting regarding client records also should be followed.

1.05 Supervisors shall adhere to current professional and legal guidelines when conducting research with human participants such as section D-1 of the ACA Ethical Standards.

1.06 Counseling supervisors are responsible for making every effort to monitor both the professional actions, and failures to take action, of their supervisees.

2. Supervisory Role

Inherent and integral to the role of supervisor are responsibilities for:

a. monitoring client welfare;
b. encouraging compliance with relevant legal, ethical, and professional standards for clinical practice;
c. monitoring clinical performance and professional development of supervisees; and
d. evaluating and certifying current performance and potential of supervisees for academic, screening, selection, placement, employment, and credentialing purposes.

2.01 Supervisors should have had training in supervision prior to initiating their role as supervisors.

2.02 Supervisors should pursue professional and personal continuing education activities such as advanced courses, seminars, and professional conferences on a regular and ongoing basis. These activities should include both counseling and supervision topics and skills.

2.03 Supervisors should make their supervisees aware of professional and ethical standards and legal responsibilities of the counseling profession.

2.04 Supervisors of postdegree counselors who are seeking state licensure should encourage these counselors to adhere to the standards for practice established by the state licensure board of the state in which they practice.

2.05 Procedures for contacting the supervisor, or an alternative supervisor, to assist in handling crisis situations should be established and communicated to supervisees.

2.06 Actual work samples via audio and/or video tape or live observation in addition to case notes should be reviewed by the supervisor as a regular part of the ongoing supervisory process.

2.07 Supervisors of counselors should meet regularly in face-to-face sessions with their supervisees.

2.08 Supervisors should provide supervisees with ongoing feedback on their performance. This feedback should take a variety of forms, both formal and informal, and should include verbal and written evaluations. It should be formative during the supervisory experience and summative at the conclusion of the experience.

2.09 Supervisors who have multiple roles (e.g., teacher, clinical supervisor, administrative supervisor, etc.) with supervisees should minimize potential conflicts. Where possible, the roles should be divided among several supervisors. Where this is not possible, careful explanation should be conveyed to the supervises as to the expectations and responsibilities associated with each supervisory role.

2.10 Supervisors should not participate in any form of sexual contact with supervisees. Supervisors should not engage in any form of social contact or interaction which would compromise the supervisor-supervisee relationship. Dual relationships with supervisees that might impair the supervisor's objectivity and professional judgment should be avoided and/or the supervisory relationship terminated.

2.11 Supervisors should not establish a psychotherapeutic relationship as a substitute for supervision. Personal issues should be addressed in supervision only in terms of the impact of these issues on clients and on professional functioning.

2.12 Supervisors, through ongoing supervisee assessment and evaluation, should be aware of any personal or professional limitations of supervisees which are likely to impede future professional performance. Supervisors have the responsibility of recommending remedial assistance to the supervisee and of screening from the training program, applied counseling setting, or state licensure those supervisees who are unable to provide competent professional services. These recommendations should be clearly and professionally explained in writing to the supervisees who are so evaluated.

2.13 Supervisors should not endorse a supervisee for certification, licensure, completion of an academic training program, or continued employment if the supervisor believes the supervisee is impaired in any way that would interfere with the performance of counseling duties. The presence of any such impairment should begin a process of feedback and remediation wherever possible so that the supervises understands the nature of the impairment and has the opportunity to remedy the problem and continue with his/her professional development.

2.14 Supervisors should incorporate the principles of informed consent and participation; clarity of requirements, expectations, roles and rules; and due process and appeal into the establishment of policies and procedures of their institution, program, courses, and individual supervisory relationships. Mechanisms for due process appeal of individual supervisory actions should be established and made available to all supervisees.

3. Program Administration Role

3.01 Supervisors should ensure that the programs conducted and experiences provided are in keeping with current guidelines and standards of ACA and its divisions.

3.02 Supervisors should teach courses and/or supervise clinical work only in areas where they are fully competent and experienced.

3.03 To achieve the highest quality of training and supervision, supervisors should be active participants in peer review and peer supervision procedures.

3.04 Supervisors should provide experiences that integrate theoretical knowledge and practical application. Supervisors also should provide opportunities in which supervisees are able to apply the knowledge they have learned and understand the rationale for the skills they have acquired. The knowledge and skills conveyed should reflect current practice, research findings, and available resources.

3.05 Professional competencies, specific courses, and/or required experiences expected of supervisees should be communicated to them in writing prior to admission to the training program or placement/employment by the applied counseling setting, and, in the case of continued employment, in a timely manner.

3.06 Supervisors should accept only those persons as supervisees who meet identified entry level requirements for admission to a program of counselor training or for placement in an applied counseling setting. In the case of private supervision in search of state licensure, supervisees should have completed all necessary prerequisites as determined by the state licensure board.

3.07 Supervisors should inform supervisees of the goals, policies, theoretical orientations toward counseling, training, and supervision model or approach on which the supervision is based.

3.08 Supervisees should be encouraged and assisted to define their own theoretical orientation toward counseling, to establish supervision goals for themselves and to monitor and evaluate their progress toward meeting these goals.

3.09 Supervisors should assess supervisees' skills and experience in order to establish standards for competent professional behavior. Supervisors should restrict supervisees' activities to those that are commensurate with their current level of skills and experiences.

3.10 Supervisors should obtain practicum and fieldwork sites that meet minimum standards for preparing students to become effective counselors. No practicum or fieldwork setting should be approved unless it truly replicates a counseling work setting.

3.11 Practicum and fieldwork classes should be limited in size according to established professional standards to ensure that each student has ample opportunity for individual supervision and feedback. Supervisors in applied counseling settings should have a limited number of supervisees.

3.12 Supervisors in university settings should establish and communicate specific policies and procedures regarding field placement of students. The respective roles of the student counselor, the university supervisor, and the field supervisor should be clearly differentiated in areas such as evaluation, requirements, and confidentiality.

3.13 Supervisors in training programs should communicate regularly with supervisors in agencies used as practicum and/or fieldwork sites regarding current professional practices, expectations of students, and preferred models and modalities of supervision.

3.14 Supervisors at the university should establish clear lines of communication among themselves, the field supervisors, and the students/ supervisees.

3.15 Supervisors should establish and communicate to supervisees and to field supervisors specific procedures regarding consultation, performance review, and evaluation of supervisees.

3.16 Evaluations of supervisee performance in universities and in applied counseling settings should be available to supervisees in ways consistent with the Family Rights and Privacy Act and the Buckley Amendment.

3.17 Forms of training that focus primarily on self-understanding and problem resolution (e.g., personal growth groups or individual counseling) should be voluntary. Those who conduct these forms of training should not serve simultaneously as supervisors of the supervisees involved in the training.

3.18 A supervisor may recommend participation in activities such as personal growth groups or personal counseling when it has been determined that a supervisee has deficits in the areas of self-understanding and problem resolution which impede his/her professional functioning. The supervisor should not be the direct provider of these activities for the supervisee.

3.19 When a training program conducts a personal growth or counseling experience involving relatively intimate self-disclosure, care should be taken to eliminate or minimize potential role conflicts for faculty and/or agency supervisors who may conduct these experiences and who also serve as teachers, group leaders, and clinical directors.

3.20 Supervisors should use the following prioritized sequence in resolving conflicts among the needs of the client, the needs of the supervisee, and the needs of the program or agency. Insofar as the client must be protected, it should be understood that client welfare is usually subsumed in federal and state laws such that these statutes should be the first point of reference. Where laws and ethical standards are not present or are unclear, the good judgment of the supervisor should be guided by the following list:

a. Relevant legal and ethical standards (e.g., duty to warn, state child abuse laws, etc.);
b. Client welfare;
c. Supervisee welfare;
d. Supervisor welfare; and
e. Program and/or agency service and administrative needs.

Ethics At Risk Test for Therapists'

Ever wonder how close you are to blundering over the ethics edge and possibly harming your clients, yourself, and/or the profession? This At Risk test may tell you. Of course, you must answer honestly. Add up your score and compare the total with the key at the end of the test. (Circle your answers.)

1. Is it true that you have never taken an academic course on ethics? No=0 Yes=1
2. Honestly, are you unfamiliar with some parts of the latest version of the Ethics Code? No=0 Yes=1
3. Do you think the Ethics Code interferes somewhat with the quality of your therapy or research? No=0 Yes=1
4. Have you ever sent a false bill for therapy to an insurance carrier? No=0 Yes=1
5. Do you feel sexually attracted to any of your present clients? No=0 Yes=1
6. Do you fantasize about kissing or touching a present client? No=0 Yes=1
7. Do you comment to a present client how attractive he or she is or make positive remarks about his or her body? No=0 Yes=1
8. Are you tempted to ask out an ex-client even though less than two years have passed since termination? No=0 Yes=1
9. Do you commonly take off your jewelry, remove shoes, loosen your tie, or become more informal during therapy sessions? No=0 Yes=1
10. Presently, do you meet a client for coffee or meals or for socializing outside of therapy? No=0 Yes=1
11. Has a present client given you an expensive gift or frequently given you inexpensive gifts? No=0 Yes=1
12. Are you stimulated by a current client's description of sexual behavior or thoughts? No=0 Yes=1
13. Are you in the midst of a difficult personal or family crisis yourself? No=0 Yes=1
14. During the past two months, have you seen clients while you were hungover or under the influence of drugs, even if only a little? No=0 Yes=1
15. Does your personal financial situation cross your mind when considering whether to terminate therapy or to refer a client? No=0 Yes=1
16. Do you feel manipulated by a current client such that you are wary of him/her or are angry and frustrated by him/her? No=0 Yes=1
17. Do you provide therapy to a current student, supervisee, or employee? No=0 Yes=1
18. Have you wanted to talk to a colleague about a current case but feared doing so would show your lack of skill or lead to an ethics case against you? No=0 Yes=1

---

²Courtesy of Gregory W. Brock, Ph.D., Department of Family Studies, University of Kentucky.

19. Are you behind on case notes?   No=0 Yes=1
20. Do you talk about clients with other clients or gossip about clients   No=0 Yes=1
     with colleagues?

Total Score

0	Excellent. You are nearly risk free.
1–2	Review your practice. Read and follow the Ethics Code.
3–4	Review your practice for problem areas. Consider needed changes.
5–7	Consult a supervisor. You are engaging in high-risk behavior.
8+	You are probably harming your clients and/or yourself. Seek therapy and supervision. Come to terms with your situation by making immediate changes.

Please send comments or questions to Dr. Brock, 315 Funkhouser Building, University of Kentucky, Lexington, KY 40506-0054, USA.

National Organizations

American Association for Marriage and Family Therapy (AAMFT)
1133 15th Street, NW, Suite 300
Washington, DC 20005-2710
Phone: (202) 452-0109
Fax: (202) 223-8310
www.aamft.org

American Counseling Association (ACA)
5999 Stevenson Avenue
Alexandria, VA 22304
Phone: (800) 347-6647
Fax: (800) 473-2329
www.counseling.org

American Psychological Association (APA)
750 First Street, NE
Washington, DC 20002-4242
(202) 336-5500
www.apa.org

National Association of Social Workers (NASW)
750 First Street, NE, Suite 700
Washington, DC 20002-4241
Phone: (202) 408-8600
Fax: (202) 336-8310
www.nasw.org

National Board for Certified Counselors, Inc. (NBCC)
3 Terrace Way, Suite D
Greensboro, NC 27403-3660
Phone: (910) 547-0607
Fax: (910) 547-0017
Email: nbcc@nbcc.org

Sample Log of Supervision Hours

Date	Client name or code	Amount of clock time	Individual	Group	Topic	Running total clock hours

Sample Generic Supervisee Evaluation Form

Date: _____

Supervisee: _____

Supervisor: _____

	Poor	Below average	Average	Above average	Excellent
Established rapport					
Structured session					
Demonstrated listening skills					
Used open-ended questions					
Used silence effectively					
Promoted positive work climate					
Demonstrated written skills (documentation, record keeping)					
Iteracted effectively with clients					
Interacted effectively with colleagues					
Interacted effectively with supervisors					
Demonstrated ethical behavior					
Was multiculturally responsive					
Demonstrated use of good judgment and counseling skills					
Provided consultation					
Provided appropriate referrals					
Accepted and learned from feedback					

Supervisee Evaluation Form
Public School Setting

Date: _____

Supervisee: _____

Supervisor: _____

	Poor	Below average	Average	Above average	Excellent
Established rapport					
Structured session					
Demonstrated active listening skills					
Used open-ended questions					
Used silence effectively					
Promoted positive school climate					
Demonstrated organizational skills with priorities and documentation					
Complied with district and camp us mandates					
Interacted effectively with students					
Interacted effectively with colleagues					
Interacted effectively with supervisors					
Demonstrated ethical behavior					
Was multiculturally responsive					
Demonstrated use of good judgment and counseling skills					
Communicated effectively with parents					
Provided consultation for staff and parents					
Provided appropriate referrals					
Accepted and learned from feedback					

Generic Evaluation Form
Supervisor's Skills & Techniques

Date: _____   Supervisee: _____

Supervisor: _____

	Not Observed	Not effective	Effective	Very effective
Structured supervisory sessions				
Provided useful feedback				
Encouraged active involvement				
Addressed session content				
Maintained focus				
Conveyed competence				
Encouraged questions				
Acted supportive				
Challenged supervisee				
Allowed self-evaluation				
Focused on behaviors				
Provided suggestions				
Maintained flexibility				
Helped with definition and achievement of goals				
Conveyed respect and acceptance				
Addressed ethical issues				
Was multiculturally responsive				

Comments:

_____   _____

Signature of Supervisee   Date

_____   _____

Signature of Supervisor   Date

Making a Genogram

A genogram is a pictorial representation of family relationships across several generations. This appendix shows some of the symbols that can be used to represent people and occurrences in a family.

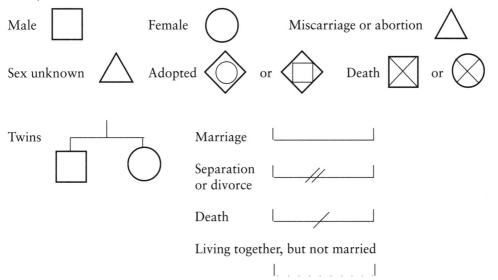

Male ☐   Female ○   Miscarriage or abortion △

Sex unknown △   Adopted ◇○ or ◇☐   Death ☒ or ⊗

Twins   Marriage

Separation or divorce

Death

Living together, but not married

Children are denoted by vertical lines. Place oldest on the left and youngest on the right.

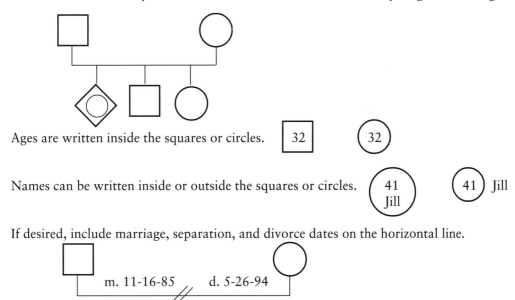

Ages are written inside the squares or circles.   32   32

Names can be written inside or outside the squares or circles.   41 Jill   41 Jill

If desired, include marriage, separation, and divorce dates on the horizontal line.

m. 11-16-85   d. 5-26-94

Additional information may include vocations, temperament, hobbies, or other pertinent attributes about each person.

Genograms may also include "feeling faces" such as happy, sad, angry, numb, and scared.

Sample Supervision Consent Form

Purpose

The purpose of this form is to acquaint you with your supervisor, to describe the supervision process, to provide structure to your supervision experience, to give you the opportunity to ask questions you may have regarding supervision, and to ensure a common understanding about the supervision process.

Professional Disclosure

I earned a Master of Education degree in counseling at the University of Houston and am licensed by the Texas State Board of Examiners of Professional Counselors to practice in this state. I am a member of the American Counseling Association, the Association for Counselor Education and Supervision, the Association for Specialists in Group Work, and the Texas Counseling Association. I have worked in higher education and agency settings for the past eight years. My experience has focused on depression, anxiety, substance dependence, and relationship issues. I have more limited experience working with battered women and abused children, as well as children with learning disabilities. I have completed coursework in clinical supervision, and have been providing individual and group supervision for the past five years. My theoretical orientation for counseling and supervision is an integration of cognitive-behavioral, humanistic, and psychodynamic theories. Throughout this supervision experience, I will take on different roles at different times—teacher, consultant, counselor, and evaluator. We will further discuss these roles in our introductory meeting.

Practical Issues

In order to fulfill the supervision requirements for LPC interns, we will meet for an hour, once a week, on Thursdays from 3:00 p.m. until 4:00 p.m. in my office. If a circumstance arises that makes it impossible for you to attend a scheduled session, contact me as soon as you know you will miss the session in order to reschedule. Payment of the $60.00 individual supervision fee is due at each session. If you need to speak to me between sessions, or in case of a client emergency, you may call me at my office or at home. If you are unable to reach me, my answering service will assist you by referring you to one of my colleagues who will be available for consultation.

Supervision Process

Supervision is an interactive process intended to monitor the quality of client care, improve clinical skills, and facilitate professional and personal growth. You can expect to receive timely feedback of your clinical interventions and to have a supportive environment in which to explore client-related

From McCarthy, P., Sugden, S., Koker, M., Lamendola, F., Maurer, S., & Renninger, S. (1995). A practical guide to informed consent in clinical supervision. *Counselor Education and Supervision, 35,* 130–138.

concerns. You will be expected to be an active participant in the supervision process, to arrive on time and be prepared for each session, and to complete all required work in a timely manner. These expectations are designed to improve your counseling conceptualization and intervention skills and to increase your sense of professional identity. Possible risks include discomfort arising from challenges to your counseling knowledge, abilities, and/or skills. The format for each session will consist of an oral case presentation combined with audio- or videotape segments highlighting any issues that you wish to discuss. I will also review your written case notes. I invite you to ask questions, explore alternatives, address ethical concerns, and receive feedback and suggestions on your therapeutic interventions. I will provide specific guidelines for oral and written requirements during our first few sessions.

Administrative Tasks and Evaluation

In my role as your supervisor, I will provide you with feedback throughout this supervision experience. Formal written evaluations will be conducted quarterly and conclude with a final evaluation at the end of your 2000 hours. Evaluation criteria include oral and written case reports, four audio- or videotapes of counseling sessions, and the degree to which you accomplish the goals set forth at the beginning of this supervision experience. Please refer to your supervision interview and goals for clarification. I will also ask you to complete a formal evaluation of my supervision at the end of this supervision experience. If you are dissatisfied with your supervision or the evaluation process, please discuss this with me. If we are unable to resolve your concerns, I will refer you to the appropriate contact.

Legal/Ethical Issues

Supervision is not intended to provide you with personal counseling or therapy. If personal issues or concerns arise, I urge you to seek counseling. The content of our sessions and evaluations are confidential, except what I share with my supervisor. Limits to confidentiality include, but are not limited to, treatment of a client which violates the legal or ethical standards set forth by professional associations and government agencies. These guidelines will be provided and discussed at our introductory meeting.

Statement of Agreement

I have read and understand the information contained in this document.

_____   _____   _____   _____
Supervisee Signature   Date   Supervisor Signature   Date

Sample Supervision Contract

Supervisor: _____

Address: _____

Telephone: _____

Supervisee: _____

Address: _____

Telephone: _____

Supervisee's Employer: _____

Address: _____

Telephone: _____

I agree to provide clinical supervision to _____ for _____ hour(s) per week of face to face supervision and _____ hour(s) per week of group supervision, if applicable, for a minimum of one or two years, as required by the licensing board. I will complete evaluation/reference forms necessary to verify this supervision and will report on the supervisee's performance during this period of time to the appropriate licensing board for purposes of state licensing and/or professional credential applications.

The purpose of this supervision is to enable _____ to satisfy the clinical supervision requirements of the _____ (state board). As the independent clinical supervisor, I am not responsible for the supervisee's job performance or for the number or types of cases assigned to him/her or for any other aspects of his/her job duties or employment agreement with _____ (employer).

Period of time: From _____ to _____

Location: _____

Fee for service: _____   Payment method: _____

Either the supervisor or supervisee may terminate this agreement with 14 days written notice.

Supervisor: _____ Date: _____

Supervisee: _____ Date: _____

REFERENCES

Altucher, N. (1967). Constructive use of the supervisory relationship. *Journal of Counseling Psychology, 14*(2), 165–170.

Anderson, S. A., Rigazio-Digio, S. A., & Kunkler, K. P. (1995). Training of family professionals: Training and supervision in family therapy-current issues and future directions. *Family Relations, 44,* 489–500.

Appelbaum, P. S., & Gutheil, T. G. (1991). *Clinical handbook of psychiatry and the law* (2nd ed.). Baltimore: Williams & Wilkins.

Arredondo, P., Toporek, R., Brown, S., Jones, J., Locke, D. C., Sanchez, J., and Stadler, H. (1996). *Operationalization of the multicultural counseling competencies.* Alexandria, VA: Association for Multicultural Counseling and Development.

Avis, J. M., & Sprunkle, D. H. (1990). Outcome research on family therapy training: A substantive and methodological review. *Journal of Marital and Family Therapy, 16*(3), 241–264.

Baldwin, M. (1983). *Satir: Step by Step.* Palo Alto, CA: Science and Behavior Books.

Bandura, A. (1986). *Social foundations of thought and action: A social cognitive theory.* Englewood Cliffs, NJ: Prentice-Hall.

Baranchok, J. S., & Kunkel, M. A. (1990). Clinical supervision training in counseling psychology. *The Counseling Psychologist, 18,* 685–687.

Barbuto, J. E. (1997). A critique of the Myers-Briggs type Indicator and its operationalization of Carl Jung's psychological types. *Psychological Reports, 80,* 611–625.

Barrow, M., & Domingo, R. A. (1997). The effectiveness of training clinical supervisors conducting the supervisory conference. *Clinical Supervisor, 16,* 55–78.

Berger, S., & Buchholz, E. (1993). On becoming a supervisee: Preparation for learning in a supervisory relationship. *Psychotherapy, 30,* 86–92.

Bergin, A. E., & Garfield, S. (1994). *Handbook of Psychotherapy and Behavior Change* (4th ed.). New York: Wiley.

Bernard, J. M. (1997). The discrimination model. In C. E. Watkins, Jr. (Ed.), *Handbook of psychotherapy supervision* (pp. 310–327). New York: Wiley.

Bernard, J. M. (1979). Supervisor training: A discrimination model. *Counselor Education and Supervision, 19,* 60–68.

Bernard, J. M., & Goodyear, R. K. (1998). *Fundamentals of clinical supervision.* Boston: Allyn and Bacon.

Blatner, A. (1991b). Imaginative interviews: A psychodramatic warm-up for developing role-playing skill. *Journal of Group Psychotherapy, Psychodrama and Sociometry, 44*(3), 115–120.

Blocher, D. H. (1983). Toward a cognitive developmental approach to counselor supervision. *The Counseling Psychologist, 11*(1), 27–34.

Bloomfield, H. (1983). *Making peace with your parents.* New York: Ballentine Books.

Borders, L. D. (1989). A pragmatic agenda for developmental supervision research. *Counselor Education and Supervision, 29,* 16–24.

Borders, L. D., Bernard, J.M., Dye, H.A., Fong, M.L., Henderson, P., & Nance, D.W. (1991). Curriculum guide for training counseling supervisors: Rationale, development, and implementation. *Counselor Education and Supervision, 31,* 61–78.

Borders, L. D., Cashwell, C. S., & Rotter, J. C. (1995). Supervision of counselor licensure applicants: A comparative study. *Counselor Education and Supervision, 35,* 54–69.

Borders, L. D., & Leddick, G. (1987). *Handbook of counseling supervision.* Alexandria, VA: Association for Counselor Education and Supervision.

Borders L. D. & Usher, C. H. (1992). Post-degree supervision: Existing and preferred practices. *Journal of Counseling and Development, 70,* 594–599.

Bordin, E. S. (1983). A working alliance based model of supervision. *The Counseling Psychologist, 11,* 35–42.

Bradley, L. (1989). *Counselor supervision.* Muncie, IN: Accelerated Development.

Bradley, L. (2000). *Counselor supervision.* Washington, DC: Accelerated Development.

Breunlin, D. C., Karrer, B. M., McGuire, D. E., & Cimmarusti, R. A. (1988). Cybernetics of videotape supervision. In H. A. Liddle, D. C. Breunlin, & R. C. Schwartz (Eds.), *Handbook of family therapy training and supervision* (pp. 194–206). New York: Guilford.

Briggs, K. C., & Myers, I. B. (1993). Myers-Briggs Type Indicator. Consulting Psychology Press. Palo Alto, CA.

Budman, S. H., & Gurman, A. S. (1988). *Theory and practice of brief therapy.* New York: Guilford.

Buhrke, R. A. (1989). Lesbian-related issues in counseling supervision. In E. Rothblum & E. Cole (Eds.). *Loving boldly: Issues facing lesbians* (pp. 195–206). New York: Haworth Press.

Burns, D. D. (1999). *Feeling good: The new mood therapy.* New York: Avon Books.

Carkhuff, R. R. (1969). *Helping and human relations, Vol. 2.* New York: Holt, Rinehart and Winston.

Carlson, J., Sperry, L., & Lewis, J. (1997). *Family therapy: Ensuring treatment efficacy.* Pacific Grove, CA: Brooks/Cole.

Carmichael, K. D. (1992, Spring). Peer rating form in counselor supervision. *Texas Association of Counseling and Development Journal,* 57–61.

Carney, C. G., & Kahn, K. B. (1984). Building competencies for effective cross-cultural counseling: A developmental view. *The Counseling Psychologist, 12*(1), 111–119.

Chagnon, J., & Russell, R. K. (1995). Assessment of supervisee developmental level and supervision environment across supervisor experience. *Journal of Counseling and Development, 73,* 553–558.

Chung, Y. B., Baskin, M. L., & Case, A. B. (1998). Positive and negative supervisory experiences reported by counseling trainees. *Psychological Reports, 82,* 762.

Claiborn, C. D., Etringer, B. D., & Hillerbrand, E. T. (1995). Influence processes in supervision. *Counselor Education and Supervision, 35,* 43–52.

Conway, P., & Ellison, M. S. (1995). The development of a behaviorally anchored rating scale for master's student evaluation of field instructors. *The Clinical Supervisor, 13,* 101–119.

Cook, D. A. (1994). Racial identity in supervision. *Counselor Education and Supervision, 34,* 132–141.

Cook, E., Berman, E., Genco, K., Repka, R., & Shrider, J. (1986). Essential characteristics of master's level counselors: Perceptions of agency administrators. *Counselor Education and Supervision, 34,* 146–152.

Corey, G. (1995). *Theory and practice of group counseling.* Pacific Grove, CA: Brooks/Cole.

Corey, G., Corey, M. S., & Callanan, P. (1993). *Issues and ethics in the helping professions* (4th ed.). Pacific Grove, CA: Brooks/Cole.

Cormier, S., & Hackney, H. (1999). *Counseling strategies and interventions* (5th ed.). Boston: Allyn & Bacon.

Corsini, R. J. (1966). *Role playing in psychotherapy.* Chicago: Aldine Publishers.

Corsini, R. J., & Wedding, D. (Ed.). (1995). *Current psychotherapies*. Itasca, IL: F. E. Peacock.

D'Andrea, M. (1989). Person-process model of supervision: A developmental approach. In L. Bradley (Ed.), *Counselor supervision*. Muncie, IN: Accelerated Development.

Daniels, T. G., Rigazio-DiGilio, S. A., & Ivey, A. E. (1997). Microcounseling: A training and supervision paradigm for the helping professions. In C. E. Watkins, Jr. (Ed.), *Handbook of psychotherapy supervision* (pp. 277–295). New York: Wiley.

DeLucia, J. L., Bowman, V. E., & Bowman, R. L. (1989). The use of parallel process in supervision and group counseling to facilitate counselor and client growth. *The Journal for Specialists in Group Work, 14*(4), 232–238.

DeShazer, S. (1985). *Keys to solution in brief therapy*. New York: Norton.

Dewald, P. A. (1997). The process of supervision in psychoanalysis. In C. E. Watkins, Jr. (Ed.), *Handbook of psychotherapy supervision Vol. 1* (pp. 31–43). New York: Wiley.

Disney, M. J., & Stephens, A. M. (1994). Legal issues in clinical supervision. In T. P. Remley (Ed.), *ACA Legal Series*. Alexandria, VA: American Counseling Association.

Doehrman, M. J. G. (1976). Parallel processes in supervision and psychotherapy. *Bulletin of the Menninger Clinic, 40*(1), 3–10.

Ecker, B. & Hully, L. (1996). *Depth oriented brief therapy*. San Francisco, CA: Jossey-Bass.

Efstation, J. F., Patton, M. J., & Kardash, C. M. (1990). Measuring the working alliance in counselor supervision. *Journal of Counseling Psychology, 37*, 322–329.

Egan, G. (1998). *The skilled helper*. Pacific Grove, CA: Brooks/Cole.

Ellis, M. V., & Ladany, N. (1997). Inferences concerning supervisees and clients in clinical supervision: An integrative review. In C. E. Watkins, Jr. (Ed.), *Handbook of psychotherapy supervision* (pp. 447–507). New York: Wiley.

Ekstein, R., & Wallerstein, R. S. (1972). *The teaching and learning of psychotherapy* (2nd ed.). New York: International Universities Press.

Feltham, C., & Dryden, W. (1994). *Developing counselor supervision*. London: Sage.

Fisher, B. (1989). Differences between supervision of beginning and advanced therapists: Hogan's hypothesis empirically revisited. *The clinical supervisor, 7*(1), 57–75.

Figley, C. R. (1995). Compassion fatigue as secondary traumatic stress disorder: An overview. In C. R. Figley (Ed.), *Compassion fatigue: Coping with secondary traumatic stress disorder in those who treat the traumatized* (pp. 1–201). New York: Brunner/Mazel Publishers.

Fowers, B. J., & Richardson, F. C. (1996). Why is multiculturalism good? *American Psychologist, 51*(6), 609–621.

Friedlander, M. L., & Ward, L. G. (1984). Development and validation of the supervisory styles inventory. *Journal of Counseling Psychology, 4*, 541–557.

Gendlin, E. T. (1996). *Focused-oriented psychotherapy: A manual of the experimental methods*. New York: Guilford.

Getz, H. G., & Protinsky, H. O. (1994). Training marriage and family counselors: A family-of-origin approach. *Counselor Education and Supervision, 33*, 183–190.

Goldberg, D. A. (1985). Process notes, audio and videotape: Modes of presentation in psychotherapy training. *Clinical Supervisor, 3*, 3–13.

Goldenberg, H., & Goldenberg, I. (1994). *Counseling today's families*. Pacific Grove, CA: Brooks/Cole.

Goldfried, M., & Newman, C. (1992). A history of psychotherapy integration. In J. C. Norcross & M. R. Goldfried (Eds.), *Handbook of psychotherapy integration*. New York: Basic Books.

Goleman, D. (1995). *Emotional intelligence*. New York: Bantam Books.

Goodyear, R., & Nelson, M. L. (1997). The major formats of psychotherapy supervision. In C. E. Watkins, Jr. (Ed.), *Handbook of psychotherapy supervision* (pp. 328–346). New York: Wiley.

Haber, R. (1996). *Dimensions of psychotherapy supervision.* New York: Norton.

Haley, J. (1985). *Problem-solving therapy.* San Francisco, CA: Jossey-Bass.

Hanna, M. A., & Smith, J. (1998). Using rubrics for documentation of clinical work supervision. *Counselor Education and Supervision, 37,* 269–278.

Hardy, K. V., & Laszloffy, T. A. (1995). The cultural genogram: Key to training culturally competent family therapists. *Journal of Marital and Family Therapy, 21*(3), 227–237.

Hawkins, P., & Shohet, R. (1989). *Supervision in the helping professions.* Milton Keynes: Open University Press.

Hendrix, D. H. (1992). Metaphors as nudges toward understanding in mental health counseling. *Journal of Mental Health Counseling, 14*(2), 234–242.

Herlihy, B., & Corey, G. (1992), *Dual relationships in counseling.* Alexandria, VA: American Association for Counseling and Development Association.

Herlihy, B. (1994). Presentation Fall 1994 Counselor Supervision Workshop. University of Houston—Clear Lake.

Hess, A. K. (Ed.). (1980). *Psychotherapy supervision: Theory, research and practice.* New York: Wiley.

Hess, A. K. (1986). Growth in supervision: Stages of supervisee and supervisor development. *Clinical Supervisor, 4*(1–2), 51–67.

Hilton, D. B., Russell, R. K., & Salmi, S. W. (1995). The effects of supervisor's race and level of support on perceptions of supervision. *Journal of Counseling and Development, 73,* 559–563.

Hogan, R. A. (1964). Issues and approaches in supervision. *Psychotherapy: Theory, Research, and Practice, 1,* 139–141.

Holloway, E. (1995). *Clinical supervision: A systems approach.* Thousand Oaks, CA: Sage.

Horney, K. (1950). *Neurosis and human growth.* New York: Norton.

Houston-Vega, M. K., Nuehring, E. M., & Daguio, E. R. (1997). *Prudent practice: A guide for managing malpractice risk.* Washington, DC: NASW Press.

Hulse-Killacky, D., & Page, B. (1994). Development of the corrective feedback instrument: A tool for use in counselor training groups. *Journal for Specialists in Group Work, 19*(4), 197–210.

Ivey, A. (1999). *Intentional interviewing and counseling: Facilitating client development in a multicultural society.* Pacific Grove, CA: Brooks/Cole.

Juhnke, G. A. (1996). Solution-focused supervision: Promoting supervisee skills and confidence through successful solutions. *Counselor Education and Supervision, 36,* 48–57.

Kagan, H., & Kagan, N. (1997). Interpersonal process recall: Influencing human interaction. In C. E. Watkins, Jr. (Ed.), *Handbook of psychotherapy supervision* (pp. 296–309). New York: Wiley.

Kagan, N. (1980a). Influencing human interaction—Eighteen years with IPR. In A. Hess (Ed.), *Psychotherapy supervision: Theory, research, and practice* (pp. 262–283). New York: Wiley.

Kagan, N. (1980b). *Interpersonal process recall: A method of influencing human interaction.* Class Workbook. Michigan State University.

Kaiser, T. (1992). The supervisory relationship: An identification of the primary elements in the relationship and an application of two theories of ethical relationships. *Journal of Marital and Family Therapy, 18*(3), 283–296.

Kaiser, T. (1997). *Supervisory relationships: Exploring the human element.* Pacific Grove, CA: Brooks/Cole.

Kaslow, F. W. (1986). *Supervision and training: Models, dilemmas, and challenges.* New York: Haworth Press.

Keirsey, D., & Bates, M. (1984). *Please understand me* (5th ed.). Del Mar, CA: Prometheus Nemesis Books.

Kirby, S. (1996). Apprentice co-therapy: Working side by side with a supervisor. In R. Haber (Ed.), *Dimensions of psychotherapy supervision: Maps and means* (pp. 202–216). New York: Norton.

Knapp, S., & Vandercreek, L. (1997). Ethical and legal aspects of clinical supervision. In C. E. Watkins, Jr. (Ed.), *Handbook of psychotherapy supervision*. New York: Wiley.

Kohut, H. (1971). *The analysis of the self*. New York: International Universities Press.

Kuehl, B. P. (1995). The solution-oriented genogram: A collaborative approach. *Journal of Marital and Family Therapy, 21*(3), 239–250.

Kushner, H. S. (1996). *How good do we have to be? A new understanding of guilt and forgiveness*. Boston: Little, Brown and Company.

Ladany, N., & Friedlander, M. L. (1995). The relationship between the supervisory working alliance and trainees' experience of role conflict and role ambiguity. *Counselor Education and Supervision, 34*, 220–231.

Ladany, N., Hill, C. E., Corbett, M. M., & Nutt, E. A. (1996). Nature, extent, and importance of what psychotherapy trainees do not disclose to their supervisors. *Journal of Counseling Psychology, 43*, 10–24.

Ladany, N., & Lehrman-Waterman, D. E. (1999). The content and frequency of supervisor self-disclosures and their relationship to supervisor style and the supervisory working alliance. *Counselor Education and Supervision, 38*, 143–160.

Ladany, N., Brittan-Powell, C. S., & Pannu, R. K. (1997). The influence of supervisory racial identity interaction and racial matching on the supervisory working alliance and supervisee multicultural competence. *Counselor Education and Supervision, 36*, 284–302.

Lambert, M. J., & Ogles, B. M. (1997). The effectiveness of psychotherapy supervision. In C. E. Watkins, Jr. (Ed.), *Handbook of psychotherapy supervision* (pp. 421–446). New York: Wiley.

Lanning, W. (1986). Development of the supervisor emphasis rating form. *Counselor Education and Supervision, 25*, 191–196.

Lanning, W., & Freeman, B. (1994). The Supervisor Emphasis Rating Form-Revised. *Counselor Education and Supervision, 33*, 294–304.

Leong, F. T., & Wagner, N. (1994). Cross-cultural counseling supervision: What do we know? What do we need to know? *Counselor Education and Supervision, 34*, 117–131.

Lerner, H. G. (1985). *The dance of anger*. New York: Harper & Row.

Lerner, H. G. (1989). *The dance of intimacy*. New York: Harper & Row.

Leveton, E. (1992). *A clinician's guide to psychodrama*. New York: Springer-Verlag.

Liddle, H. A., Becker, D., & Diamond, G. (1997). Family therapy supervision. In C. E. Watkins, Jr. (Ed.), *Handbook of psychotherapy supervision*. New York: Wiley.

Liddle, H. A., Breunlin, D. C., & Schwartz, R. C. (Eds.) (1988). *Handbook of family therapy training & supervision* (pp. 400–420). New York: Guilford.

Loganbill, C., Hardy, E., & Delworth, U. (1982). Supervision: A conceptual model. *The Counseling Psychologist, 10*(1), 3–42.

Loganbill, C., & Stoltenberg, C. (1983). The case conceptualization format: A training device for practicum. *Counselor Education and Supervision, 22*, 235–242.

Lopez, S. R. (1997). Cultural competence in psychotherapy: A guide for clinicians and their supervisors. In C. E. Watkins, Jr. (Ed.), *Handbook of psychotherapy supervision* (pp. 570–589). New York: Wiley.

Magnuson, S. (1996, October). *Investigating current practices to effectively design change*. Paper presented at the Association for Counselor Education and Supervision. Portland, OR.

Magnuson, S., & Wilcoxon, S. A. (1998). Successful clinical supervision of prelicensed counselors: How will we recognize it? *The Clinical Supervisor, 17*(1), 33–47.

Manaster, G. J., & Lyons, A. (1994). An exercise in multicultural complexity. *Texas Counseling Association Journal, 22*(2), 45–51.

Mazza, J. (1988). Training Strategic Therapists: The use of indirect techniques. In H. Liddle, D. C. Breunlin, & R. C. Schwartz (Eds.), *Handbook of family therapy training & supervision* (pp. 93–109). New York: Guilford.

McCarthy, P., Sugden, S., Koker, M., Lamendola, F., Maurer, S., & Renninger, S. (1995). A practical guide to informed consent in clinical supervision. *Counselor Education and Supervision, 35,* 130–138.

McCollum, E. E., & Wetchler, J. L. (1995). In defense of case consultation: Maybe "dead" supervision isn't dead after all. *Journal of Marital and Family Therapy, 21,* 155–166.

McGoldrick, M. (1998, March 27). *Culture, class, race, and gender: Clinical implications of our clients' context.* Presentation, University of Houston-Clear Lake, Houston, TX.

McGoldrick, M., & Gerson, R. (1985). *Genograms in family assessment.* New York: Norton.

McGoldrick, M., Giordano, J., & Pearce, J. (1996). *Ethnicity and family therapy.* New York: Guilford.

McGoldrick, M., & Green, R. J. (1998). *Re-visioning family therapy from a multicultural perspective.* New York: Guilford.

Mead, D. E. (1990). *Effective supervision: A task-oriented model for the mental health professions.* New York: Brunner/Mazel Publishers.

Middleman, R. R., & Rhodes, G. B. (1985). *Competent supervision: Making imaginative judgments.* Englewood Cliffs, NJ: Prentice Hall.

Morran, K. D., Kurpius, D. J., Brack, C. J., & Brack, G. (1995). A cognitive-skills model for counselor training and supervision. *Journal of Counseling and Development, 73,* 384–396.

Mosak, H. H. (1995). Adlerian Psychotherapy. In R. J. Corsini & D. Wedding, *Current Psychotherapies* (5th Edition). Itasca, IL: Peacock Publishers.

Myers, I. B. (1993). *Introduction to type* (3rd ed.). Palo Alto, CA: Consulting Psychologists Press.

Navin, S., Beamish, P., & Johanson, G. (1992). Ethical practices of field-based mental health counselor supervisors. *Journal of Mental Health Counseling, 15,* 243–253.

Neufeldt, S. A. (1994). Use of a manual to train supervisors. *Counselor Education and Supervision, 33,* 327–336.

Neufeldt, S. A., Beutler, L. E., & Banchero, R. (1997). Research on supervisor variables in psychotherapy supervision. In C. E. Watkins (Ed.), *Handbook of psychotherapy supervision* (pp. 508–526). New York: Wiley.

Nevill, D., & Super, D. (1985). *Values scale.* Palo Alto, CA: Consulting Psychologists Press.

Norcross, J. C., & Goldfried, M. (Eds.). (1992). *Handbook of psychotherapy integration.* New York: Basic Books.

Norcross, J. C., & Halgin, H. P. (1997). Integrative approaches to psychotherapy supervision. In C. E. Watkins, Jr. (Ed.), *Handbook of psychotherapy supervision* (pp. 203–222). New York: Wiley.

O'Hanlon, W. H., & Weiner-Davis, M. (1989). *In search of solutions: A new direction in psychotherapy.* New York: Norton.

Olk, M., & Friedlander, M. L. (1992). Role conflict and ambiguity in the supervisory experiences of counselor trainees. *Journal of Counseling Psychology, 39,* 389–397.

Patterson, C. H. (1996). Multicultural counseling: From diversity to universality. *Journal of Counseling and Development, 74,* 227–231.

Perls, F. (1969). *Gestalt therapy verbatim.* Moab, UT: Real People Press.

Peterson, F. K. (1991). Issue of race and ethnicity in supervision: Emphasizing who you are, not what you know. *Clinical Supervisor, 9*(1), 15–31.

Powell, D. J. (1993). *Clinical supervision in alcohol and drug abuse counseling: Principles, models, methods.* New York: Lexington Books.

Prochaska, J., & DiClemente, C. (1992). The transtheoretical approach. In J. Norcross & M. Goldfried (Eds.), *Handbook of psychotherapy integration* (pp. 300–304). New York: Basic Books.

Prochaska, J. O., & Norcross, J.C. (1994). *Systems of psychotherapy: A transtheoretical analysis* (3rd ed.). Pacific Grove, CA: Brooks/Cole.

Prochaska, J. O., Norcross, J. C., & DiClemente, C. (1994). *Changing for good.* New York: William Morrow.

Quick, E. K. (1996). *Doing what works in brief therapy: A strategic solution focused approach.* San Diego: Academic Press.

Raichelson, S. H., Herron, W. G., Primavera, L. H., & Ramirez, S. M. (1997). Incidence and effects of parallel process in psychotherapy supervision. *Clinical Supervisor, 15*(2), 37–48.

Rigazio-DiGilio, S. A., Anderson, S. A., & Kunkler, K. P. (1995). Gender-aware supervision in marriage and family counseling and therapy: How far have we actually come? *Counselor Education and Supervision, 34,* 344–355.

Rogers, C. R. (1951). *Client-centered therapy.* Boston, MA: Houghton Mifflin Co.

Rosenthal, H. (Ed.). (1998). *Favorite counseling and therapy techiques.* Washington, DC: Accelerated Development.

Russell, R., & Petrie, T. (1994). Issues in training effective supervisors. *Applied & Preventive Psychology, 3,* 27–42.

Satir, V. (1988) *Conjoint family therapy* (3rd ed.). Palo Alto, CA: Science and Behavior Books.

Schwartz, R. C., Liddle, H. A., & Breunlin, D. C. (1988). Muddles in live supervision. In H. A. Liddle, D. C. Breunlin, & R. C. Schwartz (Eds.), *Handbook of family therapy training & supervision* (pp. 183–193). New York: Guilford.

Shanfield, S. B., Matthews, K. L., & Hetherly, V. (1993). What do excellent psychotherapy supervisors do? *American Journal of Psychiatry, 7,* 1081–1084.

Sherry, P. (1991). Ethical issues in the conduct of supervision. *The Counseling Psychologist, 19*(4), 566-584.

Shulman, L. (1993). *Interactional supervision.* Washington, DC: NASW Press.

Smith, R. C., Mead, D. E., & Kinsella, J. A. (1998). Direct supervision: Adding computer-assisted feedback and data capture to live supervision. *Journal of Marital and Family Therapy, 24*(1), 113–125.

Stoltenberg, C. D., & Delworth, U. (1987). *Supervising counselors and therapists: A developmental approach.* San Francisco, CA: Jossey-Bass.

Stoltenberg, C. D., McNeill, B. W., & Crethar, H. C. (1994). Changes in supervision as counselors and therapists gain experience: A review. *Professional Psychology: Research and Practice, 25,* 416–449.

Stoltenberg, C. D., McNeill, B. W., & Delworth, U. (1998). *IDM supervision: An integrated development model for supervising counselors and therapists.* San Francisco, CA: Jossey-Bass.

Strupp, H., & Binder, J. L. (1984). *Psychotherapy in a new key: A guide to time-limited dynamic psychotherapy.* New York: Basic Books.

Sue, D. W., Ivey, A. E., & Pederson, P. (1996). *A theory of multicultural counseling and therapy.* Pacific Grove, CA: Brooks/Cole.

Sue, D.W., & Sue, D. (1990). *Counseling the culturally different: Theory and practice* (2nd ed.). New York: Wiley.

Sweeney, T. J. (1998). *Adlerian counseling: A practitioner's approach* (4th ed.). Washington, DC: Accelerated Development.

Teyber, E. (1997). *Interpersonal process in psychotherapy.* Pacific Grove, CA: Brooks/Cole.

Thomas, F. (1992, October). *Solution focused supervision.* Paper presented at the AAMFT Fiftieth Anniversary Conference, Atlanta, GA.

Thompson, R. A. (1996). *Counseling techniques: Improving relationships with others, ourselves, our families and our environment.* Washington, DC: Accelerated Development.

Torres, R. E. (1996, October). *Supervision from a multicultural perspective.* Paper presented at ACES Conference. Portland, OR.

Usher, C., & Borders, L. D. (1993). Practicing counselors' preferences for supervisory style and supervisory emphasis. *Counselor Education and Supervision. 33,* 66–79.

Walters, M., Carter, B., Papp, P., & Silverstein, O. (1988). *The invisible web: Gender patterns in family relationships.* New York: Guilford.

Watkins, C. E., Jr. (1993). Development of the psychotherapy supervisor: Concepts, assumptions, and hypotheses of the supervisor complexity model. *American Journal of Psychotherapy, 47,* 58–74.

Watkins, C. E., Jr. (Ed.). (1997). *Handbook of psychotherapy supervision.* New York: Wiley.

Watzlawick, P., Weakland, J. H., & Fisch, R. (1974). *Change: Principles of problem formation and problem resolution.* New York: Norton.

Webster's New World College Dictionary 4th Edition (1999). New York: Worldwide Books.

Weiner-Davis. M. (1995). *Fire your shrink: Do-it-yourself strategies for changing your life and everyone in it.* New York: Simon & Schuster.

Wessler, R. L., & Ellis, A. (1983). Supervision in counseling: Rational-emotive therapy. *The Counseling Psychologist, 11*(1), 43–49.

Wetchler, J. L., Piercy, F. P., & Sprenkle, D. H. (1989). Supervisors' and supervisees' perceptions of the effectiveness of family therapy supervisory techniques. *American Journal of Family Therapy, 17,* 35–47.

Whiffen, R. (1982). The use of videotape in supervision. In R. Whiffen & J. Byng-Hall (Eds.), *Family therapy supervision: Recent developments in practice.* New York: Academics Press.

Whiston, S. C., & Emerson, S. (1989). Ethical implications for supervisors in counseling of trainees. *Counselor Education and Supervision, 28,* 318–325.

White, M., & Russell, C. (1995). The essential elements of supervisory systems: A modified study. *Journal of Marital and Family Therapy, 21*(1), 33–53.

Williamson, D. (1991). *The intimacy paradox.* New York: Guilford.

Wong, M. L. (1996, October). *The white supervisor and cross-cultural supervision: Supervision techniques.* Paper presented at the Association for Counselor Education and Supervision Convention, Portland, OR.

Woods, P. J., & Ellis, A. (1997). Supervision in rational emotive behavior therapy. In C. E. Watkins, Jr. (Ed.), *Handbook of psychotherapy supervision* (pp. 101–113). New York: Wiley.

Worthington, E. L. (1987). Changes in supervision as counselors and supervisors gain experience: A review. *Professional Psychology: Research and Practice, 18,* 189–208.

Yalom, I. D. (1980). *Existential psychotherapy.* New York: Basic Books.

Yalom, I. D. (1985). *The theory and practice of group psychotherapy* (3rd ed.). New York: Basic Books.

Yalom, I.D. (1989). *Love's executioner and other tales of psychotherapy.* New York: Harper Perennial.

INDEX

ABOUT THE AUTHOR

Jane M. Campbell, Ph.D., NCC, ACS, has worked in the field of counseling and psychotherapy for over twenty-five years, in both private practice and academic institutions. She is certified as a licensed psychologist, a clinical member of AAMFT, and an NBCC Certified Counselor, and has recently been certified as an NCC Approved Clinical Supervisor. In 1972, she earned her M.Ed. in Counseling from Portland State University, and went on to earn her doctorate in Counseling Psychology from the University of Houston in 1988. She was a member of the counseling faculties at both the University of Houston at Clear Lake and the University of Houston, where she undertook a number of supervision responsibilities. While at the University of Houston, Dr. Campbell was the director of practicum and internship training for master's and doctoral level counseling psychology students. And while at the University of Houston—Clear Lake, she developed a training program in school and community counseling that incorporated supervision of interns and beginning counselors, in both on-campus and community settings.

Dr. Campbell is a well-known presenter both nationally and internationally, and she has offered a series of well-received workshops for counselors and other mental health professionals on topics such as supervision, ethics, brief therapy interventions, group therapy, and grief counseling. In 1994, she created and co-taught a 40-hour continuing education course for licensed professional counselors, school counselors, social workers, and marriage and family therapists in Texas on the topic of clinical supervision and state licensure.

She has provided ongoing supervision and consultation services to a number of non-profit agencies in the Houston metropolitan area. And she has volunteered to train group facilitators for the Houston Area Women's Center. In addition, she is an active member of the Houston community, having served on the Steering Committee for the Mayor's Hearing on Children and Youth, the Children's Committee of the Mental Health Association, and on the advisory boards for the Mayor's Task Force on Drugs, Harris County MADD, Vocational Guidance Service, and Widowed Persons Services. Dr. Campbell's research and private practice interests include life transitions, stress, and women's issues, as well as counselor supervision and clinical consultation. Her current focus is on personal life coaching and the use of coaching techniques in supervision.

Dr. Campbell welcomes interest and inquiries into her work. Please address all correspondence to her email address: drjmcamp@aol.com